GENERAL KNOWLEDGE WORLD

Dr. GIRISH P. PANT

ATLANTIC PUBLISHERS AND DISTRIBUTORS

Published by
ATLANTIC PUBLISHERS AND DISTRIBUTORS
B-2, Vishal Enclave, Opp. Rajouri Garden, New Delhi-27
Phones : 5413460, 5429987, 5466842

Sales Office
4215/1, Ansari Road, Darya Ganj, New Delhi-110 002
Phones : 3273880, 3285873, 3280451
Fax : 91-11-3285873
web : www.atlanticbooks.com
e-mail : info@atlanticbooks.com

ISBN 81-269-0142-X

Typeset at
APD Computer Graphics, Delhi

Printed in India at
Mehra Offset Press, Delhi

This book is meant for
Animesh, Ashesh and Ajita

PREFACE

General Knowledge has assumed considerable significance in our modern life and there is hardly a competitive examination or interview in which one can seek success without a through understanding of national and international occurrences.

Since my school days, I have been fascinated with general knowledge. I used to participate successfully in numerous general knowledge quiz contests.

Mastermind UK and Mastermind India have appealed to me greatly. The screening of *Kaun Banega Crorepati* has spurred me to write a book on general knowledge. This outcome is the product of a year of careful research.

Needless to state, all errors and omissions are entirely mine.

GIRISH P. PANT

QUIZ 1

1. The flag of Afghanistan includes two Muslim religious inscriptions in Arabic. One is *There is no god but Allah and Muhammad is the prophet of Allah.* What is the other?
   (*a*) God helps those who help themselves
   (*b*) God is great
   (*c*) Lead kindly light...one step enough for me
   (*d*) Live for god, lead for Islam.
2. James Baldaim was a black American novelist, essayist, and playwright who was born in 1924 and died in 1987. Among the following, which was his first novel?
   (*a*) *Another Country* (*b*) *Blues for Mr. Charlie*
   (*c*) *Giovanni's Room* (*d*) *Go Tell It On the Mountain.*
3. Who married Julia, daughter of Julius Caesar and Cornelia, in 59 BC?
   (*a*) Pompey (*b*) Lucius Piso
   (*c*) Mark Anthony (*d*) Marcus Junius Brutus.
4. What is the minimum age of Earth?
   (*a*) 1½ billion years (*b*) 2½ billion years
   (*c*) 3½ billion years (*d*) 4½ billion years.
5. Which European Country had a fascist party called the Arrow Cross who gained much support in the late 1930's?
   (*a*) Romania (*b*) Hungary (*c*) Albania (*d*) Bulgaria.
6. Who said, "We won the war, but only you can win the peace"?
   (*a*) Winston Churchill (*b*) John F. Kennedy
   (*c*) Bill Clinton (*d*) Charles De Gaulle.
7. What is hacienda?
   (*a*) A Church (*b*) A Movie theater
   (*c*) A library (*d*) A large farm.

8. What do you mean by dolorous?
(*a*) Languorous (*b*) Mournful (*c*) Lazy (*d*) Noisy.

9. What must an organic compound contain?
(*a*) Silicon (*b*) Carbon (*c*) Hydrogen (*d*) Oxygen.

10. In economics, of the following pairs of goods, which is an example of substitutes?
(*a*) Coats and trousers (*b*) Pen and paper
(*c*) Tea and coffee (*d*) Coffee and sugar.

11. Which is the deepest lake in the world?
(*a*) Lake Baikal (*b*) Lake Eyre
(*c*) Lake Huron (*d*) Lake Ladoga.

12. In which city was the Italian statesman and writer Niccolo Machiavelli born in 1469?
(*a*) Turin (*b*) Rome (*c*) Venice (*d*) Florence.

13. Which battle in Russia compelled the French forces under Napoleon Bonaparte to retreat in 1812?
(*a*) Battle of Friedland (*b*) Battle of Borodino
(*c*) Battle of Aspern (*d*) Battle of Austerlitz.

14. Who painted *Woman Weeping*?
(*a*) Michelangelo (*b*) Pablo Picasso
(*c*) Paul Gauguin (*d*) Robert Delaunay.

15. Where is racquetball, a fast, exciting game, mostly played?
(*a*) UK (*b*) USA (*c*) China (*d*) France.

16. Hertz is the unit used to measure frequency. How many does one hertz equal to?
(*a*) 1 vibration per second
(*b*) 10 vibrations per second
(*c*) 100 vibrations per second
(*d*) 1000 vibrations per second.

17. In which country is Waitangi Day celebrated as a holiday on February 6?
(*a*) Australia (*b*) Mexico (*c*) New Zealand (*d*) Canada.

18. Albert Einstein was offered a position in the new state of Israel in 1952. Which one?
(*a*) Prime Minister (*b*) Minister of Science and Technology
(*c*) President (*d*) Minister of Foreign Affairs.

19. What colour is iridium?

(*a*) Reddish brown (*b*) Steel gray

(*c*) Grayish purple (*d*) Ash white.

20. Which country owns the Queen Elizabeth Islands in the Arctic?

(*a*) USA (*b*) Canada (*c*) UK (*d*) France.

QUIZ 2

1. Who is often known as the 'Father of Nylon'?
   (*a*) Wallace Hume Carthers (*b*) Leo Bakeland
   (*c*) Richard Feynman (*d*) Niels Bohr.
2. With which sport is Merdeka Tournament associated?
   (*a*) Volleyball (*b*) Football (*c*) Rugby (*d*) Cricket.
3. When was the Battle of Waterloo fought?
   (*a*) 1800 (*b*) 1805 (*c*) 1810 (*d*) 1815.
4. Which famous British author used to write under the pseudonym, 'His own'?
   (*a*) Arthur Conan Doyle (*b*) Thomas Hardy
   (*c*) D.H. Lawrence (*d*) Walter Scott.
5. The Group 'Bee Gees' had a famous younger brother who died of an overdose of heroin. Name him.
   (*a*) Andy Gibb (*b*) Maurice Gibb
   (*c*) Barry Gibb (*d*) Robin Gibb.
6. Between 1535 and 1825, which Latin American City served as the capital of Spain's New World Empire?
   (*a*) La Paz (*b*) Asuncion (*c*) Bogota (*d*) Lima.
7. Who is the author of the classic *Metamorphosis* that deals with the story of a man who wakes up one morning to find that he has been changed into a giant insect?
   (*a*) Gunter Grass (*b*) Herbert George Wells
   (*c*) Franz Kafka (*d*) Jules Verne.
8. Hammurabi, the Amorite king, is well-known for his legal system. Which village did he convert into a famous capital?
   (*a*) Jerusalem (*b*) Ur (*c*) Nineveh (*d*) Babylon.
9. Who invented the ballpoint pen?
   (*a*) Whitcomb Judson (*b*) Joseph Aspdin
   (*c*) George De Mestrel (*d*) Ladislao Biro.

10. The terms *Edda* is conferred on two vital collections of literature of a certain country. Name it.
(*a*) Ireland (*b*) Iceland (*c*) Denmark (*d*) Norway.

11. Which planet lies almost flat on its axis?
(*a*) Uranus (*b*) Venus (*c*) Neptune (*d*) Mars.

12. How much water is required to flush a toilet?
(*a*) Less than 1 gallon (*b*) 2 – 4 gallon
(*c*) 5 – 7 gallon (*d*) 8 – 10 gallon.

13. What do you mean by pectoral?
(*a*) Pertaining to breast (*b*) Pertaining to lips
(*c*) Pertaining to back (*d*) Pertaining to hip.

14. What is the capital of Gabon?
(*a*) Libreville (*b*) Kinshasa (*c*) Lusaka (*d*) Harare.

15. In Hindu mythology, which female Hindu devotee entertained Ram and Laxman before they met Sugriva?
(*a*) Shakuntala (*b*) Urmila (*c*) Manthara (*d*) Sabari.

16. Which is the oldest black republic in the world and also the second oldest independent nation in the Western Hemisphere?
(*a*) Honduras (*b*) Haiti
(*c*) Dominican Republic (*d*) Jamaica.

17. In which Canadian City is the headquarters of International Civil Aviation Organization (ICAO) located?
(*a*) Toronto (*b*) Montreal (*c*) Regina (*d*) Ottawa.

18. Who discovered Newfoundland in 1498?
(*a*) Christopher Columbus (*b*) Vasco Da Gama
(*c*) John Cabot (*d*) Jacques Cartier.

19. Who believed that matter was made of earth, water, fire and air?
(*a*) Cavendish (*b*) Aristotle (*c*) Boyle (*d*) Newton.

20. Who coined the phrase 'demonstration effect'?
(*a*) Franco Modigliani (*b*) Milton Friedman
(*c*) W.W. Rostow (*d*) James Dussenberry.

QUIZ 3

1. Under whose house (period) did the Onin war begin in Japan in 1467?
(*a*) Ashikaga (*b*) Muromachi (*c*) Momoyama (*d*) Sengoku.

2. Name the body of water between India and Sri Lanka?
(*a*) Palk Strait (*b*) Strait of Messina
(*c*) Cook Strait (*d*) Bass Strait.

3. In Shakespears's *Julius Caesar*, whom does Caesar refer to as having "a lean and hungry look"?
(*a*) Cassius (*b*) Brutus (*c*) Mark Antony (*d*) Octavius.

4. What is dendrology the study of?
(*a*) Flowers (*b*) Trees (*c*) Plants (*d*) Grasses.

5. What is the meaning of the word pluvial?
(*a*) Hot (*b*) Dry (*c*) Rainy (*d*) Cold.

6. Whose portrait is depicted on the back of a modern Bank of England £ 10 note?
(*a*) Duke of Wellington (*b*) Isaac Newton
(*c*) Queen Elizabeth (*d*) Florence Nightingale.

7. When was Zulfikar Ali Bhutto executed in Pakistan?
(*a*) April 4, 1979 (*b*) June 4, 1979
(*c*) April 4, 1980 (*d*) June 4, 1980.

8. Peter Snell won the gold medal in 800 meter run in the Olympic in 1960 and 1964. Which country did he represent?
(*a*) Australia (*b*) Canada (*c*) USA (*d*) New Zealand.

9. Who wrote the following : "Better by far you should forget and smile than that you should remember and be sad"?
(*a*) Christian Rossetti (*b*) Robert Browning
(*c*) Eugene Field (*d*) Jane Austen.

10. Who invented bicycle?
(*a*) E. Torricelli (*b*) W. J. Cante
(*c*) K. Macmillan (*d*) H. W. Seeley.

11. Who was the king who ruled from 521 B.C. to 485 B.C. and made Persia a great seapower?
(*a*) Xerxes I (*b*) Cyrus (*c*) Darius (*d*) Cambyses II.

12. In 1979, the song 'Do you think I am Sexy' became a major hit. Who sang it?
(*a*) Eric Clapton (*b*) Rod Stewart
(*c*) Aerosmith (*d*) Peter Brown.

13. What is ETA?
(a) Basque Separatist Group of Spain
(b) Khemer Guerillas of Cambodia
(c) Shinning Path of Latin America
(d) Liberation Tigers of Tamil Elam (LTTE).

14. What is obtained from methyl alcohol?
(*a*) Sponge rubber (*b*) Bakelite, a hard plastic
(*c*) The rubber neoprene (*d*) The plastic, perspex.

15. Who stated : "Rent is a creation of value, not of wealth"?
(*a*) Thomas Mun (*b*) Karl Manger
(*c*) David Ricardo (*d*) A.C. Pigou.

16. Which psychiatrist introduced the ink blot test?
(*a*) Hans Geiger (*b*) Herman Rorschach
(*c*) Alfred Binet (*d*) Alfred Adler.

17. The Colossus was an electronic computer built during the Second World War and was also used by the Allies to Crack German codes. Who is credited for this feat?
(*a*) Alan Turing (*b*) Wolfgang Pauli
(*c*) Fredrick Banting (*d*) Charles Dawson.

18. What nickname was given to a 3.2 million-year-old skeleton of a new human ancestor found in Ethiopia in 1974?
(*a*) Jerry (*b*) Lucy (*c*) Tommy (*d*) Wendy.

19. In which planet did Comet Shoemaker-Levy 9 crash in 1994?
(*a*) Saturn (*b*) Venus (*c*) Jupiter (*d*) Mars.

20. Which month in the Roman calendar is named after the two — faced Greek God of Gates and Doors?
(*a*) January (*b*) March (*c*) May (*d*) July.

QUIZ 4

1. In what novel is John Loveday's trumpet 'silenced for ever upon one of the bloody battle — fields of Spain'?
   (*a*) Samuel Johnson (*b*) Thomas Hardy
   (*c*) Francis Bacon (*d*) D.H. Lawrence.

2. Name the long-distance runner who won the 5,000 and 10,000 meters and Marathon titles in the 1952 Olympics held in Helsinki.
   (*a*) Delfo Cabrera (*b*) Emil Zatopek
   (*c*) Harold Whitlock (*d*) Gaston Reiff.

3. The bowline, sheepshank and clove hitch are all classification of what?
   (*a*) Fishes (*b*) Cakes (*c*) Knots (*d*) Birds.

4. If chemical reaction is said to be exothermic, elaborate the meaning.
   (*a*) It gives off heat (*b*) It gives off vapour
   (*c*) It releases energy (*d*) It releases water.

5. This World War I battle is famous as the Battle of Jutland. What do the Germans call it?
   (*a*) Battle of the Bulge (*b*) Battle of Agincourt
   (*c*) Battle of Thermopylae (*d*) Battle of Skagersak.

6. The Hindu god Ganesh has the head of which animal?
   (*a*) Lion (*b*) Jackal (*c*) Elephant (*d*) Cow.

7. Ljubljana is the capital of which country?
   (*a*) Latavia (*b*) Estonia (*c*) Croatia (*d*) Slovenia.

8. What was Peter Dawson who died in 1960?
   (*a*) Singer (*b*) Scientist (*c*) Comedian (*d*) Cricketer.

9. Two insects were described in the poem by John Keats. One of them was a cricket. Name the other.
   (*a*) Butterfly (*b*) Grasshopper (*c*) Ant (*d*) Cockroach.

10. Which country's flag reached the moon first?
(*a*) USA (*b*) UK (*c*) France (*d*) Russia.

11. In which city was Martin Luther King, Jr. assassinated?
(*a*) Memphis (*b*) Columbus (*c*) Bismarck (*d*) Tampa.

12. Of the following, which is the heaviest substance?
(*a*) Gold (*b*) Iron (*c*) Osmium (*d*) Platinum.

13. Which is the smallest of the wood wind instruments in an orchestra?
(*a*) The Lyre (*b*) The piccolo
(*c*) The flute (*d*) The mouthorgan.

14. Name the bird, which was associated with the Greek goddess, Athena?
(*a*) Eagle (*b*) Bat (*c*) Owl (*d*) Crow.

15. Who was the last British Governor of Singapore?
(*a*) William Goode (*b*) William Farquhar
(*c*) John Butterworth (*d*) G.D. Coleman.

16. Who did Alexander the Great leave in charge of Macedonia when he embarked on his Persian campaign?
(*a*) Antipater (*b*) Nearchos (*c*) Protesilaus (*d*) Philotas.

17. Who was Napoleon Bonaparte's Chief of staff at Waterloo?
(*a*) Marshal Ney (*b*) Marshal Bernadotte
(*c*) Marshal Souet (*d*) Marshal Berthier.

18. What was the profession of Charles de Gaulle's father, Henri de Gaulle?
(*a*) Politician (*b*) Businessman (*c*) Pilot (*d*) Teacher.

19. Which cricketer achieved the first hat trick in a Test match?
(*a*) Fred Spofforth (*b*) Don Bradman
(*c*) Fred Tate (*d*) Maurice Allom.

20. Which financial institution is known as the 'soft loan window' from which developing countries can borrow in hard currencies?
(*a*) IMF (*b*) IBRD (*c*) IDA (*d*) IFC.

QUIZ 5

1. Who was the first Emperor of China?
   (*a*) Sun Yat Sen (*b*) Kublai Khan
   (*c*) Qin Shi Huangdi (*d*) Zhu Ma Hun.
2. In which Olympics and when did the Rumanian Nadia Comaneci achieve a perfect score of 10?
   (*a*) Montreal – 1976 (*b*) Munich – 1972
   (*c*) Moscow – 1980 (*d*) Mexico City – 1968.
3. Which film received the Oscar Award for the best picture in 1988?
   (*a*) Network (*b*) Rain Man
   (*c*) Out of Africa (*d*) The Accused.
4. Which body of water separates the North Island and South Island of New Zealand?
   (*a*) Bass Strait (*b*) Magellan Strait
   (*c*) Strait of Bonifacio (*d*) Cook Strait.
5. Which commandment says, "Thou Shall Not Kill"?
   (*a*) II (*b*) IV (*c*) VI (*d*) VIII.
6. To which country did the DC-10 belong which exploded in air over Niger on September 19, 1989?
   (*a*) UK (*b*) Israel (*c*) Suriname (*d*) France.
7. What is the name of the physicist who originated and developed quantum theory?
   (*a*) Albert A. Michelson (*b*) Max Planck
   (*c*) Ernest O. Lawrence (*d*) Henrich Hertz.
8. What do you mean by *sovkhoz* in Russian?
   (*a*) State farm (*b*) Collective farm
   (*c*) Museum (*d*) Cinema Hall.
9. On which sea is the island of Corfu situated?
   (*a*) Black Sea (*b*) Mediterranean Sea
   (*c*) Adriatic Sea (d) Baltic Sea.

10. What happens if glass is heated?
(*a*) It has a fixed melting point for each type of glass
(*b*) It vaporizes
(*c*) It does not melt at a fixed temperature
(*d*) It melts at only above 1000^0 C.

11. In 1916, whose writing made the Purchasing Power Parity Theory prominent?
(*a*) E. Von Bohm-Bawerk (*b*) W.S. Jevons
(*c*) Frederich List (*d*) Gustav Cassel.

12. What is the monetary unit of Nicaragua?
(*a*) Naira (*b*) Sol (*c*) Dollar (*d*) Cordoba.

13. Who was the World Grand Prix Champion in 1985 and 1986?
(*a*) Nelson Piquet (*b*) Ayrton Senna
(*c*) Alain Prost (*d*) Niki Lauda.

14. Who wrote the book *Glimpses of World History*?
(*a*) John F. Kennedy (*b*) Winston Churchill
(*c*) Dwight Eisenhower (*d*) Jawahar Lal Nehru.

15. In 560 BC, which dictator broached the 'age of the Tyrants'?
(*a*) Pisistratus (*b*) Solon (*c*) Hippias (*d*) Hipparchus.

16. What is the meaning of megalomania?
(*a*) Craving for immortality
(*b*) Delusious of grandeur
(*c*) Love for unlimited power
(*d*) Excessive preoccupation with wealth.

17. According to Time's critics, which was the best nonfiction bock and the author of the 20th century?
(*a*) *The Gulag Archipelago* by Aleksandr Solzhenitsyn
(*b*) *The Diary of a Young Girl* by Anne Frank
(*c*) *Double Helix* by James Watson
(*d*) *Lolita* by Vladimir Nabokov.

18. Who said the following : "We are driven to this. We are determined to go on with this agitation. It is our duty to make this world a better place to live."
(*a*) Helen Keller (*b*) Emmeline Pankhurst
(*c*) Harvey Milk (*d*) Maya Angelou.

19. What is the average number of hairs per square inch of scalp?
(*a*) 400 (*b*) 800 (*c*) 1,200 (*d*) 1,600.

20. The huanaco and vicuna are types of what?
(*a*) Kangaroos (*b*) Camels
(*c*) Llamas (*d*) Horses.

QUIZ 6

1. Name the number of soldiers which a Roman centurion commanded.
   (*a*) 50 (*b*) 100 (*c*) 150 (*d*) 200.
2. In cryosurgery, surgeons cool the body by 10⁰ to 15⁰. This allows them to operate on a bloodless heart for how long?
   (*a*) 8 minutes (*b*) 14 minutes
   (*c*) 20 minutes (*d*) 26 minutes.
3. In which sport does the World Championship have three classes called open, standard and 15 meters?
   (*a*) Gliding (*b*) Rowing
   (*c*) Scuba diving (*d*) Motor car racing.
4. Who played Moses in the 1956 film *The Ten Commandments*?
   (*a*) Paul Newman (*b*) Omar Shariff
   (*c*) Charlton Heston (*d*) Frank Sinarta.
5. Who sang the song 'Kiss you all over'?
   (a) Doobie Brothers (*b*) Supertramps
   (c) Dire Straits (*d*) Exile.
6. How long will an average man's face whisker grow in one year?
   (*a*) 3 ½ inches (*b*) 4 ½ inches
   (*c*) 5 ½ inches (*d*) 6 ½ inches.
7. What is the capital of Wales?
   (*a*) Gwent (*b*) Cardiff (*c*) Dyfed (*d*) Powys.
8. Who invented waterclock, an instrument that recorded time by measuring water escaping from a vessel?
   (*a*) Archimedes (*b*) Aristotle (*c*) Plato (*d*) Homer.
9. Which country produces the most wheat?
   (*a*) Russia (*b*) USA (*c*) China (*d*) India.

10. Who painted *Lady Caroline Scott*?
(*a*) Ben Nicholson (*b*) Joshua Reynolds
(*c*) Walter Silkert (*d*) Thomas Gainsborough.

11. Which three countries formed the East Africa Community in 1967?
(*a*) Tanzania, Kenya and Uganda
(*b*) Tanzania, Sudan and Uganda
(*c*) Sudan, Uganda and Egypt
(*d*) Tanzania, Egypt and Kenya.

12. Which acid has the chemical formula, $C_4H_6O_6$?
(*a*) Sulfuric acid (*b*) Nitric acid
(*c*) Tartaric acid (*d*) Hydrochloric acid.

13. Southeast Asia Treaty Organization (SEATO) was an alliance of eight nations that signed the South-East Asia Collective Defense Treaty in Manila, Philippines on September 8, 1954. It was dissolved in 1977. Of the following, which was not a member?
(*a*) Thailand (*b*) USA (*c*) New Zealand (*d*) Indonesia.

14. Whose 1939 novel *The Grapes of Wrath* won the author the 1940 Pulitzer Prize?
(*a*) James Stephens (*b*) John Steinbeck
(*c*) Douglas Stewart (*d*) A.J. Cronin.

15. Who discovered that the radiation from a body that was glowing red-hot could be explained if light came only in packets of a certain size?
(*a*) Werner Heisen Berg (*b*) Max Planck
(*c*) Paul Dirac (*d*) Erwin Schrodinger.

16. Which 20th century figure best describes the following : "He emerged as a tough, determined world leader. Finally, seizing firm control of his office, he was willing to break sharply with tradition in his privately expressed desire to make a difference in his time?"
(*a*) Richard Nixon (*b*) Mikhail Gorbachev
(*c*) Charles de Gaulle (*d*) Andrew Grove.

17. In which city was a conference held in 1945 that signed the Constitution of Food Agriculture Organisation (FAO)?
(*a*) Ottawa (*b*) San Francisco (*c*) Quebec (*d*) Philadelphia.

18. Who was the first economist to formulate the Marginal Productivity Theory of Distribution?

(*a*) George Stigler (*b*) J.B. Clark

(*c*) Bertil Ohlin (*d*) Frank H. Knight.

19. What do you mean by shibboleth?

(*a*) Mumbo Jumbo (*b*) Tenets of Faith

(*c*) Antiquated Custom (*d*) Test Word.

20. Rabbi is the title given to an ordained Jewish minister. What does this Hebrew word mean?

(*a*) My teacher (*b*) My son

(*c*) My leader (*d*) My father.

QUIZ 7

1. 'Kufic' and 'Nakshi' are the two main forms of which alphabet?
   (*a*) Arabic (*b*) Urdu (*c*) Sanskrit (*d*) Hindi.
2. In 1868, Marquis John Sholto Douglas laid down the rules for which sport?
   (*a*) Wrestling (*b*) Fencing (*c*) Boxing (*d*) Judo.
3. What colour does acid turn litmus paper?
   (*a*) Blue (*b*) Red (*c*) Brown (*d*) Black.
4. According to Hindu legend, which deity was Ved Vyasa's scribe as he dictated the story of the Mahabharat?
   (*a*) Kumar (*b*) Shiva (*c*) Vishnu (*d*) Ganesh.
5. The Mau-Mau rebellion occurred in which African Country in the 1950's?
   (*a*) Tanzania (*b*) Kenya (*c*) Uganda (*d*) Sudan.
6. Michael Jackson's autobiography *Moon Walk* was edited by a famous woman. Name her.
   (*a*) Elizabeth Taylor (*b*) Sophia Loren
   (*c*) Jacqueline Kennedy Onassis (*d*) Nancy Regan.
7. Which American City derives its name from the Greek for 'brotherly love'?
   (*a*) Philadelphia (*b*) Chicago
   (*c*) Columbus (*d*) Trenton.
8. Which culinary delight is related to the *Cave Swiflet South East Asia*?
   (*a*) Shark's Fins Soup (*b*) Chicken Noodle Soup
   (*c*) Tomato Eggdrop Soup (*d*) Bird's Nest Soup.
9. In the solar system, Triton and Nereid are the satellites of which planet?
   (*a*) Pluto (*b*) Neptune (*c*) Uranus (*d*) Jupiter.

10. Who was known as the 'Bard of Avon'?
(*a*) William Shakespeare (*b*) Charles Dickens
(*c*) D.H. Lawrence (*d*) Jonathan Swift.

11. Among the following, which is the leading rice growing country?
(*a*) Bangladesh (*b*) Indonesia (*c*) India (*d*) China.

12. When was the English rock band, *The Rolling Stones,* formed?
(*a*) 1960 (*b*) 1961 (*c*) 1962 (*d*) 1963.

13. Among the following, which is *not* a painting by Pablo Picasso?
(*a*) *Two Acrobats with Dog* (*b*) *Seated Bather*
(*c*) *Mother and Child* (*d*) *The Creation of Adam.*

14. Who became President of Chile in 1989?
(*a*) Augusto Pinochet (*b*) Salvador Allendae
(*c*) Patricio Aylwin Azocar (*d*) Carlos Andres Perez.

15. What is the meaning of ephemeral?
(*a*) Living for a short period (*b*) Celestial
(*c*) Weak interest (*d*) Temporary.

16. In economics, what is the other name for iso-product curve?
(*a*) Ridge line (*b*) Production indifference curve
(*c*) Budget line (*d*) Engel's curve.

17. Which 20th Century figure best describes the following : "His mail brings him a daily dosage of opinion in which he is by turn vilified and glorified"?
(*a*) Harry S. Truman (*b*) Ayatullah Khomeni
(*c*) Mohandas Gandhi (*d*) Martin Luther King, Jr.

18. When did Paul Newman win the Academy Award as best actor for his performance in *The Color of Money*?
(*a*) 1984 (*b*) 1986 (*c*) 1988 (*d*) 1990.

19. Who discovered natural radcoactivity in 1896?
(*a*) Albert Einstein (*b*) Ernest Rutherford
(*c*) Antoine Henri Becquerel (*d*) Otto Hahn.

20. Who painted *The Swing*?
(*a*) Jean Honore Fragonard (*b*) Nicolas Poussin
(*c*) Claesz Heda (*d*) Jan Vermeer.

QUIZ 8

1. Which vitamin is necessary for healthy skin and development of the bones and sources of which include liver, green and yellow vegetable and milk?
   (*a*) Vitamin A (*b*) Vitamin D (*c*) Vitamin E (*d*) Vitamin K.
2. Which is the largest and most important island of the Ryukyu Islands?
   (*a*) Luzon (*b*) Okinawa (*c*) Shikoku (*d*) Orkney.
3. In 1992 Olympics held in Barcelona, who win the gold medal in 100-meters?
   (*a*) Ben Johnson (*b*) Carl Lewis
   (*c*) Linford Christie (*d*) Mike Marsh.
4. Which author's pen name was George Orwell?
   (*a*) Mary Ann Evans (*b*) Charles Lamb
   (*c*) Washington Irving (*d*) Eric Arthur Blair.
5. What is the branch of physics and engineering that is concerned with the properties of light called?
   (*a*) Optics (*b*) Optometry (*c*) Opthamology (*d*) Orthopaedics.
6. In mathematics, who developed the method of exhaustion, foreshadowing integral calculus?
   (*a*) Euclid (*b*) Adelard (*c*) Vander Hoecke (*d*) Eudoxus.
7. Who was King Arthur's wife?
   (*a*) Elaine (*b*) Guenevere (*c*) Mary (*d*) Wanda.
8. Who discovered the main types of human blood — A, B, AB and O and won the 1930 Nobel Prize for medicine?
   (*a*) Karl Landsteiner (*b*) Philip Levine
   (*c*) William Harvey (*d*) Alexander Wiener.
9. Lard composes of three acids. Two of them are oleic acid and palmitic acid Name third.
   (*a*) Nitric acid (*b*) Stearic acid
   (*c*) Sulfuric acid (*d*) Formic acid.

10. What is the capital of Grenada?
(*a*) St. John's (*b*) Georgetown (*c*) St. George's (*d*) Roseau.

11. What is the monetary unit of Lesotho?
(*a*) Lat (*b*) Lek (*c*) Lev (*d*) Loti.

12. Which famous person did Mary Todd marry?
(*a*) Winston Churchill (*b*) Abraham Lincoln
(*c*) Otto Bismarck (*d*) Pierre Tradeau.

13. On which river does Vilnius, the capital and largest city of Lithuania, lie?
(*a*) Neris (*b*) Loire (*c*) Saone (*d*) Sure.

14. Who said the following : " Soul is a constant. It's cultural. It's always going to be there, in different flavours and degrees."?
(*a*) Diana, Princess of Wales (*b*) Bart Simpson
(*c*) Aretha Franklin (*d*) Imelda Marcos.

15. Who wrote *Einstein's Dreams* in 1993?
(*a*) Alan Lightman (*b*) Paul Johnson
(*c*) Roger Rosenblatt (*d*) Abraham Pais.

16. According to Times' Critics, which was the best opera and its writer of the 20th Century?
(*a*) *Wozzeck* by Alban Berg
(*b*) *Madama Butterfly* by Giacomo Puccini
(*c*) *Peter Grimes* by Benjamin Britten
(*d*) *Esplanade* by Paul Taylor.

17. When did USA space shuttle *Challenger* explode, killing all seven crewmembers abroad?
(*a*) 1982 (*b*) 1984 (*c*) 1986 (*d*) 1988.

18. In World War II, when did Germany surrender to the Russian forces at Stanlingrad?
(*a*) July 31, 1943 (*b*) May 31, 1943
(*c*) March 31, 1943 (*d*) January 31, 1943.

19. In economics, in the Cobb-Douglas production function, what is the elasticity of substitution between inputs?
(*a*) Zero (*b*) Less than Unity
(*c*) Unity (*d*) More than Unity.

20. What is the meaning of impetuous?
(*a*) Unconcerned (*b*) Nervous (*c*) Impatient (*d*) Impulsive.

QUIZ 9

1. Who invented the compound microscope in about 1590?
   (*a*) Zacharias Janssen (*b*) Charles Pravaz
   (*c*) Samuel Crompton (*d*) Albert Sabin.

2. Who was the Governor General of India between 1948-1950?
   (*a*) Fakhruddin A. Ahmed (*b*) Lord Mountbatten
   (*c*) Chakravarti Rajagopalachari (*d*) Rajendra Prasad.

3. Input-output analysis is a method of studying the complex relationships between the various parts of an economy. This method has a variety of uses in both government and business. Which economist developed it in the 1920's?
   (*a*) Paul Samuelson (*b*) James Tobin
   (*c*) Kenneth Arrow (*d*) Wassily Leontief.

4. Who became Miss Universe in 1999?
   (*a*) Sushmita Sen (*b*) Laura Dutta
   (*c*) Claudia Moreno (*d*) Mpule Kwelagobe.

5. Maria Bueno won the women's Wimbledon Tennis single title in 1959-1960 and 1964. Which country did she represent?
   (*a*) Spain (*b*) Chile (*c*) Portugal (*d*) Brazil.

6. Among the following, which is the chemical formula of Trinitrotoluene (TNT), a powerful solid explosive?
   (*a*) $CH_4C_7H_2(NO_2)_3$ (*b*) $CH_3C_6H_2(NO_2)_3$
   (*c*) $CH_7C_6H_2(NO_2)_4$ (*d*) $CH_3C_8H_3(NO_3)_2$.

7. Which country's national anthem begins with "O God Almighty"?
   (*a*) Kibrati (*b*) Fiji
   (*c*) Tonga (*d*) Papua New Guinea.

8. Which country produces the most tungsten?
   (*a*) China (*b*) Russia (*c*) Canada (*d*) Australia.

9. Name the musical group that disbanded in 1982 but regrouped in 1989 for its "25th Anniversary" tour?
(*a*) The WHO (*b*) Electric Light Orchestra
(*c*) Earth, Wind and Fire (*d*) The Rolling Stones.

10. On which date do the children dress up as witches and goblins to celebrate Halloween?
(*a*) July 31 (*b*) August 31
(*c*) October 31 (*d*) December 31.

11. In which war did the Battle of Verdun take place?
(*a*) World War I (*b*) World War II
(*c*) Crimea War (*d*) Russo-Japanese War.

12. Who was the first British writer to receive the Nobel Prize for Literature?
(*a*) T.S. Eliot (*b*) Rudyard Kipling
(*c*) John Galsworthy (*d*) George Bernard Shaw.

13. What is the probability distribution of the number of heads drawn closer and closer to the bell-shaped curve called?
(*a*) Variance (*b*) Normal distribution
(*c*) Frequency (*d*) Mode.

14. Who painted the *Potato Eaters* in 1885?
(*a*) Diego Velazquez (*b*) Pabolo Picasso
(*c*) Van Gogh (*d*) Leonardo Da Vinci.

15. Which French author wrote *Madame Bovary* in 1856?
(*a*) Alexander Dumas (*b*) Emile Zola
(*c*) Marcel Proust (*d*) Gustave Flaubert.

16. Okapi is a relative of which animal?
(*a*) Zebra (*b*) Elephant (*c*) Giraffe (*d*) Bear.

17. To which country does the Madeira Islands, of volcanic origin, which lie in the Atlantic Ocean off the northwest coast of Africa, belong?
(*a*) UK (*b*) France (*c*) Spain (*d*) Portugal.

18. What is a troglodyte?
(*a*) Prisoner of War (*b*) Clown
(*c*) Cave-man (*d*) Shepherd.

19. Which of the following is the work of Paul Samuelson?

(*a*) *Asian Drama : An Inquiry into the Causes of Poverty of Nations*

(*b*) *History of Economic Analysis*

(*c*) *The Industrial State*

(*d*) *Foundations of Economic Analysis.*

20. What is hydrology the science of?

(*a*) Heavenly bodies (*b*) Cells

(*c*) Measuring earthquakes (*d*) Flower cultivation.

QUIZ 10

1. Name the tree whose branches are the symbol of peace.
   (*a*) Oak (*b*) Pine (*c*) Olive (*d*) Teak.
2. When did Alexander the Great invade India?
   (*a*) 323-324 BC (*b*) 324-325 BC
   (*c*) 325-326 BC (*d*) 326-327 BC.
3. 'Smuck' is a group of what?
   (*a*) Jellyfish (*b*) Whale (*c*) Shark (*d*) Dolphin.
4. How many lines to a picture were there in the first television sets in widespread use in Britain?
   (*a*) 105 (*b*) 205 (*c*) 305 (*d*) 405.
5. Which ex-Beatles was the first to have Number One hit after the break-up?
   (*a*) Paul McCartney (*b*) John Lennon
   (*c*) George Harrison (*d*) Ringo Starr.
6. Which country has won Badminton's Thomas Cup most often?
   (*a*) Malaysia (*b*) Indonesia (*c*) Thailand (*d*) Philippines.
7. Which is the only European country in which a wife does not take the name of her husband after marriage?
   (*a*) Spain (*b*) Sweden (*c*) Portugal (*d*) Italy.
8. Who wrote *Kidnapped*?
   (*a*) Robert Louis Stevenson (*b*) William Shakespeare
   (*c*) Charles Dickens (*d*) D.H. Lawrence.
9. Name the star, which is nearest to the earth.
   (*a*) Sirius (*b*) Proxima Centauri (*c*) Deneb (*d*) Altair.
10. Which city in Canada is called Hogtown?
    (*a*) Ottawa (*b*) Edmonton (*c*) Toronto (*d*) Quebec.
11. Which gas is commonly used in electric bulbs?
    (*a*) Krypton (*b*) Argon (*c*) Helium (*d*) Neon.

12. Name the medical term for the pain of heart attack.
(*a*) Angina (*b*) Hypertension (*c*) Asthma (*d*) Carditis.

13. Name the five members of the Gulf Co-operation Council (GCC).
(*a*) Bahrain, Iraq, Kuwait, Oman and Saudi Arabia
(*b*) Kuwait, Oman, Qatar, Saudi Arabia and Iran
(*c*) United Arab Emirates, Bahrain, Qatar, Jordan and Yemen
(*d*) United Arab Emirates, Bahrain, Kuwait, Oman and Qatar.

14. In the Battle of Pharsalia that took place in 48 BC, who defeated whom?
(*a*) Brutus defeated Mark Antony
(*b*) Octavius Caesar defeated Mark Antomy
(*c*) Cassius defeated Octavius Caesar
(*d*) Julius Caesar defeated Pompey.

15. Who directed the film *Casablanca*?
(*a*) William Wyler (*b*) Michael Curtiz
(*c*) John Ford (*d*) Frank Capra.

16. In which sea does the River Oder outflow?
(*a*) Baltic Sea (*b*) Black Sea (*c*) Dead Sea (*d*) North Sea.

17. When did John L. Baird discover television?
(*a*) 1921 (*b*) 1926 (*c*) 1931 (*d*) 1936.

18. On August 10, 1626, the Canarsee Delaware Indians agreed to sell the 22 square miles Manhattan Island at the mouth of the Hudson River to Dutch settlers under Peter Minuit for cloth and trinkets. What has Manhattan been at least valued at the end of the 20th century?
(*a*) $ 143 billion (*b*) $ 163 billion
(*c*) $ 183 billion (*d*) $ 203 billion.

19. Who defined Economics as a science which studies human behaviour as a relationship between ends and means which have alternative uses?
(*a*) Paul Samuelson (*b*) John Hicks
(*c*) Lionel Robbins (*d*) Lester Thurow.

20. Who painted *The Night Cafe*?
(*a*) Georges Seurat (*b*) Vincent van Gogh
(*c*) Edgar Degas (*d*) Henri Matisse.

QUIZ 11

1. In which country is the volcano Erebus Located?
(*a*) Europe (*b*) Asia (*c*) Antartica (*d*) Africa.

2. Who was the inventor of the bifocal spectacles?
(*a*) Thomas Edison (*b*) Benjamin Franklin
(*c*) Joseph Aspdin (*d*) George De Mestrel.

3. What type of bird is a jackdaw?
(*a*) Crow (*b*) Owl (*c*) Sparrow (*d*) Parrot.

4. Where was Joan of Arc born?
(*a*) Nice (*b*) Domremy (*c*) Lyon (*d*) Vacouleurs.

5. Who said, "I believe it is peace in our time"?
(*a*) Winston Churchill (*b*) Charles De Gaulle
(*c*) Edouard Daladier (*d*) Neville Chamberlain.

6. Of the following, who is *not* a British painter?
(*a*) John Constable (*b*) Ben Nicholson
(*c*) George Stubbs (*d*) John Sloan.

7. Who was the British chemist who worked on atomic structure and received the 1921 Nobel Prize for Chemistry for this research?
(*a*) Francis W. Aston (*b*) Frederick Soddy
(*c*) Ernest Rutherford (*d*) Arthur Harden.

8. Among the following, which country produces the most manganese?
(*a*) Russia (*b*) South Africa (*c*) Gabon (*d*) China.

9. Who painted *The Holy Trinty*?
(*a*) Filippolippi (*b*) Correggio (*c*) Masaccio (*d*) Titian.

10. *Jamal* is an Arabic word. What is its English equivalent?
(*a*) Beauty (*b*) Well-mannered
(*c*) Docile (*d*) Prayer.

11. Who wrote *The Princess of Cleves* and *The Princess of Montpensier?*
(*a*) Emily Bronte (*b*) George Eliot
(*c*) Walter Scott (*d*) Madame De La Fayette.

12. Who was the chief writer and narrator of 'Cosmos', a popular television series?
(*a*) Norman F. Ramsey (*b*) Carl Sagan
(*c*) Stephen Hawkin (*d*) William A. Fowler.

13. In economics, among the following, which is also known as plant curves?
(*a*) Long-run average cost (LAC) curves
(*b*) Average total cost (ATC) curves
(*c*) Short-run average cost (SAC) curves
(*d*) Average variable cost (AVC) curves.

14. The signing of the Treaty of Vereeniging in May 1902 ended which war?
(*a*) Russo-Japanese War (*b*) Boer War
(*c*) Crimea War (*d*) English-Spanish War.

15. What is the language used for standard zoological nomenclatrue?
(*a*) Latin (*b*) Greek (*c*) Sanskrit (*d*) English.

16. In Hindu mythology, which of Krishna's sobriquets is earned from the fact that his mother used to tie around his belly to quell his antics?
(*a*) Govinda (*b*) Mohan (*c*) Keshab (*d*) Damodar.

17. Tennis star Yannick Noah was which country's national before becoming a French citizen?
(*a*) Algeria (*b*) Morocco (*c*) Cameroon (*d*) Kenya.

18. Which disease is called gingivitis?
(*a*) Blurring of the eye (*b*) Hallucination
(*c*) Nose bleeding (*d*) Inflammation of gums.

19. Which planet in our solar system takes the longest time to orbit the sun?
(*a*) Pluto (*b*) Neptune (*c*) Jupiter (*d*) Venus.

20. Name the ancient state in the eighth century BC which had modern Beijing as its capital.
(*a*) Yen (*b*) Ch'in (*c*) Wu (*d*) Ch'u.

QUIZ 12

1. Who wrote the following books, *The Negro in the American Revolution* (1961) and *The Negro in the Making of America* (1964)?
   (*a*) Ralph Bunche (*b*) Malcom X
   (*c*) Martin Luther King Jr. (*d*) Benjamin A. Quarles.
2. What is the atomic number of radon (Rn), a radioactive element?
   (*a*) 74 (*b*) 80 (*c*) 86 (*d*) 92.
3. If a mixture contains 5 liters of syrup and 15 liters of water, what is the ratio of syrup to water?
   (*a*) 1:2 (*b*) 1:3 (*c*) 1:4 (*d*) 1:5.
4. What is the capital of Western Australia?
   (*a*) Albamy (*b*) Perth (*c*) Bunbury (*d*) Geraldton.
5. Which playwrighter is best known for two plays, namely, *Glass Menagerie* and *A Streetcar Named Desire*?
   (*a*) William Thackeray (*b*) Malcolm Williamson
   (*c*) David Field (*d*) Tennessee Williams.
6. To which family does woodchuck, also called ground hog, belong?
   (*a*) Pig (*b*) Rat (*c*) Squirrel (*d*) Cat.
7. What is the Fifth Commandment?
   (*a*) Honour thy father and thy mother
   (*b*) Thou shalt not kill
   (*c*) Thou shalt not commit adultery
   (*d*) Thou shalt not steal.
8. Frank Sedgman won the men's single US tennis championship title in 1951 and 1952. Which country did he represent?
   (*a*) Australia (*b*) USA (*c*) UK (*d*) Canada.

9. Of the following, who is a Filipino painter?
(*a*) Joan Miro (*b*) Juan Luna
(*c*) Diego Rivera (*d*) Amado Castro.

10. In which country is the contribution of services to gross domestic product highest at around 75 per cent?
(*a*) Lebanon (*b*) Israel (*c*) Panama (*d*) USA.

11. What is the nationality of the dance-pop singer Alanis Morissette?
(*a*) American (*b*) British (*c*) French (*d*) Canadian.

12. Whom was the J. Robert Oppenheimer referring to when he said, "He was almost wholly without sophistication.... There was always with him a wonderful purity at once childlike and profoundly stubborn."?
(*a*) Louise de Broglie (*b*) Albert Einstein
(*c*) H.G. Wells (*d*) Herman Minkowski.

13. What is the third law of thermodynamics?
(*a*) Absolute zero (about — 273°C) can never be reached
(*b*) Energy in a system, which may be anything from a simple object to a complex machine, cannot be created or destroyed
(*c*) Heat will, of its own accord, flow from a hotter object to a colder object
(*d*) Total amount of energy always remains the same.

14. Which country was formerly known as French Equatorial Africa?
(*a*) Chad (*b*) Central African Republic
(*c*) Gabon (*d*) Kenya.

15. A three-member research team at Bell Laboratories invented the transistor. Two of them were William Shockley and John Bardeen. Name the third.
(*a*) Felix Bloch (*b*) Walter Brattain
(*c*) Willis E. Lamb (*d*) Donald A. Glaser.

16. Who performed the first successful coronary-artery bypass operation?
(*a*) Christian Barnard (*b*) Michael Debakey
(*c*) Robert Noyce (*d*) Edwin Land.

17. Who formulated his supply-side economic theories, which hold that reducing federal taxes spurs economic growth and, eventually, increases federal revenues?
(*a*) Milton Friedman (*b*) Simon Kuznets
(*c*) Arthur Laffer (*d*) Kenneth Arrow.

18. What was the name of the tanker that ran aground in Alaska's Prince William Sound, in 1989 spilling 11 million gallons of crude oil, the worst oil spill in US history?
(*a*) Exxon Valdez (*b*) World Glory
(*c*) Burmah Agate (*d*) Keo.

19. During the Nazi rule in Germany, who became medical chief at Auschwitz-Birkenav in 1943 and sent more than 400,000 non-Aryan prisoners to the gas chambers?
(*a*) Martin Bormann (*b*) Heinrich Himmler
(*c*) Rudolf Hess (*d*) Josef Mengele.

20. Which battle in 1945 established Indonesia resistance to Dutch colonial rule?
(*a*) Battle of Mid-way (*b*) Battle of Surabaya
(*c*) Battle of Iwo Jima (*d*) Battle of Borneo.

QUIZ 13

1. What is 'Machu Picchu'?
   (*a*) A 15th century Inca settlement high in the Peruvian Andes
   (*b*) A tent made by Red Indians
   (*c*) An offspring of red Indian and a white man
   (*d*) An animal similar to a camel.

2. When was Panama Canal, which links the Atlantic and Pacific Ocean opened for commercial traffic?
   (*a*) 1910 (*b*) 1912 (*c*) 1914 (*d*) 1916.

3. Who discovered Pluto, the ninth planet?
   (*a*) Edwin Hubble (*b*) George Hale
   (*c*) Victor Hess (*d*) Clyde Tombaugh.

4. Who developed the first effective polio vaccine?
   (*a*) Jonas Salk (*b*) Edwin Land
   (*c*) Alexander Fleming (*d*) George Wald.

5. Which country has the largest number of cities of over half a million persons?
   (*a*) India (*b*) China (*c*) USA (*d*) Russia.

6. In which African City are the headquarters of the United Nations Environment Programme (UNEP) located?
   (*a*) Addis Abba (*b*) Rabat
   (*c*) Nairobi (*d*) Algiers.

7. What would be the coefficient of price-elasticity of demand when the percentage increase in the quantity of commodity demanded is smaller than the percentage fall in its price?
   (*a*) Zero (*b*) Smaller than one
   (*c*) Greater than one (*d*) Equal to one.

8. What is the synonym for niggardly?
   (*a*) Ungrateful (*b*) Mean (*c*) Stingy (*d*) Cowardly.

9. Who is the poet who imitated the style in the opening stanza of his "The Rime of the Ancient Mariner (1798) : "It is an ancient Mariner, And he stoppeth one of three, By the long gray beard and blithering eye,"?

(*a*) Thomas Percy (*b*) W.H. Auden
(*c*) Johnny Cash (*d*) Samuel T. Coleridge.

10. Chinua Achebe, a Nigerian author, became one of the most outstanding African writers. Of the following, which is his first novel?

(*a*) *Things Fall Apart* (*b*) *Arrow of God*
(*c*) *No Longer At Ease* (*d*) *Anthills of the Savannah.*

11. What is the monetary unit of Algeria?

(*a*) Franc (*b*) Dinar (*c*) Drachma (*d*) Pound.

12. Whom did Russia defeat at the Battle of Poltava in 1709?

(*a*) Japan (*b*) Finland (*c*) Germany (*d*) Sweden.

13. Who was the first British astronaut in space?

(*a*) Michael Foale (*b*) Vance D. Brand
(*c*) Edward H. White II (*d*) John W. Young.

14. In 1496, who financed John Cabot's voyage?

(*a*) King Louis XIV of France
(*b*) King John II of Portugal
(*c*) King Ferdinand of Spain
(*d*) King Henry VII of England.

15. Who has become the Grand Prix world champion a record five times?

(*a*) Nelson Piquet (*b*) Niki Lauda
(*c*) Juan Fangio (*d*) Nigel Mansell.

16. Which castle in UK is a famous example of a castle of enceinte?

(*a*) Framlingham Castle (*b*) Beaumaris Castle
(*c*) Deal Castle (*d*) Stirling Castle.

17. There are four chief types of cerebral palsy. Three are : ataxic, athetoid, and hypotonic; name the fourth.

(*a*) Rhizotomy (*b*) Spastic
(*c*) Arteriosclerosis (*d*) Hemorrhage.

18. Who was the only president of the USA who served two terms that did not directly follow each other?

(*a*) Grover Cleveland (*b*) James Monroe

(*c*) Andrew Jackson (d) Franklin Roosevelt.

19. Bromine, chlorine, fluorine and iodine compose a family of related elements. What are they known as?

(*a*) The aromatic ring (*b*) Light gases

(*c*) Halogens (*d*) Purines.

20. Who in Roman mythology is the messenger of the Gods?

(*a*) Juno (*b*) Diana (*c*) Mercury (*d*) Penelope.

QUIZ 14

1. Who formulated the law of partial pressures in gases in 1802?
   (*a*) Henry Cavendish (*b*) John Dalton
   (*c*) Lavoisier (*d*) Robert Boyle.
2. Which strait joins the Aegean Sea with the Sea of Marmara?
   (*a*) Strait of Dardanelles (*b*) Cook Strait
   (*c*) Palk Strait (*d*) Strait of Messina.
3. What is the other name for the Battle of Arabela fought between Alexander the Great and Darius III in 331 BC?
   (*a*) Battle of Issus (*b*) Battle of Actium
   (*c*) Battle of Gaugamela (*d*) Battle of Thermopylae.
4. What was the nationality of playback singer Udit Narayan Jha before he acquired Indian citizenship?
   (*a*) Nepali (*b*) Bhutanese (*c*) Bangladeshi (*d*) Pakistani.
5. Which country is the largest producer and exporter of garments and textiles?
   (*a*) India (*b*) China (*c*) Japan (*d*) USA.
6. Statistically, if the class marks of a frequency distribution are 7, 19, 31, 43, 55, 67 then the class size is :
   (*a*) 7 (*b*) 12 (*c*) 26 (*d*) 67
7. Who is the hero in Charles Dicken's *A Tale of Two Cities*?
   (*a*) Merdle (*b*) Jeremy Bentham
   (*c*) Sidney Carton (*d*) Ebenzer Scrooge.
8. From where did 'discus throw' originate?
   (*a*) Italy (*b*) India (*c*) China (*d*) Greece.
9. Clint Eastward first gained international fame for his role as a gunman in three European-made Western films. The films were *A Fistful of Dollars* (1964), *For a Few Dollars More*

(1965), and *The Good, The Bad and The Ugly* (1966). Who directed all these films?

(*a*) Sergio Leone (*b*) George Cukor
(*c*) Mike Nichols (*d*) George R. Hill.

10. Which Australian scientist shared the 1963 Nobel Prize in medicine with British professors Alan Hodgkin and Andrew Huxley for research into nerve impulses?

(*a*) Francis Crick (*b*) Konrad E. Bloch
(*c*) John Eccles (*d*) Charles B. Huggins.

11. Among the following, which is the leading electric power producing country?

(*a*) USA (*b*) Japan (*c*) China (*d*) Canada.

12. Who built the first vacuum tubes that could detect radio signals?

(*a*) Vladimir K. Zworykin (*b*) Lee De Forest
(*c*) John A. Fleming (*d*) John Bardeen.

13. Who wrote Dictionary of the English Language?

(*a*) Laurence Sterne (*b*) Samuel Johnson
(*c*) Thomas Gray (*d*) Horace Walpole.

14. What is the monetary unit of Eritrea?

(*a*) Colon (*b*) Ringgit
(*c*) Drachma (*d*) Birr.

15. Which country's flag has three horizontal stripes, blue, black and white? To elaborate, the blue stripe at the top of the flag represents the sky; the middle stripe of black stands for the land; the white stripe at the bottom symbolizes hope in the future?

(*a*) Latavia (*b*) Lithuania (*c*) Hungary (*d*) Estonia.

16. Which explorer reached Brazilian coast and sailed around Africa to India in 1500-1501?

(*a*) Sebastian Cabot (*b*) Amerigo Vespucci
(*c*) Pedro Alvares Cabral (*d*) Martin Frobisher.

17. Who said the following "I save the best minds of my generation destroyed by madness"?

(*a*) Sigmund Freud (*b*) Margaret Sanger
(*c*) Rachel Carson (*d*) Allen Ginsberg.

18. What is the meaning of soporific?
(*a*) Sleepy (*b*) Blissful (*c*) Harmful (*d*) Congenial

19. About 30 per cent of the global population live in South Asia. What percentage of the world's poor live here?
(*a*) 40 (*b*) 46 (*c*) 52 (*d*) 58

20. Who used the metallic money since the seventh century BC and taught the Greeks how to use it?
(*a*) Ilyrians (*b*) Phoenicians
(*c*) Lydians (*d*) Scythians

QUIZ 15

1. Who received the Pulitzer in 1955 for *A Fable* and in 1963 for *The Reivers*?
   (*a*) Ernest Hemingway (*b*) William Faulkner
   (*c*) Herman Wouk (*d*) Conrad Richter.

2. Who became president of the USA on July 10, 1850 after the death of President Zachary Taylor?
   (*a*) Abraham Lincoln (*b*) James Garfield
   (*c*) Millard Fillmore (*d*) Andrew Jackson.

3. For which film did Elizabeth Taylor win the Academy Award for the best actress in 1960?
   (*a*) *Butterfield 8* (*b*) *Who's Afraid of Virginia Woolf?*
   (*c*) *Women in Love* (*d*) *Cabaret.*

4. In Greek mythology, who served as Zeus's cupbearer?
   (*a*) Opedius (*b*) Dido (*c*) Aspasia (*d*) Ganymede.

5. Who painted *The Yellow Christ*?
   (*a*) Thomas Gainsborough (*b*) Paul Gauguin
   (*c*) Pabolo Picasso (*d*) Michaelangelo.

6. What is the other name for axiom in geometry?
   (*a*) Postulate (*b*) Angle (*c*) Rhombus (*d*) Circle.

7. What was the event called in English, which referred to Nazi crowds burning down synagogues and breaking down windows of Jewish business on November 9, 1938?
   (*a*) Night of Dark (*b*) Night of Crystal
   (*c*) Night of Broken Glass (*d*) Night of Dead.

8. On which strait does Godthab, the capital of Greenland lie?
   (*a*) Bering Strait (*b*) Denmark Strait
   (*c*) Hudson Strait (*d*) Davis Strait.

9. Mikhail Gorbachev was born on March 2, 1931 in the village of Privolnoye. To which city is it nearest to?
   (*a*) Moscow (*b*) Stavropol (*c*) Vladivostok (*d*) St. Petersburg.

10. In which sport was Richard Hadlee famous?
(*a*) Rugby (*b*) Football (*c*) Cricket (*d*) Hockey.

11. Name the pigment that transports oxygen in the blood and gives blood its red colour.
(*a*) Hemoglobin (*b*) Haemolysis
(*c*) Hemophilia (*d*) Hemorrhage.

12. Whose famous oratorio is *Messiah*, one of the most popular works in music?
(*a*) W.C. Handy (*b*) Keir Hardie
(*c*) William Hazlitt (*d*) George F. Handel.

13. Which insect is referred to as *Order Isoptera*?
(*a*) Earwig (*b*) Termite (*c*) Lacewing (*d*) Silverfish.

14. Where are the headquarters of International Atomic Energy Agency (IAEA)?
(*a*) Rome (*b*) Paris (*c*) Vienna (*d*) London.

15. Who invented a weaving machine called the *flying shuttle* in 1733?
(*a*) John Kay (*b*) Thomas Edison
(*c*) Samuel Morse (*d*) Isaac Newton.

16. The Liberation Tigers of Tamil Eelam (LTTE) has been waging a war for independence in Sri Lanka. Who is its supremo?
(*a*) Ranil Wckremesinghe (*b*) Vellupillai Prabhakaraan
(*c*) Bernard Tilakratne (*d*) Russel Arnold.

17. According to the findings of the *Human Development in South Asia 1999 Report* published by Mahbub-UL-Haque Human Development Center, Islamabad, Pakistan, which South Asian country has fared the worst in social sectors?
(*a*) Bhutan (*b*) Bangladesh (*c*) Maldives (*d*) Nepal.

18. Of the following liquids, which does not dissolve in water?
(*a*) Acetic acid (*b*) Ammonia
(*c*) Kerosene (*d*) Alcohol.

19. In World War II, which of the following code name referred to the invasion of Russia by Germany?
(*a*) Barbarossa (*b*) Dynamo (*c*) Torch (*d*) Overlord.

20. Who said the following : "I can feel the sufferings of million! And yet, it I look up into the heavens, I think what it will all come right, that this cruelty will end, and that peace and tranquility will return again"?

(*a*) Billy Graham (*b*) Edmund Morris
(*c*) Jack Benny (*d*) Anne Frank.

QUIZ 16

1. In the heavyweight boxing championship, whom did Muhammad Ali defeat on September 29, 1977?
   (*a*) Earnie Shavers (*b*) Ken Norton
   (*c*) Alfredo Evangelista (*d*) Joe Fraizer.
2. Who won the first Nobel Prize in Economics in 1969?
   (*a*) Kenneth Arrow and John Hicks
   (*b*) Theodre Schultz and Arthus Lewis
   (*c*) Robert Solow and James Tolin
   (*d*) JanTinbergen and Ragnar Frisch.
3. Among the following, which was the top single album of 1989?
   (*a*) Paula Abdul, *Cold Hearted*
   (*b*) Chicago, *Look Away*
   (*c*) Janet Jackson, *MissYou Much*
   (*d*) Anita Baker, *Giving You The Best that I Got.*
4. What is the meaning of viticulture?
   (*a*) Rice-harvesting (*b*) Grape-growing
   (*c*) Orange-growing (*d*) Strawberry-growing.
5. Which republic is often called the 'emerald isle' because of its extensive pastures?
   (*a*) Ireland (*b*) New Zealand
   (*c*) Australia (*d*) Japan.
6. Which successful operation did South African surgeon, Christian Barnard perform in 1967 for the first time?
   (*a*) Kidney operation (*b*) Pancreas operation
   (*c*) Heart transplant (*d*) Complicated eye operation.
7. Which country did Sir Thomas Stamford Raffles acquire for Britain in 1819?
   (*a*) Burma (*b*) Sudan (*c*) Korea (*d*) Singapore.

8. What is 'trichophobia'?
(*a*) Morbid fear of eyes (*b*) Morbid fear of hair
(*c*) Morbid fear of ears (*d*) Morbid fear of teeth.

9. How many kingdoms are there in the modern system of classification of living things?
(*a*) Four (*b*) Five (*c*) Six (*d*) Seven.

10. What is the electrolyte in a typical dry cell?
(*a*) Sodium sulfide (*b*) Sulfuric acetate
(*c*) Ammonium chloride (*d*) Zinc chloride.

11. Who made the following statement : "Dreams are the rough road to the unconscious" ?
(*a*) Jung (*b*) Adlar (*c*) Hurlock (*d*) Freud.

12. Who wrote *Ways of Escape*?
(*a*) Jules Verne (*b*) Graham Greene
(*c*) George Eliot (*d*) Alexander Korda.

13. Who first discovered electric waves?
(*a*) Boyle (*b*) Helmholtz (*c*) Hoffman (*d*) Hertz.

14. When did the China-Vietnam war take place?
(*a*) February 1981 (*b*) February 1980
(*c*) February 1979 (*d*) February 1978.

15. Which is the planet with the most satellites?
(*a*) Saturn (*b*) Venus (*c*) Jupiter (*d*) Pluto.

16. Which two African states formed a confederation in February 1982?
(*a*) Nigeria and Zaire (*b*) The Gambia and Senegal
(*c*) Sudan and Egypt (*d*) South Africa and Namibia.

17. *Tuber Melanosporum* is a French gastronomic delicacy. By what name is it more commonly known?
(*a*) Truffle (*b*) Cake (*c*) Ice Cream (*d*) Fruit salad.

18. What is the meaning of the adjective rectilinear?
(*a*) In a curved line (*b*) In a zigzag line
(*c*) In a straight line (*d*) In a crooked line.

19. In South Africa, what is sometimes called a 'kop' or 'kopje'?
(*a*) A deserted town (*b*) A house-full cinema hall
(*c*) A famous art center (*d*) An isolated hill.

20. What is the name of James Whistler's famous painting of his mother?

(*a*) *Arrangement in Grey and Black*

(*b*) *American Gothic*

(*c*) *The Clockmaker*

(*d*) *Young Woman with a Water Jug.*

QUIZ 17

1. The Mahalanobis model was a :
(*a*) Well-known Japanese model
(*b*) Place of pilgrimage in Saudi Arabia
(*c*) Strategy of development based on the Russian experience of planning
(*d*) Famous chess-player.

2. Leo Goossens is particularly associated with which musical instrument?
(*a*) Flute (*b*) Oboe (*c*) Piano (*d*) Saxophone.

3. In 1932, two physiologists were jointly awarded a Nobel prize for their work on the nervous system. One was Charles Sherrington. Name the other.
(*a*) Thomas Morgan (*b*) Otto H. Warburg
(*c*) George Minot (*d*) Edgar Adrian.

4. Which artist painted *The Progress of Love*?
(*a*) Jean Honore Fragonard (*b*) Pabolo Picasso
(*c*) Leonardo Da Vinci (*d*) Van Gogh.

5. Who wrote *Loving and Living*?
(*a*) Henry Green (*b*) Emily Bronte
(*c*) George Eliot (*d*) G.K. Chesterton.

6. Excavations at Ephesus between 1863 and 1874 led to the discovery of the site of one of the seven wonders of the ancient world. Which one?
(*a*) Statue of Jupiter (*b*) Temple of Diana
(*c*) Hanging Gardens (*d*) Statue of Helos.

7. What war did the Treaty of Portsmouth end?
(*a*) The Boer War
(*b*) The Punic War
(*c*) The Russia-Japanese War
(*d*) The First World War.

8. Name the Roman consul, who at the end of the second century B.C., broached reforms to transform the army units into a professional force?
(*a*) Scipio (*b*) Sulla (*c*) Hadrian (*d*) Marius.

9. What game did William Morgan invent in 1895?
(*a*) Volley ball (*b*) Basket ball
(*c*) Kick ball (*d*) Base ball.

10. Film director John Ford gave the actor, Marion Morrison, his screen name. Who was the actor?
(*a*) Charles Bronson (*b*) Gregory Peck
(*c*) John Wayne (*d*) Clark Gable.

11. In which US city did Swami Vivekananda participate in the World Parliament of Religion in 1893?
(*a*) New York (*b*) Washington
(*c*) Los Angeles (*d*) Chicago.

12. The Illium, Ischius and Pubis bones fuse together to form which bone in the human body?
(*a*) Hip bone (*b*) Compact bone
(*c*) Cancellous bone (*d*) Long bone.

13. Which Australian state was called Van Diemen's land until 1856?
(*a*) Queensland (*b*) Northern Territory
(*c*) Tasmania (*d*) Western Australia.

14. Which gas, when first recognized as an element was named Azote by the French chemist Artoine Lavoiser because of its inability to support life?
(*a*) Hydrogen (*b*) Ozone (*c*) Carbon dioxide (*d*) Nitrogen.

15. Which scientist coined all the words Cathode, Anode, Ion and Electrode?
(*a*) Alfred Nobel (*b*) Michael Faraday
(*c*) Samuel Morse (*d*) Thomas Edison.

16. Which is the second largest state in Malaysia?
(*a*) Sabah (*b*) Selangor (*c*) Perak (*d*) Pahang.

17. When did Constantine Fahlberg discover saccharin?
(*a*) 1869 (*b*) 1879 (*c*) 1889 (*d*) 1899.

18. What is the meaning of parvenu?
(*a*) The lower classes (*b*) Snob
(*c*) Parasitical (*d*) Newly rich.

19. Whose toughness and rough speech earned him the nickname 'Old Blood and Guts'?
(*a*) Dwight Eisenhower (*b*) Douglas MacArthur
(*c*) George Patton Jr. (*d*) Erwin Rommel.

20. Who was the President of the Philippines between 1948-1954?
(*a*) Diosdado Macapagal (*b*) Carlos Garcia
(*c*) Ramon Magsaysay (*d*) Elpidio Quirino.

QUIZ 18

1. Which Filipino artist painted the *El Violinista* (*The Violinist*)?
   (*a*) Juan Luna (*b*) Fabian de la Rosa
   (*c*) Victorio Edades (*d*) Felix Hidalgo.
2. Name the US Poet who lived from 1819 — 1892.
   (*a*) Edgar Allan Poe (*b*) Walt Whitman
   (*c*) Henry W. Longfellow (*d*) Emily Dickinson.
3. In which county are potatoes most produced?
   (*a*) USA (*b*) China (*c*) Poland (*d*) Russia.
4. In which East European city do you find a monument to John Hus, a religious leader of the early 1400s?
   (*a*) Budapest (*b*) Warsaw (*c*) Prague (*d*) Bucharest.
5. *Don Giovanni* (1787) and *The Magic Flute* (1791) rank among the great operas of all time. Who composed them?
   (*a*) Johanna S. Bach (*b*) Wolfgang A. Mozart
   (*c*) Ludwig van Beethoven (*d*) Joseph Haydn.
6. What are *brazils*, *milds* and *robustas*?
   (*a*) Coffee (*b*) Tea (*c*) Opium (*d*) Tobacco.
7. Which South American country's flag has a yellow stripe for the golden New World, a red stripe for the bloodshed for independence, and a blue stripe for the Atlantic Ocean?
   (*a*) Ecuador (*b*) Venezuela (*c*) Peru (*d*) Colombia.
8. Name the scientist who designed one of the first successful telephones and demonstrated it at 1876 Centennial Exposition in Philadelphia.
   (*a*) Alexander G. Bell (*b*) Thomas A. Edison
   (*c*) Samuel B. Morse (*d*) Claude Chappe.
9. Cotillion was a dance in the 1600s and 1700s which was performed by four couples. From which country did this originate?
   (*a*) Poland (*b*) Hungary (*c*) France (*d*) Spain.

10. Who won an Academy Award as best actor for his performance in *Yankee Doodle Dandy* (1942) which portrayed the life of the Broadway showman, George M. Cohan?
(*a*) Paul Lukas (*b*) James Cagney
(*c*) Gary Cooper (*d*) Bing Crosby.

11. Who won the Grand Prix World Championship in 1990?
(*a*) Ayrton Senna (*b*) Nigel Mansell
(*c*) Alain Prost (*d*) Niki Lauda.

12. At what temperature does carbon disulfide boil?
(*a*) 36.5°C (*b*) 46.5°C (*c*) 56.5°C (*d*) 66.5°C.

13. Who made the following remark before her death, "Patriotism is not enough"?
(*a*) Claude Monet (*b*) Mother Teresa
(*b*) Florence Nightingale (*c*) Edith Cavell.

14. Who succeeded Yuri V Andropov as general secretary, or head of the communist party of the Soviet Union from February 1984 to March 1985?
(*a*) Leonoid Brezhenev (*b*) Mikhail Gorbachev
(*c*) Konstantin Chernenko (*d*) Boris Yeltsin.

15. Which was the last town in England to yield to William the conqueror in 1070?
(*a*) Chester (*b*) Brighton (*c*) Kent (*d*) Reading.

16. What do you mean by analgesic?
(*a*) Causing loss of consciousness
(*b*) Causing inability to feel pain
(*c*) Forgetful
(*d*) Headache pill.

17. Specify the headquarters of the United Nations Industrial Development Organization (UNIDO)?
(*a*) Paris (*b*) London (*c*) Quebec (*d*) Vienna.

18. A mixed economy means the co-existence of which sectors?
(*a*) Commercial and subsistence farming
(*b*) Foreign and domestic investments
(*c*) Public and private sectors
(*d*) Modern and traditional industries.

19. Who gave the Pacific Ocean its name?
(*a*) Ferdinand Magellan (*b*) Christopher Columbus
(*c*) Abel Tasman (*d*) Henry Hudson.

20. Which of the following was a famous theorist of naval war?
(*a*) Alfred Mahan (*b*) Antoine Jomini
(*c*) Horatio Nelson (*d*) Gebhard Bluecher.

QUIZ 19

1. The surrender of the German Sixth Army at Stalingard marked a major turning point in World War II. Who was the German commander involved?
   (*a*) Erich Von Manstein (*b*) Friedrich Von Paulus
   (*c*) Erwin Rommel (*d*) Martin Bormann.
2. What planet of the solar system has the largest moon in relation to its own size?
   (*a*) Jupiter (*b*) Neptune (*c*) Venus (*d*) Earth.
3. Which heavyweight boxer was known as the *Brown Bomber*?
   (*a*) Sonny Liston (*b*) Joe Fraizer
   (*c*) Joe Louis (*d*) Muhammad Ali.
4. In 1950, a major earthquake measuring 8.6 on the Richter Scale hit which country?
   (*a*) India (*b*) Indonesia (*c*) China (*d*) Japan.
5. When did Napoleon conquer Egypt?
   (*a*) 1797 (*b*) 1798 (*c*) 1799 (*d*) 1800.
6. How long is a micrometre?
   (*a*) $\frac{1}{10}$ millimeter (*b*) $\frac{1}{100}$ millimeter
   (*c*) $\frac{1}{1000}$ millimeter (*d*) 1 millimeter.
7. Who wrote the Nepali book *Rupmati*?
   (*a*) Moti Ram Bhatta (*b*) Bal Krishna Sama
   (*c*) Lek Nath Poudyal (*d*) Rudra Raj Pandey.
8. Name the President of Equatorial Guinea who was assassinated in 1979 after being overthrown.
   (*a*) Macias Nguema (*b*) Obiang Nguema
   (*c*) Milton Obote (*d*) Mengistu Haile — Mariam

9. Which of the following is associated with the Spanish explorer, Juan de Onate?
(*a*) Explored what is now Florida
(*b*) Explored American Southwest
(*c*) Conquered Peru, founded Lima
(*d*) Explored Amazon River.

10. Who was he referring to when critic Christopher Morley said, "Perhaps no fiction character ever created has become so charmingly real to his readers"?
(*a*) Hercule Poirot (*b*) Perry Mason
(*c*) Sherlock Holmes (*d*) Father Brown.

11. What is a 'dreadnought'?
(*a*) Airplane (*b*) Car (*c*) Battleship (*d*) Bicycle.

12. On which river does Dresden lie?
(*a*) Danube (*b*) Elbe (*c*) Vistula (*d*) Seine.

13. Who was the last of the Achaemenid kings of Persia?
(*a*) Darius I (*b*) Xerxes I (*c*) Bardiya (*d*) Darius III.

14. According to Time Magazine, which was the best painting of the 20th century?
(*a*) *The Red Studio* by Henri Matisse
(*b*) *Dog Barking at the Moon* by Joan Miro
(*c*) *Jasper's Dilemma* by Frank Stella
(*d*) *Still-Life with Chair Caning* by Pablo Picasso.

15. Where are the headquarters of the Organization of Economic Co-operation and Development (OECD) located?
(*a*) London (*b*) Rome (*c*) Paris (*d*) Berne.

16. What is an economic theory?
(*a*) A hypothesis (*b*) A tested hypothesis
(*c*) A proposition (*d*) An axiom.

17. How do you define sanctimonious?
(*a*) Immoral (*b*) Pious
(*c*) Saintly (*d*) Hypocritically devout.

18. Which Asian city is known as 'The Pearl of the Orient'?
(*a*) Singapore (*b*) Hong Kong
(*c*) Kuala Lumpur (*d*) Manila.

19. What is 'noctiphobia'?

(*a*) Morbid fear of cows (*b*) Morbid fear of night

(*c*) Morbid fear of monkeys (*d*) Morbid fear of crowd.

20. Which explorer discovered The Mississippi River?

(*a*) Christopher Columbus (*b*) John Cabot

(*c*) Hernando de Soto (*d*) Leif Ericsson.

QUIZ 20

1. According to Time magazine, which was the best album of the 20th century?
   (*a*) *Spirits Haring Flown* by Bee Gees
   (*b*) *Exodus by Bob Marley* and the Wailers
   (*c*) *Are you Experienced?* By Jimi Hendrix
   (*d*) *Kind of Blue* by Miles Davis.
2. Where was the scientist Nicolas Copernicus born?
   (*a*) Poland (*b*) Italy (*c*) Austria (*d*) Germany.
3. Who invented refrigerator?
   (*a*) Isaac Pitman (*b*) Humphrey Davy
   (*c*) J.A. Fleming (*d*) J. Perkins.
4. Name the planet which always keeps the same side towards the sun.
   (*a*) Earth (*b*) Venus (*c*) Mercury (*d*) Mars.
5. What do we call a stock that has a good record?
   (*a*) Blue chip (*b*) Red chip (*c*) Yellow chip (*d*) Green chip.
6. Where is the Aman Folk Ensemble, a notable US Dance company, located?
   (*a*) New York (*b*) Chicago (*c*) Los Angeles (*d*) Pittsburgh.
7. Who was the Prime Minister of China between 1976 — 1980?
   (*a*) Zhou Enlai (*b*) Hua Guofeng
   (*c*) Zhao Ziyong (*d*) Li Peng.
8. *Border*, *leicister* and *corriedale* are all breeds of what?
   (*a*) Donkey (*b*) Dog (*c*) Cow (*d*) Sheep.
9. How many feet are there in a chain?
   (*a*) Sixty six (*b*) Fifty (*c*) Twenty five (*d*) Ten.
10. Simon Bolivar was, in 1928, the President of three countries. Two of them were Bolivia and Peru. Name the third.
    (*a*) Paraguay (*b*) Colombia (*c*) Uruguay (*d*) Venezuela.

11. Which explorer discovered the Niger river?
(*a*) Mungo Park (*b*) Henry Stanley
(*c*) David Livingstone (*d*) Vasco da Gama.

12. What did Babe Ruth play?
(*a*) Basketball (*b*) Football (*c*) Baseball (*d*) Volleyball.

13. Who wrote : "Art seeks to disengage itself from its own medium"?
(*a*) Plato (*b*) Socrates (*c*) Cicero (*d*) Aristotle.

14. How many pints of milk are needed to make 1lb of cheddar Cheese?
(*a*) Six (*b*) Eight (*c*) Ten (*d*) Twelve.

15. To which country do the Canary Islands belong?
(*a*) Spain (*b*) France (*c*) UK (*d*) Portugal.

16. Who wrote 'The Star — spangled Banner'?
(*a*) Francis Scott Key (*b*) Robert Frost
(*c*) Paul Revere (*d*) Frank Sinarta.

17. Who invaded India seventeen times?
(*a*) Taimurlane (*b*) Chengiz Khan
(*c*) Ibrahim Lodi (*d*) Mahmud Ghazni.

18. Give a synonym for ostensible.
(*a*) Tenable (*b*) Just (*c*) Apparent (*d*) Reasonable.

19. What is the elasticity of substitution between two perfect substitutions?
(*a*) Infinity (*b*) Less than infinity
(*c*) Greater than zero (*d*) Zero.

20. When did the International Monetary Fund (IMF) start its operation?
(*a*) 1944 (*b*) 1945 (*c*) 1946 (*d*) 1947.

QUIZ 21

1. The publication of which book established Jean-Paul Sartre as the leading French existentialist?
   (*a*) *Nausea* (*b*) *Being and Nothingness*
   (*c*) *The Flies* (*d*) *Troubled Sleep*.

2. In which country, in 1959, did Mary Leakey find the fossilized skull of a human ancestor who lived 1.8 million years ago?
   (*a*) Kenya (*b*) Ethiopia (*c*) Tanzania (*d*) Sudan.

3. In which country did the discovery of a 11th century Norse settlement take place which confirmed that Europeans reached the New World centuries earlier than Columbus did?
   (*a*) Canada (*b*) USA (*c*) Mexico (*d*) Jamaica.

4. Which countries' oceanographers found the Titanic at a depth of nearly 13,000 ft. in the Atlantic in 1985?
   (*a*) French and British (*b*) Italian and British
   (*c*) Italian and Spanish (*d*) American and French.

5. Who was the mathematician who disclosed his proof for Fermat's Last Theorem, which was put forward in the 17th century?
   (*a*) Shankar Sen (*b*) Andrew Wiles
   (*c*) J. Napier (*d*) Isaac Newton.

6. Which scientist made the following remark: "People have called it a miracle. For once in my life as a scientist, I agree. It is a miracle, and it will save lives by thousands".
   (*a*) Hans Spemann (*b*) William Einthoven
   (*c*) Alexander Fleming (*d*) Jonas Salk.

7. *The Nature of the Chemical Bond* has been the most influential chemistry book of the century. Who wrote it?
   (*a*) Linus Pauling (*b*) Francis Crick
   (*c*) James Watson (*d*) Rosalind Franklin.

8. Who was the Nazi architect of the Final Solution, who escaped from an American P.O.W. camp and dodged in and out of the Middle East for several years until he settled in Argentina in 1958?
(*a*) Joachim Von Ribbentrop (*b*) Joseph Goebbels
(*c*) Martin Bormann (*d*) Adolf Eichmann

9. What is the currency of Malaysia?
(*a*) Dinar (*b*) Ringgit (*c*) Drachma (*d*) Dollar.

10. In which film did Bruce Lee debut in 1972?
(*a*) The Big Boss (*b*) Enter the Dragon
(*c*) Fist of Fury (*d*) Way of the Dragon.

11. In which Asian country is the population density the highest?
(*a*) Bangladesh (*b*) China (*c*) Indonesia (*d*) India.

12. Who won the World Food Prize in Washington in 1987?
(*a*) Norman Borlaug (*b*) T.W. Schultz
(*c*) L.S. Venkataramanan (*d*) M.S. Swaminathan.

13. Who became the fifth man to take all four Grand Slam titles in tennis?
(*a*) Boris Becker (*b*) Andre Agassi
(*c*) Stefan Edberg (*d*) Pat Cash.

14. Who was the Papua New Guinea's Prime Minister accused of diplomatically recognizing Taiwan so as to obtain a US $ 2.3 billion loan?
(*a*) Julius Chan (*b*) Michael Somare
(*c*) Bill Skate (*d*) Paias Wingti.

15. William Shakespeare wrote about the Battle of Agincourt in a certain play. Can you name it?
(*a*) Henry V (*b*) King Lear (*c*) Hamlet (*d*) Macbeth.

16. What is the recorded date of Alexander the Great's death?
(*a*) July 14, 324 BC (*b*) June 14, 324 BC
(*c*) July 13, 323 BC (*d*) June 13, 323 BC.

17. Who was the founder of the American Red Cross?
(*a*) John Berryman (*b*) Clara Barton
(*c*) Carson McCullers (*d*) Frank Norris.

18. Name the capital of the state in USA which means 'red stick'.
(*a*) Santa Fe (*b*) Des Moines
(*c*) Baton Rogue (*d*) Carson City.

19. In economics, what would be the demand curve for a Giffen good?
(*a*) Backward falling to the left
(*b*) Upward — sloping to the right
(*c*) Downward sloping to the right
(*d*) Horizontal.

20. Indicate the headquarters of World Trade Organization (WTO).
(*a*) Paris (*b*) Montreal (*c*) Vienna (*d*) Geneva.

QUIZ 22

1. Who painted *The Maids of Honour*?
(*a*) Diego Velazquez (*b*) Juan Gris
(*c*) Joan Miro (*d*) Salvador Dali.

2. In mathematics, who introduced vector analysis in three dimensions?
(*a*) Evariste Galois (*b*) George Boole
(*c*) Josiah W. Gibbs (*d*) Ernst Zermelo.

3. Who was the 'father of modern surgery' who introduced advanced surgical techniques?
(*a*) Leeuwenhoek (*b*) Pare (*c*) Harvey (*d*) Jenner.

4. Which is the largest river on the Indo-Chinese peninsula?
(*a*) Sen (*b*) Chbar (*c*) Tamyong (*d*) Mekong.

5. *Mariner 10* became the first spacecraft to study two planets. One was Venus, which was the other?
(*a*) Mars (*b*) Jupiter (*c*) Mercury (*d*) Saturn.

6. What is a 'merganser'?
(*a*) Duck (*b*) Hen (*c*) Turkey (*d*) Eagle.

7. What is the approximate diameter of the Milky Way?
(*a*) 100,000 light years (*b*) 200,000 light years
(*c*) 300,000 light years (*d*) 400,000 light years.

8. Who brought Japan under military rule by defeating the Taira at sea in 1185 AD and the Hiraizumi in 1189 AD after being exiled from his Minamoto clan?
(*a*) Kiyomori (*b*) Yoritomo (*c*) Yoshitsune (*d*) Yoshitomo.

9. How many signs of the Zodiac are there?
(*a*) Eight (*b*) Ten (*c*) Twelve (*d*) Fourteen.

10. Jon Magnusson was Prime Minister of which Scandinavian country from 1924 — 1926?
(*a*) Denmark (*b*) Norway (*c*) Sweden (*d*) Iceland.

11. Who was defeated by Richard Nixon in the US presidential election of 1968?
(*a*) Hubert Humphrey (*b*) Adlai Stevenson
(*c*) George Wallace (*d*) Barry Goldwater.

12. What is the most radiation-sensitive part of the body?
(*a*) Heart (*b*) Blood (*c*) Artery (*d*) Intestine.

13. What do you mean by 'clowder'?
(*a*) Group of bats (*b*) Group of bears
(*c*) Group of cats (*d*) Group of donkeys.

14. By what common name is acetyl-salicylic acid known?
(*a*) Cetamol (*b*) Clozapine (*c*) Nimulid (*d*) Aspirin.

15. Who captained India to cricket World Cup Victory in 1983?
(*a*) Kapil Dev (*b*) Sunil Gavaskar
(*c*) Sachin Tendulkar (*d*) Ajit Wadkar.

16. At what age did Mozart die?
(*a*) Twenty-five (*b*) Thirty-five
(*c*) Forty-five (*d*) Fifty-five.

17. What is the meaning of frugal?
(*a*) Miserly (*b*) Bare (*c*) Thrifty (*d*) Healthy.

18. When did Charles Darwin publish *Origin of Species*?
(*a*) 1854 (*b*) 1859 (*c*) 1864 (*d*) 1869.

19. Which country produces the most lemon in a year?
(*a*) Spain (*b*) Argentina (*c*) Turkey (*d*) Italy.

20. Who debated that pure profit can arise only in a dynamic economy?
(*a*) J.B. Clark (*b*) Jacob Viner
(*c*) George Stigler (*d*) Jan Tinbergen.

QUIZ 23

1. When was Sofia, the capital of Bulgaria, founded by the Roman Emperor Trajan?
   (*a*) 100's BC (*b*) 100's AD
   (*c*) 200's AD (*d*) 300's AD.
2. Among the following medium, whose speed is greatest in metres per second?
   (*a*) Steel (*b*) Aluminum (*c*) Brick (*d*) Glass.
3. Who was Prime Minister of South Africa between 1966 — 1978?
   (*a*) D.H. Verwoerd (*b*) D.F. Malan
   (*c*) Jan Smuts (*d*) B.J. Vorster.
4. What kind of spider is African and has a large two-spined head shield?
   (*a*) Fishing spider (*b*) Redback spider
   (*c*) Kite spider (*d*) Pea spider.
5. Who directed the film Jaws (1975) and *Raiders of the Lost Ark* (1981)?
   (*a*) Oliver Stone (*b*) Steven Spielberg
   (*c*) Milos Forman (*d*) Bob Fosse.
6. On the Beaufort number, 10 signifies what kind of gale?
   (*a*) Moderate gale (*b*) Fresh gale
   (*c*) Strong gale (*d*) Whole gale.
7. Who won the men's single US Tennis championship title between 1920 — 1925?
   (*a*) Bill Tilden (*b*) Rene Lacoste
   (*c*) Fred Perry (*d*) Don Budge.
8. Who said the following "I have the same recollection of Greek in youth that I have of castor oil"?
   (*a*) Robert L. Stevenson (*b*) Victor Hugo
   (*c*) William M. Thackeray (*d*) Walter Scott.

9. Rand Corporation is a non-profit research organization that studies various problem of the United States, especially those involving what?
(*a*) Agricultural products (*b*) National defense
(*c*) Transport (*d*) Aircraft.

10. Who wrote *The Ballad of Reading Gaol* in 1898?
(*a*) John Bunyan (*b*) D.H. Lawrence
(*c*) Ben Johnson (*d*) Oscar Wilde.

11. What did the Ringling brothers form in the USA?
(*a*) Circus (*b*) Baseball
(*c*) Charity organizations (*d*) YMCA.

12. What is the Golden Rule?
(*a*) God helps those who help themselves
(*b*) Early to bed and early to rise makes a man healthy, wealthy and wise
(*c*) Do unto others, as you would have them do unto you
(*d*) Do not cry over spilt milk.

13. Who painted *The Last Supper*?
(*a*) Pabolo Picasso (*b*) Leonardo Da Vinci
(*c*) Van Gogh (*d*) James Whistler.

14. Among the gospels, which is the shortest?
(*a*) Mark (*b*) John (*c*) Matthew (*d*) Luke.

15. Which record won the Grammy Award in 1983?
(*a*) George Benson, *This Masquerde*
(*b*) Christopher Cross, *Sailing*
(*c*) Michael Jackson, *Beat It*
(*d*) Paul Simon, *Graceland.*

16. Which is Nigeria's second largest city?
(*a*) Lagos (*b*) Abuja (*c*) Kano (*d*) Ibadan.

17. Which Secretary-General of the United Nations published Markings, a book of poetry, prayers and prose sayings?
(*a*) Trygve Lie (*b*) Dag Hammarskjold
(*c*) U Thant (*d*) Kurt Waldheim.

18. What is the antonym for frump?
(*a*) Unattractive woman (*b*) Woman with uncombed hair
(*c*) Vagabond (*d*) Slut.

19. Among the following, which oligopoly model is concerned with the maximization of joint profits?
(*a*) Edgeworth's model (*b*) Bertrand's model
(*c*) Collusive model (*d*) Price leadership model.

20. What are 'lycees' in France?
(*a*) Primary schools (*b*) Colleges
(*c*) Universities (*d*) Secondary schools.

QUIZ 24

1. Who won the 1934 Academy Award as best actor for his performance in *It Happened One Night*?
   (*a*) Frank Sinarta (*b*) Clark Gable
   (*c*) Richard Burton (*d*) Lee Van Clef.
2. In which city in Israel is Elijah's cave located?
   (*a*) Jerusalem (*b*) Tel Aviv (*c*) Jaffna (*d*) Haifa.
3. Which European nation was the first to drink tea?
   (*a*) Netherlands (*b*) Austria (*c*) Portugal (*d*) France.
4. What is the capital of Saudi Arabia?
   (*a*) Riyadh (*b*) Mecca (*c*) Medina (*d*) Jeddah.
5. What is the chief ingredient of *sauce lyonnaise*?
   (*a*) Potato (*b*) Bean (*c*) Onion (*d*) Radish.
6. In 1982, who attempted to assassinate President Ronald Regan?
   (*a*) Lee Harvey Oswald (*b*) John W. Hinckley Jr.
   (*c*) Charles J. Guiteau (*d*) John W. Booth.
7. Who was the founder of Saudi Arabia and its first king?
   (*a*) Faisal (*b*) Farouk (*c*) Idris (*d*) Ibn Saud.
8. Penicillin was introduced in hospitals in Nepal after 1950. Who discovered it?
   (*a*) Alexander Fleming (*b*) Charles Darwin
   (*c*) William Harvey (*d*) Thomas Morgan.
9. Which country won the World Cup football finals in 1934 and 1938?
   (*a*) Uruguay (*b*) Brazil (*c*) Italy (*d*) UK.
10. The Spingarn medal has been awarded annually since 1914 by the National Association for the Advancement of coloured people for the highest achievement by a black American. Who received the award in 1967?
    (*a*) Martin Luther king Jr. (*b*) Roy Wilkins
    (*c*) Robert C. Weaver (*d*) Sammy Davis Jr.

11. Who was the co-pilot of the ill-fated Egypt Air Flight 990 which crashed on October 31, 1999?
(*a*) Gamil El-Batouti (*b*) Adel Anwar
(*c*) Ahmed El-Habashi (*d*) Raouf Noureddin.

12. What sort of punishment was a gibbet in former days?
(*a*) Hanging (*b*) Stabbing
(*c*) Crucifying (*d*) Beheading.

13. Before becoming a disciple of Jesus, what was Matthew's occupation?
(*a*) Hunter (*b*) Sailor (*c*) Tax-collector (*d*) Soldier.

14. What is the meaning of bedrock?
(*a*) Diabolical (*b*) Pagan (*c*) Closed (*d*) Foundation.

15. What is the other name that is given to the average revenue curve?
(*a*) Indifference curve (*b*) Demand curve
(*c*) Average cost curve (*d*) Profit curve.

16. Which organic chemical bond between two carbon atoms can be early disrupted?
(*a*) A triple bond (*b*) A double bond
(*c*) A single bond (*d*) An aromatic ring.

17. What percentage of an egg's weight is the shell?
(*a*) 6 per cent (*b*) 12 per cent
(*c*) 18 per cent (*d*) 24 per cent.

18. With which organ does a snake hear?
(*a*) Teeth (*b*) Mouth (*c*) Ear (*d*) Tongue.

19. World War II started with the invasion of which country by Germany?
(*a*) Czechoslovakia (*b*) Austria (*c*) Poland (*d*) Hungary.

20. Who was described as the following : "He had perfect pitch and perfect rhythm. His improvised melodies and singing could be as lofty as a moon flight or as low down as the blood drops of a sweet thug dying in the gutter"?
(*a*) Louis Armstrong (*b*) Igor Stravinsky
(*c*) Coco Chanel (*d*) Lucille Ball.

QUIZ 25

1. In the election of 1953. Eisenhower and Nixon defeated the Democratic candidates Adlai E. Stevenson and Whom?
   (*a*) Lyndon B. Johnson (*b*) John J. Sparkman
   (*c*) George Wallace (*d*) Edmund Muskie.
2. Elbe River is one of the most important commercial waterways of central Europe. From which country's western part does it rise?
   (*a*) Austria (*b*) Hungary (*c*) Switzerland (*d*) Czech Republic.
3. A man is standing on a weighing machine in a lift. His weight will be maximum when the lift is moving :
   (*a*) Upward at uniform speed
   (*b*) Upward with uniform acceleration
   (*c*) Downward with uniform acceleration
   (*d*) In a free fall.
4. When did Henry VIII unite England and Wales?
   (*a*) 1516 (*b*) 1526 (*c*) 1536 (*d*) 1542.
5. Diverticulitis is a common disease of what?
   (*a*) Liver (*b*) Colon (*c*) Skin (*d*) Pancreas.
6. Cable is a unit of nautical measurement. How long is a British cable?
   (*a*) 155 meters (*b*) 165 meters (*c*) 175 meters (*d*) 185 meters.
7. Name the British Prime Minister whose autobiography is titled Time and Chance?
   (*a*) James Callaghan (*b*) Clement Atlee
   (*c*) Winston Churchill (*d*) Edward Heath.
8. Who served as Governor General of Australia from 1965 — 1969?
   (*a*) John Gray Gorton (*b*) James Scullin
   (*c*) Richard Gardiner Casey (*d*) Arthur Fadden.

9. During the reign of Charlemagne, what was the capital of Austrasia?
(*a*) Barcelona (*b*) Aachen (*c*) Pavia (*d*) Bordeaux.

10. Name the planet which has the highest atmosphere.
(*a*) Saturn (*b*) Jupiter (*c*) Uranus (*d*) Neptune.

11. Who discovered insulin?
(*a*) Alexander Fleming (*b*) William Harvey
(*c*) Frank Whittle (*d*) Frederick Banting.

12. By how many year was Mahatma Gandhi older than Jawahar Lal Nehru?
(*a*) 5 years (*b*) 10 years (*c*) 15 years (*d*) 20 years.

13. Which gland in the human body secretes the hormone, *cortisone*?
(*a*) The pineal gland (*b*) The adrenal gland
(*c*) The thyroid gland (*d*) The prostate gland.

14. *Riksdag* is the parliament of which North European country?
(*a*) Denmark (*b*) Norway (*c*) Sweden (*d*) Finland.

15. In which country was 'Negus' a title of the sovereign or king?
(*a*) Ethiopia (*b*) Central African Republic
(*c*) Saudi Arabia (*d*) Jordan.

16. In geometry, which angle is called a reflex angle?
(*a*) A straight line (*b*) An angle less than 90°
(*c*) An angle exactly equal to 90°
(*d*) An angle greater than a straight line.

17. Which poet has said "Nature is the art of god"?
(*a*) Goethe (*b*) Dante (*c*) Henry Longfellow (*d*) Oscar Wilde.

18. Who painted the Swing?
(*a*) Nicolas Poussin (*b*) Claesz Heda
(*c*) Jean Honore Fragonard (*d*) Jan Vermeer.

19. What is larceny?
(*a*) Theft (*b*) Rape (*c*) Murder (*d*) Robbery.

20. Identify Irving Fisher's work from the following :
(*a*) *The Affluent Society* (*b*) *The Economics of Labour*
(*c*) *Money, Credit and Commerce*
(*d*) *The Making of Index Numbers*.

QUIZ 26

1. When Marich Man Singh Shrestha became Prime Minister of Nepal in June 1986, who became the Minister for Forest and Soil Conservation?
   (*a*) Hem Bahadur Malla Thakuri
   (*b*) Ramananda Prasad Yadav
   (*c*) Tejendra Bahadur Khadka
   (*d*) Parsu Narayan Chaudhary.
2. *Economics* by Paul Samuelson has been a best seller. Recently, it is being co-authored with another American economist. Name him.
   (*a*) Lester Thurow (*b*) William Nordhaus
   (*c*) Thomas Sargent (*d*) Richard Quandt.
3. Who played the male leading role in the film, *The Grapes of Wrath*?
   (*a*) Clark Gable (*b*) Gary Cooper
   (*c*) Marlon Brando (*d*) Henry Fonda.
4. Who wrote two autobiographies named Daybreak and and a Voice to Sing With?
   (*a*) Charles Perrault (*b*) Thornton N. Wilder
   (*c*) Joan Baez (*d*) Sean O'Casey.
5. Which river is considered to be the chief commercial waterway of the Balkans?
   (*a*) Moravo (*b*) Vardar (*c*) Maritsa (*d*) Danube.
6. On October 15, 1783, a French scientist became the first person to make a balloon ascent by rising about 25 meter in a captive Montgolfier balloon. Name him.
   (*a*) Jean Francois Pilatre De Rozier
   (*b*) Jacques Alexandre Charles
   (*c*) Marie-Noel Robert
   (*d*) Andre Garnerin.

7. Who painted *The Artist's Studio*?
(*a*) Anton Van Dyck (*b*) Gustave Courbet
(*c*) Diego Velazquez (*d*) Rembrandt.

8. South Africa has two official languages. One is Afrikaans, what is the other?
(*a*) Belgian (*b*) Dutch (*c*) English (*d*) French.

9. How much perspiration does an average pair of feet give off daily?
(*a*) ½ pint (*b*) 1 pint (*c*) 1½ pints (*d*) 2 pints.

10. Approximately what percentage of the earth's surface is covered by glaciers?
(*a*) 5 per cent (*b*) 10 per cent (*c*) 15 per cent (*d*) 20 per cent.

11. Which county's currency is said to be the most difficult to counterfeit?
(*a*) France (*b*) Thailand (*c*) USA (*d*) Japan.

12. Which country is the world's greatest producer of jute?
(*a*) Sri Lanka (*b*) Malaysia (*c*) Bangladesh (*d*) India.

13. With which outdoor game is Rovers cup associated?
(*a*) Volleyball (*b*) Basketball
(*c*) Badminton (*d*) Football.

14. Which position did Nepal adopt in the Arab-Israel conflict?
(*a*) Remained neutral (*b*) Declined to take part
(*c*) Supported Israelis (*d*) Supported Arabs.

15. Who invented photography?
(*a*) Lippman (*b*) L. Daguerre
(*c*) Henry Baqoeral (*d*) M. M. Curie.

16. When is Teacher's Day celebrated?
(*a*) September 5 (*b*) September 10
(*c*) September 15 (*d*) September 20.

17. What are lines joining places with the similar barometric pressures known as?
(*a*) Ballistic (*b*) Isogenics (*c*) Isobars (*d*) Isotherm.

18. When did USA enter World War II?
(*a*) September 7, 1941 (*b*) October 7, 1941
(*c*) November 7, 1941 (*d*) December 7, 1941.

19. Who said, "Thank God, I have done my duty"?

(*a*) Mahatma Gandhi (*b*) Adolf Hitler

(*c*) Otts Bismark (*d*) Horatio Nelson.

20. What do you mean by verdant?

(*a*) Well — wooded (*b*) Green

(*c*) Fragrant (*d*) Sonorous.

QUIZ 27

1. In which country do Walloons live?
   (*a*) France (*b*) Spain (*c*) UK (*d*) Belgium.
2. How many inches does 1 span make?
   (*a*) 3 inches (*b*) 6 inches (*c*) 9 inches (*d*) 12 inches.
3. When did Uruguay gain Independence?
   (*a*) 1824 (*b*) 1828 (*c*) 1832 (*d*) 1836.
4. Name the scientific satellite that conducted radio astronomy research on the far side of the moon.
   (*a*) Nimbus-7 (*b*) Explorer-49 (*c*) Heao-3 (*d*) OS0-1.
5. Of which nationality was the painter Murillo?
   (*a*) Spanish (*b*) French (*c*) British (*d*) Italian.
6. Squid is a marine mollusc (animal with a soft, boneless body) that is similar to the octopus, nautilus and cuttlefish. How many arms does a squid have?
   (*a*) Four (*b*) Six (*c*) Eight (*d*) Ten.
7. What is a 'stonechat'?
   (*a*) An animal (*b*) An insect (*c*) A tree (*d*) A bush.
8. For which film did Meryl Streep receive an Academy Award for the best supporting actress in 1982?
   (*a*) *The Deer Hunter* (*b*) *Out of Africa*
   (*c*) *Kramer vs Kramer* (*d*) *A Cry in the Dark.*
9. Two major countries remained neutral in both World War I and World War II. Switzerland is one. Which is the other?
   (*a*) Norway (*b*) Sweden (*c*) Holland (*d*) Denmark.
10. When was the Argnad lamp invented?
    (*a*) 1720s (*b*) 1740s (*c*) 1760s (*d*) 1780s.
11. Which is the largest island in the Philippines?
    (*a*) Luzon (*b*) Mindanao (*c*) Cebu (*d*) Palawan.

12. Who wrote *The Scarlet Letter* in 1850?
(*a*) Herman Melville (*b*) Mark Twain
(*c*) Nathaniel Hawthorne (*d*) Henry James.

13. In nuclear energy, what is an electrically uncharged particle in a nucleus called?
(*a*) Proton (*b*) Neutron (*c*) Electron (*d*) Isotope.

14. Which embassy did the Iranian revolutionaries take over on November 4, 1979 and seized its citizens as hostages?
(*a*) France (*b*) USA (*c*) UK (*d*) Canada.

15. Which vitamin is also known as thiamine?
(*a*) Vitamin B_{12} (*b*) Vitamin B_6
(*c*) Vitamin B_2 (*d*) Vitamin B_1

16. Who was the chief god in Norse mythology?
(*a*) Odin (*b*) Ve (*c*) Vili (*d*) Ymir.

17. In which track and field event are the Western Roll and Scissors methods used?
(*a*) Long Jump (*b*) Javelin (*c*) High Jump (*d*) Shot-put.

18. How many letters are there in the Greek alphabet?
(*a*) Twenty-two (*b*) Twenty-four
(*c*) Twenty-six (*d*) Twenty-eight.

19. What do you mean by tergiversate?
(*a*) Contradict (*b*) Make excuses
(*c*) Hesitate (*d*) Change Loyalties.

20. With which money is fiat money associated?
(*a*) International money (*b*) Quasi money
(*c*) Legal money (*d*) Token money.

QUIZ 28

1. Name the code of the Anglo-American military operation of the June 1944 Normandy landings.
   (*a*) Operation Overlord (*b*) Operation Counterspy
   (*c*) Operation Desert Storm (*d*) Operation Desert Calm.
2. Which European power administered the Nicobar Islands before the British took over in 1868?
   (*a*) Spain (*b*) Portugal (*c*) Denmark (*d*) Netherlands.
3. What is the more common name for the malaise *circardian rhythm stress*?
   (*a*) Motor car lag (*b*) Jet lag (*c*) Ship lag (*d*) Train lag.
4. Which game that became popular in England in the mid-nineteenth century takes its name from the French for 'little hook'?
   (*a*) Snooker (*b*) Billiards (*c*) Pool (*d*) Croquet.
5. Who was the first Russian Emperor to use the imperial title Tzar?
   (*a*) Ivan the Terrible (*b*) Peter the Great
   (*c*) Alexander II (*d*) Nicholas II.
6. In ancient Indian history, by what name do we better know the former dacoit, Ratnakar?
   (*a*) Dronacharya (*b*) Valmiki
   (*c*) Vishwamitra (*d*) Basistha.
7. Of what creature are *tiger* and *sand* types?
   (*a*) Tigers (*b*) Crocodiles (*c*) Sharks (*d*) Buffaloes.
8. Which musical instrument was invented by Italian harpsichord maker Bartolemeo Christoforic in Florence in 1709?
   (*a*) The Piano (*b*) The Guitar
   (*c*) The Harmonium (*d*) The Drum.

9. By what name was Belgian born Oscar winning screen star and one time UNICEF Goodwill Ambassador Eda Von Heemstra better known?

(*a*) Elizabeth Taylor (*b*) Audrey Hepuburn
(*c*) Sophia Loren (*d*) Julie Andrews.

10. In which European city was a treaty of eight communist European countries under a unified military command signed in 1955?

(*a*) Prague (*b*) Budapest (*c*) Sofia (*d*) Warsaw.

11. Which scientist has been called the 'Father of Modern Physics'?

(*a*) Albert Einstein (*b*) Joseph Thomson
(*c*) Isaac Newton (*d*) Stephen Hawking.

12. To whom is the Latin phrase *caveat emptor* a warning?

(*a*) A purchaser (*b*) A producer
(*c*) A seller (*d*) A retailer.

13. According to St. Matthew, Jesus said : "Among them that are born of women there hath not risen a greater than…" Who?

(*a*) Lazarus (*b*) Peter (*c*) John the Baptist (*d*) Saul.

14. Saturn has ten moons. What is the largest called?

(*a*) Rhea (*b*) Dione (*c*) Titan (*d*) Phoebe.

15. What general physical distinction was common to these literary characters : Pantagruel, Despair and Cormoran?

(*a*) They were all midgets (*b*) They were all giants
(*c*) They were all deaf (*d*) They were all blind.

16. Shylock is found in which of Shakespeare's plays?

(*a*) *The Merchant of Venice*
(*b*) *Two Gentlemen of Verona*
(*c*) *A Midsummer Night's Dream*
(*d*) *Love's Labour's Lost.*

17. Who invented dynamo?

(*a*) Michael Faraday (*b*) Alfred Nobel
(*c*) Thomas Edison (*d*) Samuel Morse

18. In the eighteenth century, Hester Bateman mainly worked in a metal. Which was it?

(*a*) Gold (*b*) Platinum (*c*) Copper (*d*) Silver.

19. Which constellation has both a belt and a sword?
(*a*) Andromeda (*b*) Cassiopeia
(*c*) Orion (*d*) Perseus.

20. Who is usually associated with the cash transactions approach to the quantity theory of money?
(*a*) Don Patinkin (*b*) Milton Friedman
(*c*) Irving Fisher (*d*) M.L. Bursten.

QUIZ 29

1. If Lawn Tennis takes place in Wimbledon in England, where is it held in the USA?
   (*a*) Forest Hill (*b*) Rodger Kingdom
   (*c*) Madison Square Garden (*d*) Brooklyn.
2. Which of the following is true about energy?
   (*a*) Can be neither created nor destroyed
   (*b*) Can be converted from one form to another
   (*c*) Can be destroyed
   (*d*) Can be created.
3. Who was the author of *Candide*?
   (*a*) Thomas Hardy (*b*) D.H. Lawrence
   (*c*) Voltaire (*d*) Ernest Hemingway.
4. The name 'Greek' is associated with which industry?
   (*a*) Paper goods (*b*) Electrical goods
   (*c*) Garment (*d*) Lenses.
5. Who discovered the solar system?
   (*a*) Galileo (*b*) Descartes (*c*) Copernicus (*d*) Kepler.
6. What do all insects have?
   (*a*) Wings
   (*b*) Potential to harm
   (*c*) Three pairs of jeweled appendages
   (*d*) Four pairs of jeweled appendages.
7. Sound waves cannot travel in :
   (*a*) Vacuum (*b*) Gases (*c*) Liquids (*d*) Solids.
8. To which country does the Xinhua News Agency belong?
   (*a*) Korea (*b*) China (*c*) Vietnam (*d*) Thailand.
9. Who is the creator of the 'Bonnet Family' in fiction?
   (*a*) George Eliot (*b*) Emily Bronte
   (*c*) Boris Pasternak (*d*) Jane Austen.

10. Who said, "The old order changeth yielding place to the new"?
(*a*) Alfred Tennyson (*b*) Thomas Hardy
(*c*) Alexander Pope (*d*) John Milton.

11. Which is the hottest place in the world?
(*a*) Tiratsvi, Israel (*b*) 'Al' Az'ziyah, Libya
(*c*) Seville, Spain (*d*) Death Valley, California.

12. When did the battle of Bosworth Field which ended 'The War of Roses' take place?
(*a*) 1487 (*b*) 1486 (*c*) 1485 (*d*) 1484.

13. Who received the Nobel Prize for literature in 1970?
(*a*) Yasunari Kawabata (*b*) Boris Pasternak
(*c*) William Golding (*d*) Aleksandr Solzhenitsyn.

14. Which sun-goddess do the Japanese claim legendary descent of their emperors?
(*a*) Amatresu (*b*) Himiko (*c*) Izanagi (*d*) Dainichi.

15. Which flower is the symbol of secrecy?
(*a*) Lotus (*b*) Pansy (*c*) Gomphrena (*d*) Rose.

16. Cete is the collective name of what?
(*a*) Bees (*b*) Badgers (*c*) Otters (*d*) Wolves.

17. Tabso is the airline of which country?
(*a*) Albania (*b*) Serbia (*c*) Bulgaria (*d*) Romania.

18. Who plays the fictitious heir to the British throne in the 1976 film Seven Nights in Japan?
(*a*) Michael York (*b*) Kirk Douglas
(*c*) Robert Mitchum (*d*) Richard Burton.

19. In what is a herpetologist interested?
(*a*) Whales (*b*) Birds (*c*) Men (*d*) Reptiles.

20. When was the Asian Development Fund (ADF) launched by the ADB with a view to provide concessional credit to needy members formed?
(*a*) 1978 (*b*) 1976 (*c*) 1974 (*d*) 1972.

QUIZ 30

1. Who were 'Wali Sanga'?
   (*a*) Muslim saints (*b*) Buddhist saints
   (*c*) Hindu saints (*d*) Christian saints.
2. Which is the largest country in the world?
   (*a*) Canada (*b*) USA (*c*) Liechtenstein (*d*) Russia.
3. During World War II, when did the allied forces invade Sicily?
   (*a*) July 10, 1941 (*b*) June 10, 1942
   (*c*) July 10 1943 (*d*) June 10, 1944.
4. In 1932 Olympic games, who set three world records in 80-meter hurdles, the javelin throw and the high jump?
   (*a*) Tilly Fleischer (*b*) Babe Didrikson Zaharias
   (*c*) Trebisonda Valla (*d*) Ibolya Csak.
5. Songhai Empire was a black trading state in Africa that reached its peak in the 1400s and 1500s. What was its capital?
   (*a*) Gao (*b*) Walata (*c*) Tekedda (*d*) Kano.
6. Who launched the first successful liquid-propellant rocket in 1926 that burned petrol and liquid oxygen?
   (*a*) Albert Einstein (*b*) Robert H. Goddard
   (*c*) F.A. Tsander (*d*) Wernher Von Braun.
7. What is a 'lammergeier'?
   (*a*) Owl (*b*) Kingfisher (*c*) Sparrow (*d*) Vulture.
8. How did the French chemist, Antoine L. Lavoisier, die?
   (*a*) Typhoid (*b*) Suicide (*c*) Execution (*d*) Accident.
9. Sesotho, a Bantu language, is one of the two official languages of Lesotho. What is the other language?
   (*a*) French (*b*) English (*c*) Portuguese (*d*) German.

10. In newspaper terms, *scoop* refers to a story obtained by a newspaper without the knowledge of its competitors. What is another name for *scoop*?
(*a*) Exclusive (*b*) Squib (*c*) Masthead (*d*) Beat.

11. Which African country has the national anthem, 'Arise, O Compatriots'?
(*a*) Libya (*b*) Sudan (*c*) Kenya (*d*) Nigeria.

12. Who is sometimes described as 'one of the greatest names in the history of human thought' because of his great contribution to mathematics, physics and astronomy?
(*a*) Robert Boyle (*b*) Albert Einstein
(*c*) Isaac Newton (*d*) Thomas A. Edison.

13. Who wrote *The Expedition of Humphry Clinker* in 1771?
(*a*) Henry Felding (*b*) Tobias Smollett
(*c*) Samuel Richardson (*d*) Daniel Defoe.

14. When was Harvard College founded in USA?
(*a*) 1636 (*b*) 1646 (*c*) 1656 (*d*) 1666.

15. In opera, who composed *Bomarzo* in 1967?
(*a*) Karl — Birger Blomdahl (*b*) Alberto Ginastera
(*c*) Benjamin Britten (*d*) Virgil Thomson.

16. What is the meaning of the German word 'jager'?
(*a*) Sailor (*b*) Politician (*c*) Fisherman (*d*) Hunter.

17. Name the Swedish diplomat who saved about 100,000 Hungarian Jews from being massacred during World War II.
(*a*) Birgit Nilsson (*b*) Gustavus Vasa
(*c*) Raoul Wallenberg (*d*) Claes Oldenburg.

18. In mathematics, who developed a tiling made up of two types of rhombuses that has no repeating patterns?
(*a*) Emmy Noether (*b*) Roger Penrose
(*c*) Kurt Godel (*d*) Allan Turing.

19. Who stated that bad money drives good money out of circulation?
(*a*) Thomas Gresham (*b*) David Ricardo
(*c*) Adam Smith (*d*) Thomas Malthus.

20. What is the meaning of somatology?

(*a*) Study of abnormal psyche

(*b*) Study of microorganisms

(*c*) Study of the life cycle of diseases

(*d*) Study of the structure and function of the body.

QUIZ 31

1. Which is the largest city in South America?
   (*a*) Santiago (*b*) Rio de Janeiro (*c*) Lima (*d*) Sao Paulo.
2. Timgad, part of the giant Roman Empire, was built around 100 AD. In which present — day country does it fall?
   (*a*) Algeria (*b*) Libya (*c*) Tunisia (*d*) Morocco.
3. Who wrote *The Decline of the West* (1918-1922)?
   (*a*) Arnold Toynbee (*b*) Oswald Spengler
   (*c*) George W.F. Hegel (*d*) Winston Churchill.
4. Who produced *Poeme Electronique*, the first major work of electronic music?
   (*a*) Edgard Varese (*b*) Johannes Brahms
   (*c*) Arnold Schoenberg (*d*) Hector Berlioz.
5. How did Robert Clive, the British administrator and military leader who brought India into the British Empire, die?
   (*a*) Assassination (*b*) Execution (*c*) Suicide (*d*) Accident.
6. Which country produces the most coconut?
   (*a*) Sri Lanka (*b*) India (*c*) Philippines (*d*) Indonesia.
7. In which year did the British physicist James C. Maxwell report his theory of electromagnetism, which led to radio?
   (*a*) 1854 (*b*) 1864 (*c*) 1874 (*d*) 1884.
8. What is the cube root of 216?
   (*a*) 3 (*b*) 4 (*c*) 5 (*d*) 6.
9. Where was Muhammad, prophet of Islam, born in Saudi Arabia?
   (*a*) Madina (*b*) Mecca (*c*) Jidda (*d*) Riyadh.
10. Who is the goddess of mercy in Chinese Buddhism?
    (*a*) Guanyin (*b*) Aizen Myo-o (*c*) Nataraja (*d*) U ta

11. Who first isolated selenium, a chemical element, in 1817?
(*a*) Robert Boyle (*b*) Hans Selye
(*c*) Jons J. Berzelius (*d*) Nikolai N. Semenov.

12. In *Julius Caesar*, who said these words "Friends, Romans, countrymen, lend me you ears"?
(*a*) Brutus (*b*) Augustus (*c*) Cassius (*d*) Mark Antony.

13. Who directed the films *Lawrence of Arabia* and *Dr. Zhivago* in which Omar Sharif played the leading role?
(*a*) David Lean (*b*) Frank Capra
(*c*) William Wyler (*d*) Tony Richardson.

14. What is a 'pava'?
(*a*) Cat (*b*) Rodent (*c*) Dog (*d*) Bear.

15. Among the following, which country produces the most paper and paperboard?
(*a*) China (*b*) Canada (*c*) Japan (*d*) USA.

16. In World War II, in which country did the Battle of the Bulge take place?
(*a*) France (*b*) Italy (*c*) Belgium (*d*) Germany.

17. Which sport does the pelota resemble?
(*a*) Handball (*b*) Volleyball (*c*) Basketball (*d*) Kickball.

18. There are only two mammals that reproduce by laying eggs. Spiny anteater is one, which is the other?
(*a*) Kangaroo (*b*) Koala (*c*) Wombat (*d*) Platypus.

19. In which region has the number of poor increased between 1985 and 2000?
(*a*) East Asia (*b*) Sub-Saharan Africa
(*c*) Eastern Europe (*d*) Central America.

20. What do you mean by ekistics?
(*a*) The study of extremely backward tribes
(*b*) The study of human settlements
(*c*) The study of animals in their natural habitat
(*d*) The study of the patterns of suburban settlements.

QUIZ 32

1. Which country is known as the *Sickman of Europe*?
   (*a*) Greece (*b*) Turkey (*c*) Cyprus (*d*) Albania.
2. What is a group of peacocks called?
   (*a*) Husk (*b*) Pride (*c*) Muster (*d*) Gaggle.
3. What is the capital of Finland?
   (*a*) Helsinki (*b*) Stockholm (*c*) Oslo (*d*) Copenhagen.
4. Who won the gold medal in the men 100-meter breaststroke in the 1972 Olympics?
   (*a*) Mark Spitz (*b*) Nobutaka Taguchi
   (*c*) Don Mckenzie (*d*) Duncan Goodhew.
5. In which island is the Auyuittuq National Park located?
   (*a*) Staten Island (*b*) Caribbean Islands
   (*c*) Borneo Island (*d*) Baffin Island.
6. Who created the ballads, namely, *Prince Igor*, *The Firebird* and *Petrouchka*?
   (*a*) Michael Fokine (*b*) Marius Petipa
   (*c*) George Balanchine (*d*) August Bournonville.
7. In the New Testament of the Bible, whom did Jesus identify as Satan?
   (*a*) Devil (*b*) Joshua (*c*) Beelzebub (*d*) Ezekiel.
8. Which county is the leading producer of bauxite?
   (*a*) India (*b*) Brazil (*c*) Jamaica (*d*) Australia.
9. Ngultrum is the monetary unit of which country?
   (*a*) China (*b*) Bhutan (*c*) Malaysia (*d*) Kampuchea.
10. Who became the Chairman of the Presidium of Supreme Soviet in 1965?
    (*a*) Nikolai V. Podgorny (*b*) Nikita S. Khrushchev
    (*c*) Leonid I. Brezhnev (*d*) Alexsei N. Kosygin.

11. In bridge, what is the failure to make a contract called?
(*a*) Overcall (*b*) Board (*c*) Rubber (*d*) Sel.

12. Bromine was first prepared in 1826 almost simultaneously by Antoine J. Balard, a French Chemist and a German Chemist. Name the German.
(*a*) Georg Buchner (*b*) Richard Kuhn
(*c*) Carl J. Lowig (*d*) Otto Hahn.

13. Who wrote the satirical novel *Erewhon* in 1872 which ridicules English institutions and customs through the eyes of a traveler in a strange new world?
(*a*) Jonathan Swift (*b*) Samuel Butler
(*c*) Daniel Defoe (*d*) Walter Scott.

14. Which American President was known as 'Man of the People'?
(*a*) Andrew Jackson (*b*) George Washington
(*c*) Abraham Lincoln (*d*) John F. Kennedy.

15. Which vitamin is called the 'antisterility' vitamin?
(*a*) Vitamin B (*b*) Vitamin C (*c*) Vitamin D (*d*) Vitamin E.

16. Who is the author of *King Lear*?
(*a*) Charles Dickens (*b*) Geofrey Chaucer
(*c*) William Shakespeare (*d*) Alfred Tennyson.

17. When did Wilhelm Roentgen discover X-ray?
(*a*) 1890 (*b*) 1895 (*c*) 1900 (*d*) 1905.

18. Who said the following, "I fall, I stand still.... I trudge on, I gain a little.... I get more eager and climb higher and begin to see the widening horizon. Every struggle is a victory."
(*a*) Helen Keller (*b*) Tenzing Norgay
(*c*) Napoleon Bonaparte (*d*) Annette Funicello.

19. In which growth model was the capital-output ratio employed for development planning?
(*a*) Sen model (*b*) Hicks model
(*c*) Kaldor model (*d*) Harrod-Domar model.

20. In which village in North China does the painted pottery culture of late Neolithic period show its presence?
(*a*) Yang Shao (*b*) Lan-T'ien
(*c*) Pan-P'o (*d*) Ch'ang-An.

QUIZ 33

1. La Paz is the highest capital in the world. Which is the second highest capital in South America?
   (*a*) Quito (*b*) Asuncion (*c*) Bogota (*d*) Santiago.
2. What is the colour of an emu's egg?
   (*a*) White (*b*) Green (*c*) Yellow (*d*) Brown.
3. Who wrote the *Middlemarch* (1871 — 1872)?
   (*a*) Emily Bronte (*b*) Joseph Conrad
   (*c*) Matthew Arnold (*d*) George Eliot.
4. Whose most important accomplishment was introducing screw propellers for use in place of paddle wheels on ships?
   (*a*) Leif Ericsson (*b*) Bjarni Herjulfsson
   (*c*) John Ericsson (*d*) Christopher Columbus.
5. What are *kayaks* and *umiaks*?
   (*a*) Boats (*b*) Light houses
   (*c*) Elephants (*d*) Art Galleries.
6. Which of the following is associated with the Scottish explorer, James Bruce?
   (*a*) Explored the Congo River
   (*b*) Reached Lake Tanganyika and Lake Victoria
   (*c*) Rediscovered source of he Blue Nile
   (*d*) Explored course of the Niger River.
7. Who was the first person of Jewish ancestry to becomes Prime Minister of Great Britain?
   (*a*) Lloyd George (*b*) Neville Chamberlain
   (*c*) Edward Heath (*d*) Benjamin Disraeli.
8. John Herbert Dillinger was one of the most notorious criminals in USA history. Where was he born?
   (*a*) Salt Lake City (*b*) Houston
   (*c*) Santa Fe (*d*) Indianapolis.

9. In dog terminology, what is a 'litter'?
(*a*) Dog less than 1 year old
(*b*) Group of puppies born at one time
(*c*) Group of puppies born at different time
(*d*) Dog whose parents are of mixed descent.

10. Who was elected President of El Salvador on June 1, 1984?
(*a*) Jose Napoleon Duarte (*b*) Daniel Ortega
(*c*) Marco Vinicio Cerezo (*d*) Amilcar Cabral.

11. What is the atomic number of dysprosium, a chemical element with symbol, Dy?
(*a*) 56 (*b*) 60 (*c*) 66 (*d*) 70.

12. Of the Channel Islands in the English channel, which is the largest?
(*a*) Guernsey (*b*) Lihou (*c*) Herm (*d*) Jersey.

13. Who was the world chess champion between 1866 — 1894?
(*a*) Alexander A. Alekhine (*b*) William Steinitz
(*c*) Max Euwe (*d*) Emanuel Larker.

14. Which musician, popularly known as the Maestro founded the Singapore Symphony Orchestra in 1979?
(*a*) Choo Hoey (*b*) Bob Gibson
(*c*) George M. Cohan (*d*) Lorenz Hart.

15. Who made the following remark, "Genius is 95% perspiration and 5% inspiration"?
(*a*) Samuel Morse (*b*) Alexander G. Bell
(*c*) Thomas A. Edison (*d*) Albert Einstein.

16. Which two countries are divided by the 49th parallel?
(*a*) France and Spain (*b*) India and Pakistan
(*c*) North Korea and South Korea (*d*) USA and Canada.

17. In which country does the volcano release mud and not fire and brimstone?
(*a*) Italy (*b*) New Zealand (*c*) Japan (*d*) Paraguay.

18. Who invented the toilet paper, the poison gas and the decimal point?
(*a*) The Chinese (*b*) The Spanish
(*c*) The Indian (*d*) The British.

19. In economics, what would be the income elasticity of demand of an inferior good?

(*a*) Infinite (*b*) Negative (*c*) Zero (*d*) Positive.

20. What do you mean by pulchritude?

(*a*) Sensuality (*b*) Tearfulness

(*c*) Beauty (*d*) Fatness.

QUIZ 34

1. In which country, during the 1600's and 1700's, were ballets often used as intermezzos between the acts of opera?
   (*a*) UK (*b*) Spain (*c*) France (*d*) Austria.
2. Which is a major industrial city in northwestern South Korea and the nation's second largest port?
   (*a*) Seoul (*b*) Pusan (*c*) Inchon (*d*) Taegu.
3. One of the worst global epidemics of influenza occurred in 1918 — 1919. How many people died?
   (*a*) 5 million (*b*) 10 million (*c*) 15 million (*d*) 20 million.
4. What is the specialist in heart diseases called?
   (*a*) Neurologist (*b*) Cardiologist
   (*c*) Endocrinologist (*d*) Ophthalmologist.
5. Which country publishes the most daily newspapers?
   (*a*) Japan (*b*) USA (*c*) India (*d*) China.
6. What is 'onyx'?
   (*a*) Oyster (*b*) Metal (*c*) Gas (*d*) Gem.
7. What is the atomic number of germanium, a chemical element?
   (*a*) 28 (*b*) 30 (*c*) 32 (*d*) 34.
8. Who was the British caricaturist who drew satirical and humorous sketches of Napoleon, Horatio Nelson, and George III, among others.
   (*a*) James Gillray (*b*) Eric Gill
   (*c*) John Updike (*d*) George Vancouver.
9. What was a band of men who followed Jason in his quest for the Golden Fleece called?
   (*a*) Sailors (*b*) Pirates (*c*) Argonauts (*d*) Astronauts.
10. Who won the 1983 Nobel Prize for Literature?
    (*a*) Wole Soyinka (*b*) Jaroslav Siefert
    (*c*) Claude Simon (*d*) William Golding.

11. What is sometimes called grape-sugar?
(*a*) Glucose (*b*) Molasses (*c*) Saccharin (*d*) Sucrose.

12. Who wrote the poem, *The Deserted Village*, which details country life and depicts the evil that spawns when people underscore too much on money and luxury?
(*a*) Robert Browning (*b*) Oliver Goldsmith
(*c*) Eugene Field (*d*) James Whitcomb Riley.

13. At what degree centigrade does one gram contain about as much mass as 1 cubic centimeter of water?
(*a*) 2°C (*b*) 3°C (*c*) 4°C (*d*) 5°C.

14. On December 24, 1999, an airbus Flight no. IC 814 was hijacked as it was on its route from Kathmandu to where?
(*a*) Amritsar (*b*) New Delhi (*c*) Lahore (*d*) Dubai.

15. In tennis, who won the women's single US championship title between 1923 — 1925 and 1927 — 1929?
(*a*) Helen Wills (*b*) Alice Marble
(*c*) Molla B. Mallory (*d*) Betty Nuthall.

16. Of the following, which is the smallest state (area-wise) in the world?
(*a*) Tonga (*b*) Kibrati (*c*) Monaco (*d*) Vatican City.

17. Name the dynasty of Prince Rainer III, monarch of Monaco.
(*a*) Alawi (*b*) Bourbon (*c*) Grimaldi (*d*) Chakri.

18. What is a farrier?
(*a*) Goldsmith (*b*) Blacksmith
(*c*) Silversmith (*d*) Coppersmith.

19. Who was Prime Minster of Australia three times — from 1908 to 1909, from 1910 to 1913, and from 1914 to 1915?
(*a*) Andrew Fisher (*b*) William M. Hughes
(*c*) Joseph A. Lyons (*d*) Harold E. Holt.

20. Which country first employed multiple exchange rates?
(*a*) Germany (*b*) Brazil (*c*) Ecuador (*d*) France.

QUIZ 35

1. Who defeated whom in the World Cup football final match in 1970 in Mexico City?
   (*a*) Uruguay defeated Argentina (4-2)
   (*b*) Brazil defeated Italy (4-1)
   (*c*) West Germany defeated Hungary (3-2)
   (*d*) Argentina defeated Netherlands (3-1).

2. Who painted The Madonna of Humility?
   (*a*) Fra Angelico (*b*) Frank Stella
   (*c*) El Greco (*d*) Vincent Van Gogh.

3. Who ruled France between 1422 — 1461?
   (*a*) Charles IV (*b*) Charles V
   (*c*) Charles VI (*d*) Charles VII.

4. Who was the second wife of Priam, the King of Troy, in Greek mythology?
   (*a*) Diana (*b*) Helen (*c*) Hecuba (*d*) Jocasta.

5. Which country's flag has five stars representing five Central American republics that formed a union in the early 1800s?
   (*a*) Honduras (*b*) Haiti (*c*) Nicaragua (*d*) El Salvador.

6. What is a 'palomino'?
   (*a*) Lion (*b*) Hyena (*c*) Horse (*d*) Mouse.

7. Which is the third largest city in Sweden?
   (*a*) Umea (*b*) Malmo (*c*) Goteborg (*d*) Gavle.

8. Two small satellites (moons) travel around Mars. One is called Phobos, what is the other?
   (*a*) Charon (*b*) Janus (*c*) Umbriel (*d*) Deimos.

9. The book *Society in America* attacked slavery. Who wrote it?
   (*a*) Martin Luther King, Jr. (*b*) Harriet Martineau
   (*c*) Ralph Bunche (*d*) Harriet B. Stowe.

10. What is the other name for ENT, the diagnosis and treatment of diseases of the ear, nose and throat?
(*a*) Geriatrics (*b*) Ophthalmology
(*c*) Otolaryngology (*d*) Orthopedics.

11. What is a 'mesquite'?
(*a*) Shrub (*b*) Insect (*c*) Cactus (*d*) Animal.

12. What is moccasin, a soft item, originally won by North American Indians?
(*a*) Jacket (*b*) Cap (*c*) Glove (*d*) Shoe.

13. What is the monetary unit of Papua New Guinea?
(*a*) Kina (*b*) Naira (*c*) Balboa (*d*) Guarani.

14. When did British troops remove an Argentinean invasion force from the Falkland Islands in the South Atlantic?
(*a*) 1974 (*b*) 1978 (*c*) 1982 (*d*) 1986.

15. About how many species of living fish are known?
(*a*) 15,000 (*b*) 19,000 (*c*) 23,000 (*d*) 27,000

16. Which was the first James Bond film?
(*a*) Goldfinger (*b*) Dr. No
(*c*) Thunderball (*d*) From Russia with Love.

17. Which colour is worth five points at snooker?
(*a*) Black (*b*) Green (*c*) Pink (*d*) Blue.

18. A polymer is shaped when simple, chemical units :
(*a*) Combine to form long chain
(*b*) Combine to form circles
(*c*) Become round, complex shapes
(*d*) Break up.

19. Give the antonym of promiscuous.
(*a*) Mixed up (*b*) Chaste
(*c*) Holding great promise (*d*) Sexually irregular.

20. For which sector has the highest percentage of the World Bank's total loans been provided?
(*a*) Health (*b*) Education (*c*) Energy (*d*) Transport.

QUIZ 36

1. When was the League of Nations established?
   (*a*) 1919 (*b*) 1920 (*c*) 1921 (*d*) 1922.
2. All the evidence of Java man's existence comes from fossils found in ancient streams and volcanic deposits on the island of Java. Who, in 1891, was the first to discover the fossils?
   (*a*) Eugene Dubois (*b*) Heinrich Schliemann
   (*c*) Johanna J. Winckelmann (*d*) Leonard Woolley.
3. In which country does the Kalahari Desert stretch the most?
   (*a*) Namibia (*b*) South Africa (*c*) Angola (*d*) Botswana.
4. What is a 'katydid'?
   (*a*) Mouse (*b*) Insect (*c*) Cat (*d*) Dog.
5. After the death of Josef Stalin in March 1953, who became Prime Minister of he Soviet Union?
   (*a*) Nikolai Bulganin (*b*) Nikita Khrushchev
   (*c*) Georgi Malenkov (*d*) Vyacheslav Molotov.
6. Who was born on November 10, 1483?
   (*a*) Martin Luther (*b*) Edmond Halley
   (*c*) Lope de Vega (*d*) Nicholas Copernicus.
7. Which vitamin is necessary for proper clotting of the blood?
   (*a*) Vitamin A (*b*) Vitamin C
   (*c*) Vitamin D (*d*) Vitamin K.
8. What was the specialization of Rudolf Nureyev, who lived from 1938 to 1993?
   (*a*) Economist (*b*) Ballet dancer
   (*c*) Politician (*d*) Medical doctor.
9. Among the following, which country produces the most olive?
   (*a*) Italy (*b*) Greece (*c*) Spain (*d*) Turkey.
10. In which state in USA is Mount Hood located?
   (*a*) Ohio (*b*) Oregon (*c*) Arizona (*d*) California.

11. Litharge is a poisonous yellow or reddish-yellow solid, a compound of lead and oxygen and is made by heating lead or certain of its compounds in air. What is its other name?
(*a*) Lead Monoxide (*b*) Lead dioxide
(*c*) Lead oxide (*d*) Lead trioxide.

12. Name the communication satellite that broadcasted first voice message from space.
(*a*) Project Score (*b*) Syncom 2 (*c*) Arik 1 (*d*) Comstar D.

13. Christina Stead, one of the best known novelists, wrote *The Salzburg Tales*. What was her nationality?
(*a*) American (*b*) Canadian (*c*) Australian (*d*) British.

14. What is the name of the strait between the Stewart Island and thed South Island of New Zealand called?
(*a*) Cook Strait (*b*) Bass Strait
(*c*) Palk Strait (*d*) Foveaux Strait.

15. About three-fourth of the mass of the sun consists of which element?
(*a*) Oxygen (*b*) Nitrogen (*c*) Hydrogen (*d*) Helium.

16. During World War II, when did USA marines capture Iwo Jima?
(*a*) March 16, 1946 (*b*) March 16, 1945
(*c*) March 16, 1944 (*d*) March 16, 1943.

17. Which Indian city was given as a dowry to Charles II of England in 1661?
(*a*) Mumbai (*b*) Banglore (*c*) Delhi (*d*) Calcutta.

18. Apart from the sun and the moon, what is the brightest object in the sky?
(*a*) Mars (*b*) Mercury (*c*) Venus (*d*) Jupiter.

19. What is the opposite of laconic?
(*a*) Loquacious (*b*) Informal (*c*) Uninterested (*d*) Polite.

20. Which economist first advocated the 'big-push' strategy of development?
(*a*) Charles Kindleberger (*b*) W.W. Rostow
(*c*) Robert Solow (*d*) P.N. Rosenstein-Rodan.

QUIZ 37

1. The Roman Emperor Gaius Caesar adopted his name from the Latin for 'little boot'. What was it?
   (*a*) Caligula (*b*) Nero (*c*) Antony (*d*) Cassius.
2. Which monkey possesses a blood factor otherwise found only in human?
   (*a*) Gorilla (*b*) Rhesus (*c*) Sloth (*d*) Chimpanzee.
3. Which comic character was created by Jerry Siegal and Joe Schuster for Action Comics in June 1938?
   (*a*) Batman (*b*) Superman
   (*c*) Richie Rich (*d*) Spiderman.
4. In 1957, which Indian film was nominated for an Oscar as the Best Foreign Language film?
   (*a*) *Awara* (*b*) *Chaaya*
   (*c*) *Tere Ghar Ke Samane* (*d*) *Mother India*.
5. Robert Frost recited his poem, *The Gift Outright*, at a swearing in ceremony of which US president?
   (*a*) Harry Truman (*b*) Dwight Eisenhower
   (*c*) John F. Kennedy (*d*) Lyndon B. Johnson.
6. What is the present name of the west African nation formerly called Dahomey?
   (*a*) Benin (*b*) Guinea-Bissau
   (*c*) Nigeria (*d*) Ghana.
7. A name was given to the antigravity matter used to propel the spaceship in H.G. Wells' *The First Men in The Moon*. What was it?
   (*a*) Mercury (*b*) Cavorite (*c*) Gemini (*d*) Apollo.
8. Name the fruit that gives the liquer Grand Marnier its distinctive flavour.
   (*a*) Apples (*b*) Grapes (*c*) Oranges (*d*) Cherries.

9. How is an oral examination called in Latin?
(*a*) *Quid pro quo* (*b*) *Veni, vedi, veci*
(*c*) *Bete noire* (*d*) *Viva voce.*

10. What were the calends in the ancient Roman calendar?
(*a*) The first day of any month
(*b*) The second day of any month
(*c*) The third day of any month
(*d*) The last day of any month.

11. 'Schnauzer' is a breed of what kind of animal?
(*a*) Dog (*b*) Deer (*c*) Horse (*d*) Jackal.

12. Name the first Negro to hold the heavyweight boxing championship of the world.
(*a*) Joe Louis (*b*) Jack Johnson
(*c*) Sonny Liston (*d*) Muhammad Ali.

13. In which Shakespearian play do Hermia and Helena both appear?
(*a*) *Two Gentlemen of Verona* (*b*) *As You Like it*
(*c*) *A Midsummer Night's Dream* (*d*) *Hamlet.*

14. Spain was one of the two countries bound by the Treaty of Tordesillas of 1494. Name the other.
(*a*) England (*b*) France (*c*) Italy (*d*) Portugal.

15. Where was the Organization of African Unity (OAU) founded in 1963?
(*a*) Lagos (*b*) Addis Ababa (*c*) Nairobi (*d*) Accra.

16. What did G.K. Chesterton describe as 'the devil's walking parody'?
(*a*) The donkey (*b*) The horse
(*c*) The mule (*d*) The unicorn.

17. Where do cryophytes grow?
(*a*) On soil (*b*) On desert (*c*) On snow (*d*) On water.

18. Name the acid that was initially made from red ants.
(*a*) Nitric (*b*) Sulfuric (*c*) Formic (*d*) Hydrochloric.

19. Which of the following is the true measure of the degree of monopoly power, according to M. Kalecki?
(*a*) Price charged by the monopolist minus marginal cost of production

(*b*) Cross-elasticity of demand for the product of the monopolist
(*c*) Extent of monopolistic profit enjoyed by the monopolist
(*d*) Ratio between price and marginal cost.

20. What is the opposite of seductive?
(*a*) Repulsive (*b*) Horrific
(*c*) Puritanical (*d*) Chaste.

QUIZ 38

1. What is the popular name of the plant *nymphaea abba*?
(*a*) Water lily (*b*) Lotus (*c*) Chrysanthemum (*d*) Poppy.

2. Whom did the Turks defeat at the Battle of Mohacs in 1526?
(*a*) Greeks (*b*) Italians (*c*) Serbs (*d*) Hungarians.

3. To which Scandinavian country did Willy Brandt flee and was granted citizenship after the Nazis came to power in Germany?
(*a*) Denmark (*b*) Norway (*c*) Sweden (*d*) Finland.

4. Over which country did the House of Savoy rule until the abdication of the King in 1946?
(*a*) Portugal (*b*) Greece (*c*) Italy (*d*) Finland.

5. Which film star sang 'Over the Rainbow' in the 1939 film *The Wizard of Oz*?
(*a*) Judy Garland (*b*) Greta Garbo
(*c*) Julie Andrews (*d*) Elizabeth Taylor.

6. On an Ordance Survey 1 : 5000 Land ranger Map, what does a red triangle represent?
(*a*) A hospital (*b*) An university
(*c*) A youth hostel (*d*) A department store.

7. What is a 'peccary'?
(*a*) Panther (*b*) Pig (*c*) Deer (*d*) Dog.

8. How many days after Easter does Ascension Day fall?
(*a*) Twentieth day (*b*) Thirtieth day
(*c*) Fortieth day (*d*) Fiftieth day.

9. Erno Rubic invented the Rubic Cube. What was his nationality?
(*a*) Austrian (*b*) Romanian (*c*) Czech (*d*) Hungarian.

10. Of which metal is pearl ash a carbonate?
(*a*) Copper (*b*) Potassium (*c*) Cement (*d*) Gypsum.

11. Dr. Konard Adenauer was the founder of the German Christan Democratic Party. When did he die?
(*a*) 1967 (*b*) 1969 (*c*) 1971 (*d*) 1973.

12. Which is the brightest star of the constellation Orion?
(*a*) Betelgeuse (*b*) Bellatrix (*c*) Rigel (*d*) Saiph.

13. Name the European capital which is situated on River Tagus.
(*a*) Madrid (*b*) Lisbon (*c*) Vienna (*d*) Paris.

14. In which Olympics did women's events first make their appearance?
(*a*) Antwerp — 1920 (*b*) Paris — 1924
(*c*) Amsterdam — 1928 (*d*) Los Angeles — 1932.

15. What is archery called in Japanese?
(*a*) *Ikebana* (*b*) *Sayonara* (*c*) *Sumo* (*d*) *Yabusame.*

16. *Jude the Obscure* was the last novel of which famous writer?
(*a*) George Eliot (*b*) D.H. Lawrence
(*c*) Thomas Hardy (*d*) George Orwell.

17. Which English King was born at Caernarvon castle in 1284?
(*a*) Edward I (*b*) Edward II
(*c*) George I (*d*) George II.

18. Which famous personality was drowned — lost in the cruiser 'Hampshire' off the Orkneys in 1916?
(*a*) Lloyd George (*b*) Henry Hudson
(*c*) Raymond Poincare (*d*) Lord Kitchener.

19. Open market operations refer to the buying and selling of what?
(*a*) Government securities (*b*) Gold
(*c*) Foreign currencies (*d*) Commercial bills.

20. Give a synonym for eccentric.
(*a*) Peripatetic (*b*) Perverse
(*c*) Whimsical (*d*) Unreasonable.

QUIZ 39

1. Who authored the play *The Passing of the Third Floor Back*?
   (*a*) Henrik Ibsen (*b*) Jerome K. Jerome
   (*c*) F.C. Burnand (*d*) Beethoven.
2. Sileve Donard is the highest mountain in which part of UK?
   (*a*) Wales (*b*) Scotland
   (*c*) Northern Ireland (*d*) Channel Islands
3. Where was Charles VII crowned in 1429 with the help of Joan of Arc?
   (*a*) Paris (*b*) Nice (*c*) Reims (*d*) Burgundy.
4. On June 17, 1944, Iceland declared itself independent from which country?
   (*a*) Denmark (*b*) Norway (*c*) Finland (*d*) Sweden.
5. Of which country did Wafsi Tal become Prime Minister?
   (*a*) Iraq (*b*) Egypt (*c*) Syria (*d*) Jordan.
6. What is the more common name of *pulex irritans*, a parasitic insect?
   (*a*) Mosquito (*b*) Housefly (*c*) Human flea (*d*) Cockroach.
7. Who stated : "Some books are to be tasted, others to be swallowed, and some few to be chewed and digested"?
   (*a*) Samuel Johnson (*b*) Francis Bacon
   (*c*) Geoffrey Chaucer (*d*) Ernest Hemingway.
8. Which British University was the first to admit women to degrees?
   (*a*) London University (*b*) Leeds University
   (*c*) Oxford University (*d*) Reading University.
9. In which calendar would the year 1974 be numbered 1394?
   (*a*) Hindu (*b*) Moslem (*c*) Jew (*d*) Sikh.
10. Which is the chemical element found in all proteins?
    (*a*) Hydrogen (*b*) Helium (*c*) Oxygen (*d*) Nitrogen.

11. Who was the French journalist, essayist, novelist and playwright who was associated with the existentialist movement and won the 1957 Nobel Prize for Literature?
(*a*) Albert Camus (*b*) Jean Paul Sartre
(*c*) Roger Martin Du Gard (*d*) Henri Bergson.

12. Which country provides about one-fourth of the world's supply of cassiterite, a tin ore?
(*a*) Thailand (*b*) Indonesia (*c*) Malaysia (*d*) Philippines.

13. What is the capital of St. Lucia, an island country in the Caribbean Sea?
(*a*) Hamilton (*b*) Castries (*c*) Kingston (*d*) Funafuti.

14. Willa Cather was one of America's finest novelists. Among the following, which is not the novel written by her?
(*a*) *My Antonia* (*b*) *Death Comes for the Archbishop*
(*c*) *Alexander's Bridge* (*d*) *The Stricken Deer.*

15. Who is often called the 'Father of Modern Aeronautics'?
(*a*) Wilbur Wright (*b*) Charles Lindbergh
(*c*) George Cayley (*d*) Orville Wright.

16. What is a 'dik-dik'?
(*a*) Antelope (*b*) Lion (*c*) Bear (*d*) Hyena.

17. Which famous explorer was called by the Spaniards a name meaning *The Dragon*?
(*a*) Ferdinand Magellan (*b*) Francis Drake
(*c*) Vasco Da Gama (*d*) Christopher Columbus.

18. What is the actual name of Bob Dylan?
(*a*) Robert Zimmerman (*b*) Maurice Gibb
(*c*) Jeremy Twit (*d*) Boy George.

19. How do you define collude?
(*a*) Contest (*b*) Co-operate (*c*) Conclude (*d*) Conspire.

20. What is the market for very short-term loan known as?
(*a*) Discount market (*b*) Stock market
(*c*) Money market (*d*) Capital market.

QUIZ 40

1. Approximately, how much surface area of the earth in percentage is covered by water?
   (*a*) 60 per cent (*b*) 65 per cent
   (*c*) 70 per cent (*d*) 75 per cent.

2. Which element did William Wollaston discover?
   (*a*) Palladium (*b*) Platinum (*c*) Plutonium (*d*) Polonium.

3. Who wrote *The Birthday Party* (1958) and *The Homecoming* (1965)?
   (*a*) T.S. Eliot (*b*) Harold Pinter
   (*c*) Doris Lessing (*d*) J.R.R. Tolkien.

4. Which famous North American explorer was probably the first white person to reach Great Salt Lake?
   (*a*) James Bridger (*b*) William Clark
   (*c*) Pike Zebulon (*d*) John C. Fremont.

5. In which country was electroconvulsive therapy (ECT) — controlled electric shocks that cause temporary loss of consciousness and seizure — was first used on mental patients?
   (*a*) USA (*b*) UK (*c*) France (*d*) Italy.

6. When was the atom bomb dropped on Nagasaki?
   (*a*) August 6, 1945 (*b*) August 9, 1945
   (*c*) August 12, 1945 (*d*) August 15, 1945.

7. British ethologist Jane Goodall started studying the behavior of a certain monkey in Tanzania. Which one?
   (*a*) Gorilla (*b*) Sloth (*c*) Chimpanzee (*d*) Orang-utan.

8. In 1974, near which city did farmers discover an army of life-size terra-cotta human figures in a 3rd century BC Chinese Emperor's tomb?
   (*a*) Shanghai (*b*) Beijing (*c*) Xian (*d*) Nanking.

9. In which American University did researchers clone human embryos and nurtured them in vitro for several days?
(*a*) Harvard University (*b*) University of Minnesota
(*c*) Stanford University (*d*) George Washington University.

10. What is epistemology?
(*a*) The theory of knowledge (*b*) The theory of aircrafts
(*c*) The theory of sound (*d*) The theory of stars.

11. Who was the mathematical genius who committed suicide on June 7, 1954 by eating an apple laced with cyanide?
(*a*) John Von Neumann (*b*) Alan Turing
(*c*) Clifford Bell (*d*) John Atanasoff.

12. Who remarked "Well, we shall write our memoirs. Work is the scythe of time"?
(*a*) Napoleon Bonaparte (*b*) Horatio Nelson
(*c*) Otto Bismark (*d*) Benito Mussolini.

13. Who released his first film *Sanshiro Sugata* in 1943?
(*a*) Zhang Yimori (*b*) Akiro Kurosawa
(*c*) Ishiro Honda (*d*) Takashi Shimura.

14. In which month in 1999 did the Melissa Virus spread through more than 300 corporate networks?
(*a*) January (*b*) February (*c*) March (*d*) April.

15. Name the archaeologist who found grim evidence of the sacrificial rites of the ancient Inca on Mount Llullaillaco in the Argentine Andes.
(*a*) Arthur J. Evans (*b*) Howard Carter
(*c*) Johan Reinhard (*d*) Michael G. Ventris.

16. Who won the men's 400 metre in Seville in 1999?
(*a*) Michael Johnson (*b*) Ben Johnson
(*c*) Maurice Grenne (*d*) Linford Christie.

17. Who is the owner of the musical album *Supernatural*?
(*a*) Bee Gees (*b*) Santana
(*c*) The Culture Club (*d*) Brad Mehldau.

18. Name the report produced by a congressman that investigated allegations that China systematically stole American nuclear secrets.
(*a*) Cox Report (*b*) Church Report
(*c*) Watergate Report (*d*) Tower Report.

19. Among the following, who is associated with the homohypallagic production function?

(*a*) Paul Samuelson (*b*) A.K. Sen

(*c*) James Meade (*d*) B.S. Minhas.

20. What is the meaning of cohort?

(*a*) Group Leader (*b*) Assistant

(*c*) Group of soldiers (*d*) Gangster's mate.

QUIZ 41

1. Which country won the World Series Cup one-day cricket competition at Melbourne in February 1986?
   (*a*) West Indies (*b*) Pakistan (*c*) India (*d*) Australia.
2. Initially, which country vetoed the entry of Bangladesh into United Nations?
   (*a*) Russia (*b*) China (*c*) UK (*d*) France.
3. During 1965-76, while diplomatic relations between India and Pakistan remained suspended, which country's embassy carried out diplomatic activities between the two countries?
   (*a*) Canada (*b*) Nepal (*c*) Switzerland (*d*) Russia.
4. What is the monetary unit of Bangladesh?
   (*a*) Rupee (*b*) Rupiah (*c*) Dinar (*d*) Taka.
5. Deficiency of vitamin C causes the disease scurvy which is characterized by :
   (*a*) Weakening and aching of bones and loosening of tooth
   (*b*) Hallucination
   (*c*) Heart problem
   (*d*) Loss of weight and general weakness.
6. Who explored Arabia and East Africa and reached Lake Tanganyika in 1853 — 1858?
   (*a*) Richard Burton (*b*) David Livingstone
   (*c*) Emin Pasha (*d*) Hugh Clapperton.
7. How did Sigmund Freud die?
   (*a*) Pneumonia (*b*) Mouth cancer
   (*c*) Suicide (*d*) Car accident.
8. Who invented the polygraph machine better known as the lie detector?
   (*a*) Max Planck (*b*) Karl Landsteiner
   (*c*) James Mackenzie (*d*) Henri Becquerel.

9. Where was Madam Maria Curie born?
(*a*) France (*b*) Poland (*c*) Germany (*d*) Austria.

10. Who is the author of the novel *Bone by Bone*?
(*a*) Arthur Conan Doyle (*b*) Rachel Carson
(*c*) Agatha Christie (*d*) Peter Matthiessen.

11. Which 20th century figure best suits the following description: "He is obsessed with the idea that some day it may be possible to write a message on a pad at one's desk or beside and have it instantaneously transmitted to addresses anywhere on earth."
(*a*) Haile Selassie (*b*) Owen Young
(*c*) Andrew Grove (*d*) Harry S. Truman.

12. Name the planet which has a moon that revolves backwards.
(*a*) Neptune (*b*) Saturn (*c*) Earth (*d*) Pluto.

13. When was General A.A. Guevara elected president of Guatemala?
(*a*) 1978 (*b*) 1980 (*c*) 1982 (*d*) 1984.

14. Who revived the Olympic games in modern time on April 6, 1896?
(*a*) Walter Tewksbury (*b*) Thomas Burke
(*c*) Edwin Flack (*d*) Pierre de Coubertin.

15. What is omophagia?
(*a*) Eating raw flesh (*b*) Eating raw eggs
(*c*) Eating raw vegetables (*d*) Eating raw fruits.

16. Which country was formerly known as Portuguese East Africa?
(*a*) Madagascar (*b*) Mozambique
(*c*) Chad (*d*) Cape Verde.

17. What do we get when steam is blown over white-hot coke?
(*a*) Inert gas (*b*) Carbon dioxide
(*c*) Ammonia (*d*) Water gas.

18. Who was the Chilean President whose policies of nationalism and social reform was undermined by the Great Depression in 1927?
(*a*) Juan Peron (*b*) Carlos Ibanez
(*c*) Salvador Allende (*d*) Augusto Pinochet.

19. Among Organization of Petroleum Exporting countries, which is the largest oil exporter?
(*a*) Iraq (*b*) Iran (*c*) Saudi Arabia (*d*) Qatar.

20. What is the antonym of encomium?
(*a*) Criticism (*b*) Excellence (*c*) Eulogy (*d*) Salary.

QUIZ 42

1. Where in Africa is Lake Assal which is 155 meters below sea level?
(*a*) Ghana (*b*) Chad (*c*) Djibouti (*d*) Comoros.

2. Which aviator made the first official circular flight of 1 kilometre and also flew 27 kilometres in the first cross — country flight?
(*a*) Glenn H. Curtiss (*b*) Henri Farman
(*c*) John Alcock (*d*) Richard E. Byrd.

3. When did Hammurabi rule Babylon?
(*a*) 1792 to 1750 BC (*b*) 1892 to 1850 BC
(*c*) 1992 to 1950 BC (*d*) 2092 to 2050 BC.

4. In which of James Barrie's play does the meek wife of a politician secretly guides her husband's successful career?
(*a*) *What Every Woman Knows* (*b*) *Mary Rose*
(*c*) *Dear Brutus* (*d*) *A Kiss for Cinderella.*

5. Paul-Henri Spaak served as the first President of the United Nations General Assembly. Which country did he represent?
(*a*) Netherlands (*b*) Austria (*c*) France (*d*) Belgium.

6. What do you mean by 'shanking'?
(*a*) Fish (*b*) Exercise (*c*) Dance (*d*) Bear.

7. Who wrote the Nepali national anthem?
(*a*) Leknath Poudyal (*b*) Chakrapani Chalise
(*c*) Madhav Ghimire (*d*) Laxmi Prasad Devkota.

8. This person won gold medals in super heavyweight boxing in three consecutive Olympics. Name him.
(*a*) Joe Fraizer (*b*) George Foreman
(*c*) Tyrell Biggs (*d*) Lennox Lewis.

9. Who painted *Woman Weeping*?
(*a*) Michelangelo (*b*) Pablo Picasso
(*c*) Paul Gauguin (*d*) Robert Delaunay.

10. In Greek mythology, Paris was a son of Priam, King of Troy. Who was his mother?
(*a*) Hecuba (*b*) Oenone (*c*) Cassandra (*d*) Hera.

11. Where was prince Philip of UK born?
(*a*) Sicily (*b*) Corsica (*c*) Cyprus (*d*) Corfu.

12. Which planet was named after the Roman god of the lower world?
(*a*) Jupiter (*b*) Mercury (*c*) Mars (*d*) Pluto.

13. What is the capital of St. Christopher and Nevis?
(*a*) Kingston (*b*) Hamilton
(*c*) Basseterre (*d*) Bandar Seri Begwan

14. University of San Marcos is the oldest university in South America. In which capital city is it located?
(*a*) Santiago (*b*) Lima (*c*) La Paz (*d*) Asuncion.

15. What is the amount of revenue-producing space of a ship called?
(*a*) Net tonnage (*b*) Deadweight tonnage
(*c*) Gross tonnage (*d*) Displacement tonnage.

16. Ur was one of the first cities founded by the Sumerians in about 3500 BC. Where is it located now?
(*a*) Jordan (*b*) Syria (*c*) Iran (*d*) Iraq.

17. Who was the first to reach South Pole overland and flew over North Pole?
(*a*) Robert F. Scott (*b*) Umberto Nobile
(*c*) William E. Parry (*d*) Roald Amundsen.

18. Lemon, orange, peppermint and ginger oils are used for flavoring food and sweets which can be acquired from plant sources by using what kind of solvents?
(*a*) Vinegar (*b*) Water (*c*) Alcohol (*d*) Ammonia.

19. Which of the following is an instrument of quantitative credit control?
(*a*) Consumer credit regulation (*b*) Variable reserve ratio
(*c*) Prescribing margin requirements (*d*) Credit rationing.

20. What is the opposite of exhume?
(*a*) Display (*b*) Destroy (*c*) Bury (*d*) Burn.

QUIZ 43

1. Who was the Premier of Quebec who led unsuccessful fight to separate from Canada?
   (*a*) Rene Levesque (*b*) Arthur Meighen
   (*c*) Pierre Tradeau (*d*) Joe Clark.

2. The National Planning Commission (NPC) in Nepal formulates the nation's Five-Year plan; but whose approval is required before the Plan can commence?
   (*a*) The National Development Council
   (*b*) Parliament
   (*c*) The Prime Minister (*d*) The Council of Ministries.

3. Which is the country closest to the Gulf of San Jorge?
   (*a*) Chile (*b*) Argentina (*c*) Uruguay (*d*) Brazil.

4. Which American doctor pioneered the pill — a mixture of two hormones that suppress ovulation — in 1954?
   (*a*) John F. Enders (*b*) Frederick C. Robbins
   (*c*) Thomas H. Weller (*d*) Gregory Pincus.

5. According to a survey of the 1997/98 season by the accountants Deloitte and Touche, which is the richest soccer club in the world?
   (*a*) Juventus, Italy (*b*) Bayern Munich, Germany
   (*c*) Real Madrid, Spain (*d*) Manchester United, UK.

6. Who is the author of the book *Horn of the Hunter*?
   (*a*) James Herriot (*b*) Walt Disney
   (*c*) Robert Ruark (*d*) Joy Adamson.

7. Who made the famous statement "Don't fire until you see the whites of their eyes"?
   (*a*) Robert Lee (*b*) Charles Cornwallis
   (*c*) Thomas Jeffreson (*d*) Israel Putnam.

8. From which country did the USA purchase Louisiana in 1803?
   (*a*) France (*b*) Russia (*c*) Spain (*d*) UK.

9. What was a surtout in the nineteenth century?
(*a*) A leather jacket (*b*) An overcoat
(*c*) A woolen shirt (*d*) A pullover.

10. From which South American country was Pilin Leon who won the Miss World Contest in 1981?
(*a*) Brazil (*b*) Argentina (*c*) Venezuela (*d*) Peru.

11. With which instrument is the American jazz musician Benny Goodman associated?
(*a*) Drum (*b*) Flute (*c*) Guitar (*d*) Clarinet.

12. What is the common name of the fruit of the tree citrus paradisi?
(*a*) Grapefruit (*b*) Lemon (*c*) Orange (*d*) Apricot.

13. In which mythology were Osiris, Horus and Irus major deities?
(*a*) Ancient Greece (*b*) Ancient Rome
(*c*) Ancient India (*d*) Ancient Ehypt.

14. In the Bible, which sea is said to have closed in upon the Egyptian army pursuing the Israelites?
(*a*) Dead Sea (*b*) Red Sea
(*c*) Black Sea (*d*) Sea of Marmara.

15. In Troy weight, how many grains are there in a pennyweight?
(*a*) 8 (*b*) 16 (*c*) 24 (*d*) 32.

16. What does a phillumentist collect?
(*a*) Stamps (*b*) Coins
(*c*) Matchbox labels (*d*) Cigarette labels.

17. What must an organic compound contain?
(*a*) Silicon (*b*) Carbon (*c*) Hydrogen (*d*) Oxygen.

18. Who initiated and ordered the building of the famous 'Hanging Garden of the Babylon'?
(*a*) Nebuchandnezzar (*b*) Gudea
(*c*) Hammurabi (*d*) Ashurbanipal.

19. What is the present percentage contribution of agriculture in the USA to the country's gross domestic product?
(*a*) 11 (*b*) 8 (*c*) 5 (*d*) 2.

20. What is the meaning of supplicate?
(*a*) Repeatedly insist (*b*) Petition humbly
(*c*) Request earnestly (*d*) Beg favor.

QUIZ 44

1. Which USA president was also called the 'Sage of Monticello'?
   (*a*) George Washington (*b*) Thomas Jeffreson
   (*c*) Andrew Jackson (*d*) James Garfield

2. Three major rivers flow in the Baltic Sea. Two of them are Oder and Vistula; name the third.
   (*a*) Neva (*b*) Volga (*c*) Danube (*d*) Seine.

3. In money terms, what is a monkey in sterling pounds?
   (*a*) £100 (*b*) £500 (*c*) £1,000 (*d*) £5,000.

4. Which director described actors as cattle?
   (*a*) Lewis Milestone (*b*) Frank Lloyd
   (*c*) Alfred Hitchcock (*d*) Norman Taurag.

5. How many faces has an icosahedron?
   (*a*) Fourteen (*b*) Sixteen
   (*c*) Eighteen (*d*) Twenty.

6. In 1964 more than 300 people were killed during a riot following an Olympic qualifying football match in which country?
   (*a*) Italy (*b*) Peru (*c*) Paraguay (*d*) Brazil.

7. 'Salopettes' are types of what?
   (*a*) Jackets (*b*) Shirts (*c*) Trousers (*d*) Half-pants.

8. With which group was Keith Moon the drummer?
   (*a*) Bay City Rollers (*b*) The WHO (*c*) Exile (*d*) Wings.

9. How many calories are there in a half pint of milk?
   (*a*) 260 (*b*) 220 (*c*) 180 (*d*) 140.

10. With which country is the *The Soldier's Song* associated?
    (*a*) Ireland (*b*) USA (*c*) Australia (*d*) Canada.

11. Which country is the leading producer of nickel?
    (*a*) Brazil (*b*) India (*c*) Canada (*d*) USA.

12. Who discovered neutron?
(*a*) Rutherford (*b*) Dalton (*c*) Thompson (*d*) Chadwick.

13. When did the Indian Security Forces enter the Golden Temple in Punjab?
(*a*) June 3, 1984 (*b*) July 3, 1984
(*c*) August 3, 1984 (*d*) September 3, 1984.

14. Cleopatra, Queen of Egypt, married many times and knew a lot of men. Who was her last husband?
(*a*) Julius Caesar (*b*) Octavius Caeser
(*c*) Mark Antony (*d*) Ptolemy XIV.

15. The world's longest man-made canal is the Grand canal with a length of 1600 km. In which city is it located?
(*a*) Bangkok (*b*) Venice (*c*) Amsterdam (*d*) Beijing.

16. What is the name of the instrument which can even measure the intensity of pain?
(*a*) Lactometer (*b*) Algometer (*c*) Achimeter (*d*) Poinemeter.

17. Who was the founder of the Chou dynasty who established it by revolting against the tyrannical Shang ruler in 1122 BC?
(*a*) Wu Wang (*b*) Chou Kung (*c*) Shun (*d*) Wen Wang.

18. "A weak, electrical combination is formed if a piece of zinc and a piece of copper are brought into contact." Who made this statement and when?
(*a*) Volta in medieval tines (*b*) Albert Einstein in 1927
(*c*) Alfred Nobel in 1885 (*d*) Humphrey Davy in 1812.

19. Which economist used the term *consumption capital for consumers'* goods?
(*a*) John K. Galbraith (*b*) Thomas Malthus
(*c*) Alfred Marshall (*d*) M.E. L. Walras.

20. What is freebooter?
(*a*) One who rides roughshod over others
(*b*) Freedom fighter in Latin America
(*c*) Collector of free handouts
(*d*) One who lives off plunder.

QUIZ 45

1. Who invented 2-stroke petrol engine?
   (*a*) Dugald Clerk (*b*) Rudolf Diesel
   (*c*) Christopher Cockerell (*d*) Anton Van Leeuwenhoek.

2. Who wrote *The Last Days of Hitler*?
   (*a*) Larry Collins (*b*) Hugh Trevor-Roper
   (*c*) Erich Maria Remarque (*d*) Dominique Lapierre.

3. For which country did Stan McCabe play cricket?
   (*a*) South Africa (*b*) UK (*c*) Australia (*d*) New Zealand.

4. Who was the assassin who gunned down Archduke Francis Ferdinand of Austria-Hungary in Sarajevo on June 28, 1914 that led to the outbreak of World War I?
   (*a*) Lee Harvey Oswald (*b*) Robert Nivelle
   (*c*) Luigi Cadorna (*d*) Gavrilo Princip.

5. Which country produces the most zinc?
   (*a*) Peru (*b*) Australia (*c*) Russia (*d*) Canada.

6. Where are the Soo Canals located?
   (*a*) USA-Canada Border (*b*) Russia-Finland Border
   (*c*) China-Korea Border (*d*) India-Pakistan Border.

7. Who was the first of the three Greek writers of tragedy who favoured presentation of trilogies (groups of three related plays)?
   (*a*) Sophocles (*b*) Aeschylus (*c*) Euripides (*d*) Aristotle.

8. Which is the second brightest star?
   (*a*) Arcturus (*b*) Vega (*c*) Rigel (*d*) Canopus.

9. What is the first name of the author, D.H. Laurence?
   (*a*) Dwight (*b*) Donald (*c*) David (*d*) Duncan.

10. Which chemical element has its atomic number as 28 and atomic weight as 58.69?
    (*a*) Nickel (*b*) Nitrogen (*c*) Gold (*d*) Aluminum.

11. Which Indian city is walled and surrounded on three sides by hills?
(*a*) Bombay (*b*) Madras (*c*) Srinagar (*d*) Jaipur.

12. When did Louis Bleriot make the first airplane flight across the English Channel?
(*a*) 1905 (*b*) 1909 (*c*) 1913 (*d*) 1917.

13. When did the extremist Roman Catholics try to kill James I in the Gunpowder Plot?
(*a*) 1595 (*b*) 1605 (*c*) 1615 (*d*) 1625.

14. Among the following, which is the world's largest manufacturing industry?
(*a*) Toyota Motor (*b*) Royal Dutch/Shell Group
(*c*) General Motors (*d*) Daimler-Benz.

15. What is tokay?
(*a*) French wine (*b*) Spanish wine
(*c*) Romanian wine (*d*) Hungarian wine.

16. How much would a matchbox weigh if it were filled with material from the center of the star Sirius B?
(*a*) About 10 tons (*b*) About 30 tons
(*c*) About 50 tons (*d*) About 70 tons.

17. If you have chlorosis, what colour does your skin go?
(*a*) White (*b*) Green (*c*) Red (*d*) Purple.

18. Name the God of the Dead who had overpowering influence on Egyptian society, mentality and culture.
(*a*) Osiris (*b*) Ra (*c*) Horus (*d*) Seth.

19. When was the world's first set of traveler's cheques issued by the American Express Company?
(*a*) 1876 (*b*) 1881 (*c*) 1886 (*d*) 1891.

20. Give a synonym for tardy.
(*a*) Mean (*b*) Unwilling (*c*) Slow (*d*) Stingy.

QUIZ 46

1. What is 'hacienda'?
   (*a*) A church (*b*) A movie theater
   (*c*) A library (*d*) A large farm.

2. Who is ranked by historians almost unanimously as the weakest president of USA?
   (*a*) Warren G. Harding (*b*) James Monroe
   (*c*) Gerald Ford (*d*) Jimmy Carter.

3. Among the following, which is the oldest university?
   (*a*) University of Heidelberg (*b*) Oxford University.
   (*c*) Harvard University (*d*) University of Manitoba.

4. When did Sri Lanka gain its Independence?
   (*a*) February 4, 1948 (*b*) February 4, 1949
   (*c*) February 4, 1950 (*d*) February 4, 1951.

5. Where is Mount Tomanivi, which is 1, 323m high, located?
   (*a*) Tonga (*b*) Kibrati (*c*) Fiji (*d*) Papua New Guinea.

6. Which film won the Academy Award as best picture in 1959?
   (*a*) Ben Hur (*b*) Gigi
   (*c*) The Bridge on the River Kwai (*d*) The Apartment.

7. How did Grigori Efimovich Rasputin die in 1916?
   (*a*) Suicide (*b*) Natural death
   (*c*) Horse accident (*d*) Assassination.

8. Who built the first copper-rolling mill in the USA?
   (*a*) Joseph Warren (*b*) Paul Revere
   (*c*) William Daives (*d*) Samuel Prescott.

9. What is the emblem of Germany?
   (*a*) Pansy (*b*) Marigold (*c*) Com flower (*d*) Rose.

10. Leaves appear green because they :
    (*a*) Absorb and reflect green light (*b*) Absorb green light
    (*c*) Reflect green light (*d*) None of the above.

11. Who invented the telegraph?
(*a*) Samuel Morse (*b*) Thomas Edison
(*c*) Alexander Graham Bell (*d*) Michael Farady.

12. Who is the author of the novel *Gone With the Wind*?
(*a*) Pearl S. Buck (*b*) Margaret Mitchell
(*c*) Victoria Holt (*d*) Harper Lee.

13. To the nearest ounce, what does a tennis-ball weigh?
(*a*) 5 ounces (*b*) 4 ounces (*c*) 3 ounces (*d*) 2 ounces.

14. What are *brick*, *fontina*, and *port* salut?
(*a*) Butter (*b*) Cheese (*c*) Milk (*d*) Yogurt.

15. Who was *Time* magazine's 'Man of the Year' for 1938?
(*a*) Franklin Roosevelt (*b*) Benito Mussolini
(*c*) Adolf Hitler (*d*) Francisco Franco.

16. 'Jewish penicillin' means a type of soup. What is it?
(*a*) Chicken soup (*b*) Mushroom soup
(*c*) Prawn soup (*d*) Vegetable soup.

17. What happens to camphor when it is heated?
(*a*) Boils (*b*) Reacts (*c*) Melts (*d*) Sublimes.

18. Who ruled over China from 1279 till the Ming dynasty and dislodged the Mongols?
(*a*) Mangu (*b*) Kublai (*c*) Hulagu (*d*) Batu.

19. When was the International Development Association (IDA), an affiliate of the World Bank, established?
(*a*) 1954 (*b*) 1956 (*c*) 1958 (*d*) 1960.

20. What is the meaning of turgid?
(*a*) Bombastic (*b*) Confused
(*c*) Turbulent (*d*) Unclear.

QUIZ 47

1. Which USA President was nicknamed 'Old Rough and Ready'?
   (*a*) Herbert Hoover (*b*) Theodore Roosevelt
   (*c*) Zachary Taylor (*d*) Abraham Lincoln.
2. Who won the women's Wimbledon tennis single title between 1920-1923?
   (*a*) Kitty Mckane (*b*) Helen Wills
   (*c*) Suzanne Lenglen (*d*) Cilly Aussem.
3. Which historian won two Pulitzer prizes for general non-fiction, namely, *The Guns of August and Stilwell and the American Experience in China*, 1911 — 1945?
   (*a*) Barbara Tuchman (*b*) Jane Austen
   (*c*) John Steinback (*d*) Ernest Hemingway.
4. Who won the Academy Award for best actress in 1967?
   (*a*) Julie Andrews (*b*) Katharine Hepburn
   (*c*) Sophia Loren (*d*) Diana Keaton.
5. What is a 'gadwall'?
   (*a*) Cat (*b*) Dog (*c*) Pig (*d*) Duck.
6. To which country do the Galapagos Islands belong?
   (*a*) Chile (*b*) Ecuador (*c*) Venezuela (*d*) Brazil.
7. What was Judy Garland's real name?
   (*a*) Mary Ann Evans (*b*) Samuel L. Clemens
   (*c*) Frances Gumm (*d*) Emily Bronte.
8. Which gland disorder makes a giant abnormally tall?
   (*a*) Pituitary gland (*b*) Adrenal gland
   (*c*) Thyroid gland (*d*) Salivary gland.
9. Gorgons were three sisters in Greek mythology. They have been described as monstrous creatures whose ugliness had the

power to turn a viewer to stone. What kind of hands did they have?
(*a*) Golden (*b*) Bronze (*c*) Copper (*d*) Silver.

10. Among the following land measurements in acres, which would be closest to 100 hectares?
(*a*) 245 acres (*b*) 225 acres (*c*) 205 acres (*d*) 185 acres.

11. When did cockpit flight recorders become a compulsory instrument in commercial aircraft?
(*a*) 1964 (*b*) 1965 (*c*) 1966 (*d*) 1967.

12. What is a substance which helps in a chemical change without itself undergoing any change called?
(*a*) Enzyme (*b*) Reducing agent
(*c*) Oxidizing agent (*d*) Catalyst.

13. What is hemophilia?
(*a*) Incurable disease (*b*) Infectious disease
(*c*) Inheritable disease (*d*) Deficiency disease.

14. Which city does Changi airport serve?
(*a*) Hong Kong (*b*) Seoul (*c*) Singapore (*d*) Taipei.

15. The flag of which country is split horizontally, bottom half red, top half white?
(*a*) Poland (*b*) Slovakia (*c*) Madagascar (*d*) Gabon.

16. Skulk is a terminology used for which group of animals?
(*a*) Lions (*b*) Foxes (*c*) Wolves (*d*) Bears.

17. Which Malaysian port is associated with a walking cane?
(*a*) Pekan (*b*) Penang (*c*) Pattani (*d*) Malacca.

18. Who was this Pala ruler who fought with the Rashtrakutas in the eighth century AD?
(*a*) Mahipala (*b*) Gopala (*c*) Dharmapala (*d*) Jayapala.

19. Which country leads in terms of *per capita* aid receipts?
(*a*) Israel (*b*) Bangladesh (*c*) Egypt (*d*) Ethiopia.

20. What is the antonym of wither?
(*a*) Procrastinate (*b*) Proliferate
(*c*) Hibernate (*d*) Rejuvenate.

QUIZ 48

1. In which French city is the headquarters of International Bureau of Weights and Measures located?
(*a*) Nice (*b*) Lyons (*c*) Paris (*d*) Sevres.

2. Which disease is commonly called 'flu'?
(*a*) Small pox (*b*) Chicken pox (*c*) Influenza (*d*) Measles.

3. Who invented printing?
(*a*) Johannes Gutenberg (*b*) Jethro Tull
(*c*) Evangelista Torricelli (*d*) Hans Lippershey.

4. Who won the Academy Award for the best performance by an actor in a supporting role in 1970?
(*a*) Jack Albertson (*b*) John Mills
(*c*) Walter Matthau (*d*) Joel Grey.

5. Jaroslav Drobny won the men's Wimbledon tennis single title between 1920 — 1923. Which African country did he represent?
(*a*) Sudan (*b*) Ethiopia (*c*) Egypt (*d*) Kenya.

6. What is the capital of Daghestan?
(*a*) Tashkent (*b*) Noukachott
(*c*) Baku (*d*) Makhachkala.

7. Who wrote *The International Anarchy* in 1926?
(*a*) Goldsworthy L. Dickinson (*b*) Ernest Hemingway
(*c*) D. H. Lawrence (*d*) Emily Dickinson.

8. What do you call the tube connecting kidney with the bladder?
(*a*) Renal pelvis (*b*) Medullary plexus
(*c*) Loop of henle (*d*) Ureter.

9. In which unit is electric current measured?
(*a*) Volts (*b*) Amperes (*c*) Dynes (*d*) Kilowatts.

10. In which continent is the mountain, Vinson Massif located?
(*a*) Asia (*b*) Antarctica (*c*) Europe (*d*) Africa.

11. In which year did the German chemist, Hans Fischer, receive the Nobel Prize?
(*a*) 1928 (*b*) 1929 (*c*) 1930 (*d*) 1931.

12. How many years after Waterloo did Napoleon die?
(*a*) Four (*b*) Five (*c*) Six (*d*) Seven.

13. Which country's flag has three equal vertical stripes of green, white and orange?
(*a*) Ireland (*b*) France (*c*) Spain (*d*) Italy.

14. What colour is an amethyst?
(*a*) Green (*b*) Red (*c*) Blue (*d*) Purple.

15. An incredible gambling mania began in Holland in 1634 centered on which flower?
(*a*) Rose (*b*) Pansy (*c*) Lotus (*d*) Tulip.

16. In ancient Greece, what was a 'hoplite'?
(*a*) Soldier (*b*) Politician (*c*) Gladiator (*d*) Slave.

17. Which of the following is not a natural dye of either vegetable or animal origin?
(*a*) Azo dye (*b*) Tyrian purple (*c*) Indigo (*d*) Saffron.

18. From where did Abbot Odo reform all aspects of Western European Christianity and the Benedictine order?
(*a*) Strasbourg (*b*) Cluny (*c*) Frankfurt (*d*) Cologne.

19. Among the following countries, which has the largest *per capita* daily calorie intake?
(*a*) Turkey (*b*) Norway
(*c*) United Arab Emirates (*d*) France.

20. What do you mean by oblique?
(*a*) Obscure (*b*) Sophisticated
(*c*) Opposite (*d*) Indirect.

QUIZ 49

1. When was Memphis, ancient Egypt's first capital, which stood near the site of present-day Cairo, founded?
   (*a*) 4100 BC (*b*) 3600 BC (*c*) 3100 BC (*d*) 2600 BC.
2. Laos is a land-locked country in Asia which shares border with a number of countries. Of the following, which does not share border with Laos?
   (*a*) Vietnam (*b*) Thailand (*c*) Indonesia (*d*) Kampuchea.
3. Whose books of verse include *Speak with the Sun* (1949) and *The Branch of Dodona* (1970)?
   (*a*) Robert Campbell (*b*) Patrick Campbell
   (*c*) Donald Campbell (*d*) David Campbell.
4. What is a 'carob'?
   (*a*) Tree (*b*) Bird (*c*) Cat (*d*) Cheese.
5. Carolingian art was a style of art created during the late 700's and the 800's primarily in two countries. One was Germany, which was the other?
   (*a*) Spain (*b*) Austria (*c*) Italy (*d*) France.
6. Who won the Academy Award for best actor in 1987?
   (*a*) Paul Newman (*b*) Michael Douglas
   (*c*) Dustin Hoffman (*d*) Tom Hanks.
7. Who won the Professional Golfer's Association (PGA) tournament in 1974 and 1984?
   (*a*) Arnold Palmer (*b*) Lee Trevino
   (*c*) Gary Player (*d*) Jack Nickalus.
8. Before the Royal Bengal Tiger, which was the national animal of India?
   (*a*) Leopard (*b*) Panther (*c*) Lion (*d*) Cow.
9. Which terrorist group was responsible for the Munich Olympic massacre of 1972?
   (*a*) Black September (*b*) Hizibollah
   (*c*) The Shining Path (*d*) ETA.

10. In a healthy body, what should be the daily quantity of urine production?
(*a*) 1 liter (*b*) 1.5 liters (*c*) 2 liters (*d*) 2.5 liters.

11. What have the following in common : Sheraton and Hepplewhite?
(*a*) All types of owl (*b*) All pears
(*c*) All chair designs (*d*) All varieties of cheese.

12. Which gas fills electric lamps after they are sealed?
(*a*) Nitrogen (*b*) Ozone (*c*) Carbon dioxide (*d*) Argon.

13. Who founded the Indian National Congress?
(*a*) A.O. Hume (*b*) Subas Chandra Bose
(*c*) J.L. Nehru (*d*) Mahatma Gandhi.

14. What is Baden Powell known for?
(*a*) Being the pioneer of jazz
(*b*) Being a world famous guitarist
(*c*) Being a staunch supporter of Pakistan's movement
(*d*) Being the founder of boy scouts and girl guides.

15. Where would you find a *parlor*, a *scriptorium*, a *dorter* and a *cellarium*?
(*a*) Monastery (*b*) Police station (*c*) Restaurant (*d*) Court.

16. What colour are laburnum flowers?
(*a*) Red (*b*) Purple (*c*) Yellow (*d*) White.

17. Of which island group is Viti Levu the largest?
(*a*) Fiji (*b*) Seychelles (*c*) Falkland (*d*) Caribbean.

18. The Third Legion constructed this Roman colony in North Africa as protection against desert tribes, and as a senate house. Name it.
(*a*) Aswan (*b*) Thamagudi (*c*) Nimes (*d*) Alexandria.

19. Among the following low-income countries, where is the crude birth rate the highest?
(*a*) Egypt (*b*) Burundi (*c*) Kenya (*d*) Malawi.

20. What is the meaning of immaculate?
(*a*) Completely honest (*b*) Perfect (*c*) Spotless (*d*) Sad.

QUIZ 50

1. What is the capital of Wales?
   (*a*) Gwent (*b*) Cardiff (*c*) Dyfed (*d*) Powys.
2. Who wrote *The New Machiavelli*?
   (*a*) H.G. Wells (*b*) Jules Verne
   (*c*) Daniel Defoe (*d*) Walter Scott.
3. Which country produces the most wine?
   (*a*) Argentina (*b*) France (*c*) Spain (*d*) Italy.
4. When did the Act of Union join England and Wales with Scotland to form Great Britain?
   (*a*) May 1, 1707 (*b*) June 1, 1707
   (*c*) July 1, 1707 (*d*) August 1, 1707.
5. Which UN organization received the 1965 Nobel Peace Prize?
   (*a*) UNESCO (*b*) WHO (*c*) UNICEF (*d*) ILO.
6. When did Nepal become a member of the United Nations?
   (*a*) 1951 (*b*) 1953 (*c*) 1955 (*d*) 1957.
7. What is a 'Japanese chin'?
   (*a*) Dog (*b*) Cat (*c*) Mouse (*d*) Cow.
8. Where is the newspaper the *Mainichi Shimbun* published?
   (*a*) China (*b*) Republic of Korea (*c*) Singapore (*d*) Japan.
9. What do you mean by a *khotia* in Lesotho?
   (*a*) Toilet (*b*) Kitchen (*c*) Bedroom (*d*) Meeting place.
10. Where is Simpson Desert?
    (*a*) Canada (*b*) Australia (*c*) USA (*d*) China.
11. What is the meaning of the drink 'Mother's Ruin'?
    (*a*) Vodka (*b*) Whiskey (*c*) Gin (*d*) Brandy.
12. For which film did Gene Hackman win the award for best actor in 1971?
    (*a*) *The French Connection* (*b*) *Unforgiving*
    (*c*) *Harry and Tonto* (*d*) *Raging Bull.*

13. Anita Lizana won the women's single US tennis championship title in 1937. Which country did she represent?
(*a*) Mexico (*b*) Argentina (*c*) Spain (*d*) Chile.

14. What is the diameter of a basketball ring?
(*a*) 16 inches (*b*) 17 inches (*c*) 18 inches (*d*) 19 inches.

15. What was the world's approximate population at the time of Christ?
(*a*) 150 million (*b*) 250 million
(*c*) 350 million (*d*) 450 million.

16. Soto and Rinzai are the two main branches of which religion?
(*a*) Hinduism (*b*) Islam (*c*) Jainism (*d*) Buddhism.

17. Who was the first European author said to have used a typewriter?
(*a*) Leo Tolostoy (*b*) D.H. Lawrence
(*c*) Alexander Dumas (*d*) Ben Travers.

18. During excavation at San Lorenzo Tenochtitlan were unearthed many pieces of monumental sculpture in volcanic stone-giant heads deliberately defaced, then buried. Who were their creators?
(*a*) Aztecs (*b*) Incas (*c*) Olmecs (*d*) Mayans.

19. Which country has made the largest use of International Monetary Fund (IMF) credit?
(*a*) Ecuador (*b*) Mexico (*c*) China (*d*) India.

20. What do you mean by apnoea?
(*a*) Inability to sleep (*b*) Inability to swallow
(*c*) Inability to breathe (*d*) Inability to stand up.

QUIZ 51

1. The Kumbh Mela at Nasik, India is held on the bank of which river?
(*a*) Hooghly (*b*) Goodavari (*c*) Ganges (*d*) Brahmaputra.

2. Which famous singing group made their respective acting debuts in the film, *Anmie Hall and Catch* 22?
(*a*) Culture Club (*b*) Simon and Garfunkel
(*c*) Bee Gees (*d*) Queen

3. By what name is the disease, *varicella*, more commonly known?
(*a*) Small Pox (*b*) Chicken Pox (*c*) Measles (*d*) Mumps.

4. Name the Russian Nobel laureate who coined the term 'conditioned reflex'?
(*a*) Lev D. Landau (*b*) Nikolai N. Semenov
(*c*) Igor Y. Tamm (*d*) Ivan P. Pavlov.

5. Tarsals and Metatarsals are found in which part of the body?
(*a*) Arms (*b*) Heart (*c*) Feet (*d*) Lungs.

6. Arnold Smith, Sridath Ramphal and Emeka Anyaoke have all held top posts in which global organization?
(*a*) United Nations Children Fund
(*b*) International Labour Organization
(*c*) Commonwealth
(*d*) United Nations Fund for Population Activities.

7. Where did kick-boxing originate?
(*a*) Japan (*b*) Thailand (*c*) China (*d*) Korea.

8. Who won the Academy Award as the best achiever in directing in 1981?
(*a*) Warren Beatty (*b*) Robert Redford
(*c*) Michael Cimino (*d*) Woody Allen.

9. On August 26-28, 1883, a volcano named Krakatau erupted which killed almost 35,000 people. Where is this volcano located?
(*a*) Ecuador (*b*) Bolivia (*c*) Philippines (*d*) Indonesia.

10. In which country was the ban on the works of Aristotle, Shakespeare and Dickens lifted in 1968?
(*a*) Bulgaria (*b*) China (*c*) Poland (*d*) Hungary.

11. About what proportion of a man's body weight is the weight of his blood?
(*a*) 16 per cent (*b*) 12 per cent (*c*) 8 per cent (*d*) 4 per cent.

12. When did Charles Dickens die?
(*a*) 1840 (*b*) 1850 (*c*) 1860 (*d*) 1870.

13. Which element's name is derived from the Greek word meaning 'lazy'?
(*a*) Argon (*b*) Aluminum (*c*) Zinc (*d*) Gold.

14. If you suffer from cynanthropy, what do you think you are?
(*a*) Cat (*b*) Dog (*c*) Cow (*d*) Horse.

15. Name the sea having no coast.
(*a*) North Sea (*b*) Dead Sea (*c*) Red Sea (*d*) Sargasso Sea.

16. What is the length of a hockey pitch?
(*a*) 110 yards (*b*) 105 yards (*c*) 100 yards (*d*) 95 yards.

17. There were three kings who were the founders and consolidators of the Gupta dynasty : Kumaragupta, Samudragupta and somebody else. Can you name the third king?
(*a*) Chandragupta II (*b*) Samudragupta II
(*c*) Skandagupta (*d*) Rudradaman.

18. Who wrote *Mathematical Analysis for Economists*?
(*a*) William Nordhaus (*b*) R.G. Lipsey
(*c*) Richard Quandt (*d*) A. Chiang.

19. Which country has the world's largest cattle population?
(*a*) Canada (*b*) Australia (*c*) India (*d*) China.

20. What is the meaning of cloaca?
(*a*) A sewer
(*b*) Sticky and smelly matter
(*c*) Animal refuse in a slaughterhouse
(*d*) Entrails of animals.

QUIZ 52

1. What is the disease that crippled the efforts of many sea explorers in the fifteenth and sixteenth centuries?
(*a*) Typhoid (*b*) Measles (*c*) Scurvy (*d*) Dysentery.

2. Where is the 'Valley of Kings' located?
(*a*) Syria (*b*) Egypt (*c*) Jordan (*d*) Iraq.

3. Who wrote about Faust or Doctor Faustus?
(*a*) Goethe (*b*) Berlioz (*c*) Liszt (*d*) Wagner.

4. What is the other name of the 'Battle of the Three Emperors'?
(*a*) Battle of Nile (*b*) Battle of Trafalgar
(*c*) Battle of Austerlitz (*d*) Battle of Waterloo

5. When did the French establish the Fifth Republic?
(*a*) 1963 (*b*) 1958 (*c*) 1953 (*d*) 1948.

6. If you lapidated somebody,what would you be doing to him?
(*a*) Kissing (*b*) Embracing (*c*) Surrounding (*d*) Stoning.

7. Who was the British Prime Minister who enacted national health and nationalized many industries?
(*a*) Winston Churchill (*b*) Stanley Baldwin
(*c*) Harold Wilson (*d*) Clement Attlee.

8. With the launching of which satellite on October 4, 1957 did the space age begin?
(*a*) Apollo 2 (*b*) Soyuz 1 (*c*) Sputnik 1 (*d*) Vostok 1.

9. What was the real name of Sri Ramakrishna, the god-man of modern India?
(*a*) Gadadhar (*b*) Ram Kumar
(*c*) Mathur Babu (*d*) Keshab Chandra Sen.

10. Who led the US delegation in hammering out a deal with China for its entry into World Trade organization (WTO)?
(*a*) Charlene Barshefsky (*b*) Madeleine Albright
(*c*) Julia V. Taft (*d*) Karl Inderfuth.

11. For which film did Kevin Costner win the Academy Award for best achievement in directing?
(*a*) The Silence of the Lambs (*b*) Unforgiven
(*c*) Dances with Wolves (*d*) Rainman.

12. Who won the men's Wimbledon tennis single title between 1976-1980?
(*a*) Arthur Ashe (*b*) Bjorn Borg
(*c*) Rod Laver (*d*) John McEnroe.

13. Turning an ordinary number into a power of 10 creates what?
(*a*) Logarithm (*b*) Antilogarithm
(*c*) Square root (*d*) Exponential.

14. Approximately, how many times thicker is blood than water?
(*a*) 2 times (*b*) 4 times (*c*) 6 times (*d*) 8 times.

15. What kind of fruit is a 'kumquat'?
(*a*) Apple (*b*) Pear (*c*) Mango (*d*) Orange.

16. Which planet is called the 'Horned Planet'?
(*a*) Venus (*b*) Mars (*c*) Earth (*d*) Saturn.

17. Which of the following depicts silica gel as a very useful agent?
(*a*) Solvent (*b*) Raw material for soap
(*c*) Drying agent (*d*) Wetting agent.

18. A vast number of Indus seals in this place of the Middle East proves the existence of Harappan and Sumerian trade connection. What is it called?
(*a*) United Arab Emirates (*b*) Bahrain
(*c*) Kuwait (*d*) Qatar.

19. Which school was founded by Wilhelm Roscher?
(*a*) Mathematical School (*b*) Historical School
(*c*) Cambridge School (*d*) Austrian School.

20. What do you mean by admonition?
(*a*) Disapproval (*b*) Prohibition (*c*) Anger (*d*) Warning.

QUIZ 53

1. Terbium, an element, was discovered by Carl Mosander in 1843. What was his nationality?
(*a*) Denmark (*b*) Finland (*c*) Norway (*d*) Sweden.

2. Many scholars consider *Pamela* (1740) to be the first true novel in English. Who wrote it?
(*a*) Henry Felding (*b*) Samuel Richardson
(*c*) Alexander Pope (*d*) Joseph Addison

3. On which sea is Odessa situated?
(*a*) The Black Sea (*b*) The Red Sea
(*c*) The Adriatic Sea (*d*) The Caspian Sea.

4. The terms 'fumaroles' and 'solfaterres' are associated with which natural phenomenon?
(*a*) Landslides (*b*) Earthquakes
(*c*) Typhoon (*d*) Volcanoes.

5. Prince Albert expired at the age of 42 in 1861. What was the cause?
(*a*) Plague (*b*) Typhoid (*c*) Suicide (*d*) Horse accident.

6. Who was the first King of unified Nepal?
(*a*) Rana Bahadur Shah (*b*) Pratap Singh Shah
(*c*) Prithibi Narayan Shah (*d*) Nara Bhupal Shah.

7. In which year did the film *Gandhi* win an Academy Award as best picture?
(*a*) 1982 (*b*) 1983 (*c*) 1984 (*d*) 1985.

8. Which is the largest city in Africa?
(*a*) Algiers (*b*) Lagos (*c*) Kinshasa (*d*) Cairo.

9. *The Firebird*, a ballet, was first performed in 1910. Who wrote it?
(*a*) Allan Berg (*b*) Elliott Carter
(*c*) Dimitri Shostakovich (*d*) Igor Stravinsky.

10. Who discovered electron in 1897?
(*a*) Niels Bohr (*b*) J.J. Thomson
(*c*) Richard Feynman (*d*) Albert Einstein.

11. James Monroe was elected the President of the USA in 1816. Which one?
(*a*) Third (*b*) Fifth (*c*) Seventh (*d*) Ninth.

12. Carapace is the upper body part of which creature?
(*a*) Alligator (*b*) Dog (*c*) Tortoise (*d*) Elephant.

13. According to Greek mythology, which musical instrument did Hermes present to Apollo?
(*a*) Lyre (*b*) Flute (*c*) Trumpet (*d*) Mouthorgan.

14. When did Harold Macmillan made his famous 'wind of change' speech in Cape Town to both houses of the South African parliament?
(*a*) January 3,1960 (*b*) February 3, 1960
(*c*) March 3, 1961 (*d*) April 3, 1961.

15. King Zog belonged to which country?
(*a*) Italy (*b*) Ethiopia (*c*) Nepal (*d*) Albania.

16. In darts, what is the height from the floor to the center of the bull?
(*a*) 5 ft. (*b*) 5 ft. 4 inches (*c*) 5 ft. 8 inches (*d*) 6 ft.

17. Pneumonia is a disease of what?
(*a*) Lungs (*b*) Heart (*c*) Pancreas (*d*) Gall bladder.

18. Which insect is called the 'croton bug' in New York?
(*a*) Cricket (*b*) Cockroach (*c*) Caterpillar (*d*) Cranefly.

19. In which year was Francis Quensay's *Tableu Economique* published?
(*a*) 1758 (*b*) 1762 (*c*) 1766 (*d*) 1770.

20. What do you mean by masochist?
(*a*) One who derives pleasure from giving other pain
(*b*) One who indulges in abnormal sex practices
(*c*) A woman paid to whip her client
(*d*) One who derives pleasure from pain.

QUIZ 54

1. Of which group of islands is Mahe the main island?
   (*a*) The Seychelles (*b*) The Bahamas
   (*c*) The Canary Islands (*d*) The Channel Islands.
2. The 'Stresa Front' of 1935 was a union of Britain, France and Italy, against which country?
   (*a*) Spain (*b*) Germany (*c*) Portugal (*d*) Austria.
3. According to Dr. Johnson, claret is the liquor for boys, port for men, but he who aspires to be a hero must drink what?
   (*a*) Gin (*b*) Vodka (*c*) Brandy (*d*) Rum.
4. What shape is a lunette in architecture?
   (*a*) Triangular (*b*) Circular
   (*c*) Rectangular (*d*) Trapezeium-like
5. Who filed the first patent for a jet engine in 1930?
   (*a*) Charles Lindbergh (*b*) Wilbur Wright
   (*c*) Orville Wright (*d*) Frank Whittle.
6. Which Chinese leader once described himself as 'just an ordinary Chinese — but with a bad temper'?
   (*a*) Mào Zedong (*b*) Li Peng
   (*c*) Zhu Rongji (*d*) Wang Xiaodong.
7. Who was the Finish athlete to win the 5,000 meter and 10,000 meter run in both the Olympics, that is, Munich (1972) and Montreal (1976)?
   (*a*) Lasse Viren (*b*) Gunnar Hockert
   (*c*) Miruts Yifter (*d*) Willi Ritola.
8. What is a young turkey called?
   (*a*) Cygnet (*b*) Pullet (*c*) Joey (*d*) Poult.
9. Among the following, who was killed on February 28, 1986?
   (*a*) Indira Gandhi (*b*) Olof Palme
   (*c*) Rashid Karami (*d*) Khalil Wazir.

10. What is the original name of the pop singer, Alice Cooper?
(*a*) Vincent Furnier (*b*) Robert Zimmerman
(*c*) Jacob Cohen (*d*) John Freund.

11. What is the judicial capital of South Africa?
(*a*) Cape Town (*b*) Pretoria (*c*) Bloemfontein (*d*) Durban.

12. Who were the members of the Second Triumvirate formed in Rome in 43 BC?
(*a*) Caesar, Pompey and Antomy
(*b*) Octavianus, Antonius and Lepidus
(*c*) Brutus, Cassius and Antomy
(*d*) Brutus, Pompey and Lepidus.

13. In stock market, what do you mean by a bear market?
(*a*) A market in which prices are rising
(*b*) A market in which prices are stable
(*c*) A market in which prices are fluctuating
(*d*) A market in which prices are falling.

14. Name the Syrian town where an earthquake killed 250,000 people on May 20, 526 AD.
(*a*) Antioch (*b*) Damascus (*c*) Aleppo (*d*) Hama.

15. All horses have one official birthday. When does it fall?
(*a*) January 1 (*b*) February 1
(*c*) March 1 (*d*) April 1.

16. What is chromophobia?
(*a*) Fear of caves (*b*) Fear of clothes
(*c*) Fear of cows (*d*) Fear of colours.

17. What is the maximum legal weight of a bowling ball?
(*a*) 10 pounds (*b*) 12 pounds (*c*) 14 pounds (*d*) 16 pounds.

18. What is the smallest state of the USA?
(*a*) Hawaii (*b*) Rhode Island (*c*) Minnesota (*d*) Texas.

19. Which gas is utilized for disinfecting the air in underground railways?
(*a*) Ozone (*b*) Nitrogen (*c*) Oxygen (*d*) Chlorine.

20. What do you mean by lupine?
(*a*) Like a kangaroo (*b*) Like a fish
(*c*) Like a wolf (*d*) Like a bear.

QUIZ 55

1. Who was the second Prime Minister of Malaysia?
   (*a*) Tun Abdul Razak (*b*) Tunku Abdul Rahman
   (*c*) Mahatir Mohammed (*d*) Abdullah Abdurahman.
2. Which Australian city is known as the 'City of Churches'?
   (*a*) Brisbane (*b*) Perth (*c*) Sydney (*d*) Adelaide.
3. In basketball, how do you define the attacking team's half of the court?
   (*a*) Back court (*b*) Front court (*c*) Lay-up (*d*) Turnover.
4. James K. Baxter was a gifted poet who first gained international recognition in 1958 when Oxford University published a volume of his poems entitled *In Fires of No Returns*. Which country did he represent?
   (*a*) UK (*b*) Canada (*c*) Australia (*d*) New Zealand.
5. Who founded the influential party, *Perserikatan Nasional Indonesia*?
   (*a*) Sukarno (*b*) Suharto
   (*c*) Abdurrahman Wahid (*d*) Megawati Sukarnoputri.
6. Who remarked, "The people will build the happiest country in the world — a country of the people, by the people, for the people"?
   (*a*) Mao Zedong (*b*) John F. Kennedy
   (*c*) Martin Luther King Jr. (*d*) Sun Yat-Sen.
7. Name the sister-in-law of John F. Kennedy Jr. who died in the plane crash with him in July 1999.
   (*a*) Caroline Kennedy (*b*) Tatum O'Neal
   (*c*) Lauren Bessette (*d*) Brook Shields.
8. Name the architect who won the 1999 Pritzker prize.
   (*a*) Richard Rogers (*b*) Norman Foster
   (*c*) Zaha Hadid (*d*) Hugh Hardy

9. Which mathematician invented logarithm?
(*a*) Isaac Newton (*b*) John V. Neumann
(*c*) John Napier (*d*) G. Lebenitz.

10. Which European city was founded in 1050, destroyed by fire in 1624, and rebuilt?
(*a*) Copenhagen (*b*) Oslo (*c*) Prague (*d*) Vienna.

11. Name the Goddess of Knowledge in Indian mythology.
(*a*) Agni (*b*) Laxmi (*c*) Parbati (*d*) Sarswati.

12. Luxembourg uses two languages. Name them,
(*a*) French and German (*b*) Italian and German
(*c*) English and French (*d*) English and Italian.

13. Approximately, how many inches of snow are equal to 1 inch of rain?
(*a*) 8 inches (*b*) 10 inches (*c*) 12 inches (*d*) 14 inches.

14. For what is a platinum record awarded?
(*a*) An LP selling 10 million
(*b*) An LP selling 5 million
(*c*) An LP selling 1 million
(*d*) An LP selling ½ million.

15. About how many times its own weight can an ant pull?
(*a*) Five times (*b*) Ten times
(*c*) Fifteen times (*d*) Twenty times.

16. What is a blue-grey gnatcatcher?
(*a*) An insect (*b*) A vegetable
(*c*) An animal (*d*) A bird.

17. Which king split the series of Norman monarchies in 1154, to establish the Plantagenet line?
(*a*) William III (*b*) Richard III
(*c*) Stephen (*d*) Henry II.

18. Ferric sulfate is obtained when x-rays are passed though a solution of ferrous sulfate. This law is utilized for measuring radiation emitted by radioactive substances in an instrument. What is it called?
(*a*) Oscilloscope (*b*) Cloud Chamber
(*c*) Dosimeter (*d*) Geiger — Muller Counter.

19. When did Milton Friedman receive the Nobel Prize in Economics?
(*a*) 1976 (*b*) 1977 (*c*) 1978 (*d*) 1979.

20. What do you mean by yahoo?
(*a*) Brute in human shape (*b*) Uncultivated person
(*c*) A ghost (*d*) Foreigner.

QUIZ 56

1. Among the following, which is the busiest airport in the world?
   (*a*) O'Hare airport, Chicago
   (*b*) Heathrow airport, London
   (*c*) Orly airport, Paris
   (*d*) Changi airport, Singapore.
2. In which country is vinegrower's day celebrated as a holiday?
   (*a*) Switzerland (*b*) Brazil (*c*) Bulgaria (*d*) Israel.
3. Who was the Prime Minister of UK from 1908 — 1916?
   (*a*) Arthur J. Balfour (*b*) Henry Campbell-Bannerman
   (*c*) Herbert H. Asquith (*d*) David Lloyd George.
4. Who was the world Chess champion between 1975 — 1985?
   (*a*) Gary Kasparov (*b*) Anatoly Karpov
   (*c*) Bobly Fischer (*d*) Boris Spassky.
5. In Nepal, which periodic plan lasted for only three years?
   (*a*) The First Plan (*b*) The Second Plan
   (*c*) The Fourth Plan (*d*) The Seventh Plan.
6. Who was Benito Mussolini's mistress?
   (*a*) Eva Braun (*b*) Josephanie Bonaparte
   (*c*) Rosalyn Carter (*d*) Clara Petaci.
7. Samson was a folk hero of ancient Israel, famed for his great strength. Name his second wife.
   (*a*) Deliah (*b*) Delphi (*c*) Daupheny (*d*) Dolly.
8. Who completed the statue of '*A Shepherd Boy*'?
   (*a*) Bertel Thorvaldsen (*b*) Antoine Coysevox
   (*c*) Gian Lorenzo Bernini (*d*) Benvenuto Cellini.
9. Who wrote *The Devil's Disciple and Caesar and Cleopatra*?
   (*a*) William Shakespeare (*b*) Ernest Hemingway
   (*c*) D.H. Lawrence (*d*) George Bernard Shaw.

10. In 1917, which ship exploded in Halifax, Nova Scotia, Canada killing 1,635 persons?
(*a*) Eastland (*b*) Mont Blanc (*c*) Curaco (*d*) Hobson.

11. When did Gotlieb of Germany invent carburetor?
(*a*) 1876 (*b*) 1880 (*c*) 1884 (*d*) 1888.

12. *Epidermal appendages* compose of three elements. Hairs and glands are two; which is the third?
(*a*) Scalp (*b*) Finger (*c*) Toes (*d*) Nails.

13. Who was referred to as "he looked like a magician and his playing justified his looks"?
(*a*) Winston Churchill (*b*) Benjamin Disraeli
(*c*) Niccolo Paganini (*d*) Franklin Roosevelt.

14. Which Louis was the King of France at the time of the French Revolution and was executed?
(*a*) Louis XVIII (*b*) Louis XVI
(*c*) Louis XV (*d*) Louis XIV.

15. Which is the longest river in Europe?
(*a*) Tagus (*b*) Loire (*c*) Volga (*d*) Liffey.

16. Of the following, which is not a member of G-8?
(*a*) Switzerland (*b*) Japan (*c*) UK (*d*) Canada.

17. The Baltic domination of the Hanseatic League percolated different levels of culture and politics in Europe. It included Wendish, Lithuanians and what?
(*a*) Poles (*b*) Estonians (*c*) Latavians (*d*) Bohemians.

18. Nitrobenzene is used for making aniline, an important chemical used in :
(*a*) Fast-drying varnish (*b*) The making of glue
(*c*) The dyeing industry (*d*) The crimping of wool.

19. Which country has the largest Gross Domestic Product (GDP) in the world?
(*a*) France (*b*) USA (*c*) Japan (*d*) Germany.

20. What is the meaning of concomitant?
(*a*) Accompanying (*b*) Committed
(*c*) Inferior (*d*) Logical.

QUIZ 57

1. What is an instrument for measuring quantities of heat called?
   (*a*) Ammeter (*b*) Chronometer
   (*c*) Calorimeter (*d*) Galvanometer.

2. Who was the President of India between 1974 — 1977?
   (*a*) Fakhruddin Ali Ahmad (*b*) V.V. Giri
   (*c*) Neelam S. Reddy (*d*) Zail Singh.

3. In which city in Italy was John Cabot, the famous explorer, born?
   (*a*) Venice (*b*) Genoa (*c*) Turin (*d*) Rome.

4. Which group of people were probably the first to adopt a mainly solar calendar?
   (*a*) The Greeks (*b*) The Babylonians
   (*c*) The Egyptians (*d*) The Romans.

5. In 1967, Denis Hulme was the Grand Prix World Champion. What was his nationality?
   (*a*) Australian (*b*) Argentinean
   (*c*) Italian (*d*) New Zealander.

6. What is 'cassava'?
   (*a*) A small shrub native to South America
   (*b*) A kind of camel found in Saudi Arabia
   (*c*) The territorial line separating India and Nepal
   (*d*) A seaport of Morocco.

7. What is the chief peak of Caucasus Mountains?
   (*a*) Mt. Blanc (*b*) Mt. Elbrus (*c*) Mt. Etna (*d*) Mt. K-2.

8. Who earned the sobriquet 'Maimed of Lepanto'?
   (*a*) Paul Cezanne (*b*) Mark Chagall
   (*c*) Walter Scott (*d*) Miguel de Cervantes.

9. What are sparkling wines from Italy called?
   (*a*) Sekt (*b*) Cava (*c*) Spumantc (*d*) Champagne.

10. Name the chemist who identified carbon dioxide in 1750s.
(*a*) Joseph Black (*b*) Henry Cavendish
(*c*) Carl Scheele (*d*) Joseph Priestly

11. What are australorp, cornish and dorking, breeds of?
(*a*) Duck (*b*) Chicken (*c*) Horse (*d*) Jaguar.

12. Which country produces the most amount of cacao beans in a year?
(*a*) Malaysia (*b*) Ghana (*c*) Brazil (*d*) Ivory Coast.

13. When was Joseph Stalin born?
(*a*) 1859 (*b*) 1869 (*c*) 1879 (*d*) 1889.

14. Where did badminton originate?
(*a*) UK (*b*) Japan (*c*) France (*d*) India.

15. Who was the first singer to sell a million records?
(*a*) Tina Turner (*b*) Enrico Caruso
(*c*) Michael Jackson (*d*) Donna Summers.

16. A nectarine is a cross of which two fruits?
(*a*) A peach and a plum (*b*) A peach and a pear
(*c*) A plum and a pear (*d*) An orange and an apricot.

17. Which is the only state in the USA over which no foreign flag has ever flown?
(*a*) Idaho (*b*) Minnesota (*c*) Texas (*d*) California.

18. Who wrote the following essays : *Poor Relations and My First Play*?
(*a*) Geofrey Chaucer (*b*) Samuel Johnson
(*c*) Charles Lamb (*d*) Oscar Wilde.

19. Among the low-income countries in Africa, expenditure on education as a percentage of total expenditure is highest where?
(*a*) Rwanda (*b*) Ghana (*c*) Eritrea (*d*) Sudan.

20. Give a synonym for emulate.
(*a*) Expatiate (*b*) Rival (*c*) Liquefy (*d*) Imitate.

QUIZ 58

1. Which country was formerly named South West Africa?
(*a*) Botswana (*b*) Namibia (*c*) Angola (*d*) Lesotho.
2. When did Cook circumnavigate New Zealand?
(*a*) 1749 (*b*) 1759 (*c*) 1769 (*d*) 1779.
3. Which country is known as the 'Sugar Bowl of the World'?
(*a*) Cuba (*b*) Haiti (*c*) Honduras (*d*) El Salvador.
4. A group of scientists headed by the Italian-born physicist Enrico Fermi produced the world's first artificially created chain reaction at a certain American University in 1942. Name it.
(*a*) California Institute of Technology (Caltech)
(*b*) Harvard University
(*c*) Princeton University
(*d*) University of Chicago.
5. With which sport do you associate Jahangir Khan?
(*a*) Tennis (*b*) Table tennis (*c*) Cricket (*d*) Squash.
6. Jenne is a small city in which African country?
(*a*) Malawi (*b*) Mali (*c*) Sudan (*d*) Egypt.
7. Approximately, how many earths would it take to fill up the volume of Jupiter?
(*a*) 2,000 (*b*) 1,500 (*c*) 1,000 (*d*) 500.
8. Who became Prime Minister of UK in 1955?
(*a*) Anthony Eden (*b*) Clement Attlee
(*c*) Winston Churchill (*d*) Harold Macmillan.
9. Which British King ascended the throne at the mere age of ten?
(*a*) Edward VIII (*b*) Edward VI
(*c*) Edward IV (*d*) Edward II

10. Who were the first to observe that a snowflake possesses six sides?
(*a*) The Indians (*b*) The Danes
(*c*) The Portuguese (*d*) The Chinese.

11. Whose work was *Madonna of the Rocks*?
(*a*) Van Gogh (*b*) Pabolo Picasso
(*c*) Leonardo Da Vinci (*d*) Rembrandt.

12. Of the following, which is the earliest renowned American Symphony Orchestra?
(*a*) New York Philharmonic Orchestra
(*b*) Chicago Symphony Orchestra
(*c*) Los Angeles Philharmonic Orchestra
(*d*) Boston Symphony Orchestra.

13. What is the other name for 'laughing gas'?
(*a*) Hydrogen sulfide (*b*) Argon
(*c*) Nitrous oxide (*d*) Calcium Oxide

14. What are *homeguard* and *ulster chieftain*?
(*a*) Tomatoes (*b*) Potatoes (*c*) Onions (*d*) Brinjals.

15. Of what is 'widgeon' a wild variety?
(*a*) Crane (*b*) Swan (*c*) Flamingo (*d*) Duck.

16. Which well-known drink did Dr. John S. Pemberton invent in 1866?
(*a*) Tea (*b*) Coffee (*c*) Cider (*d*) Coca-cola.

17. Which was the first country with women MPs?
(*a*) Finland (*b*) England (*c*) Norway (*d*) Denmark.

18. Approximately, how long does sunlight take to reach the earth?
(*a*) 6 minutes (*b*) 8 minutes
(*c*) 10 minutes (*d*) 12 minutes.

19. Which is the country is the world that has the lowest death rate?
(*a*) USA (*b*) Singapore (*c*) Kuwait (*d*) Korea.

20. What do you mean by venal?
(*a*) Corruptible (*b*) Condonable (*c*) Lewd (*d*) Guilty.

QUIZ 59

1. Which is the longest river in Canada?
   (*a*) Mackenzie (*b*) Slave (*c*) Albany (*d*) Fraser.
2. Among the following, which country has the most doctor per 1000?
   (*a*) USA (*b*) UK (*c*) Italy (*d*) Israel.
3. Mermaid was a mythical creature that lived in the sea. According to popular belief, mermaids had bodies that were half human and half what?
   (*a*) Fish (*b*) Whale (*c*) Shark (*d*) Dolphin.
4. Among the following, which is considered to be John Milton's greatest work?
   (*a*) *Paradise Regained*
   (*b*) *Paradise Lost*
   (*c*) *Samson Agonistes*
   (*d*) *On the Morning of Christ's Nativity.*
5. What was a 'moa'?
   (*a*) Duck (*b*) Insect (*c*) Cat (*d*) Bird.
6. What is the monetary unit of Iceland?
   (*a*) Lempira (*b*) Krona (*c*) Schilling (*d*) Tughrik.
7. Which country produces the most wool?
   (*a*) Australia (*b*) Russia (*c*) New Zealand (*d*) China.
8. Who is the scientist and science fiction writer who coined the term 'robotics'?
   (*a*) Luis Alvarez (*b*) Eugene P. Wigner
   (*c*) Isaac Asimov (*d*) Emilio G. Serge.
9. Which compound also called saltpetre is used in the mixture of gunpowder?
   (*a*) Sodium chloride (*b*) Sulfur dioxide
   (*c*) Ammonium sulfate (*d*) Potassium nitrate.

10. What is the current name of land known as Caledonia till the eleventh A.D.?
(*a*) Ireland (*b*) Scotland (*c*) Wales (*d*) England.

11. In which bird family would you find the species shivering and great horned?
(*a*) Owls (*b*) Swallows (*c*) Eagles (*d*) Pigeons.

12. Which island country gets its name from the Spanish for 'shallow water'?
(*a*) Jamaica (*b*) Tonga (*c*) Bahamas (*d*) Mauritius.

13. Whom did India beat in the final to win its Olympic hockey gold medal in 1980?
(*a*) Pakistan (*b*) Australia (*c*) Holland (*d*) Spain.

14. The name of which animal translates into 'Old Man of the Woods'?
(*a*) Orangutan (*b*) Baboon (*c*) Chimpanzee (*d*) Gorilla.

15. What is the symbol of the World Wildlife Fund (WWF)?
(*a*) Elephant (*b*) Panda (*c*) Tiger (*d*) Bear.

16. Which conqueror was called the 'Scourge of God'?
(*a*) Batu Khan (*b*) Attila, King of Huns
(*c*) Charlemange (*d*) Julius Caesar.

17. Who is the creator of the comic strip character *Peanut*?
(*a*) Wall Disney (*b*) Al Capp
(*c*) Charles Schulz (*d*) Joseph Barbera.

18. What is the name of the mosquito which is a carrier of malaria?
(*a*) Aedes aegypti (*b*) Anopheles (*c*) Culex (*d*) Worker.

19. Approximately, what percentage of the globe's aggregate oil-reserves have been discovered in West Asia?
(*a*) 55 (*b*) 60 (*c*) 65 (*d*) 70.

20. Give a synonym for moribund.
(*a*) Stagnant (*b*) Corrupt (*c*) Indebted (*d*) Stationary.

QUIZ 60

1. To which country does Aruba belong?
(*a*) UK (*b*) USA (*c*) Netherlands (*d*) Portugal.

2. The *Garda Siochana* is the police force of which country?
(*a*) UK (*b*) Ireland (*c*) Italy (*d*) France.

3. Which metallic chemical element has the atomic number 27 and atomic weight 58.9332?
(*a*) Manganese (*b*) Cobalt (*c*) Tungsten (*d*) Platinum.

4. In 1868, three American inventors patented the first practical typewriter. Two of them were Carlos Glidden and Christopher L. Sholes; name the third.
(*a*) Samuel W. Soule (*b*) Friedrich Koenig
(*c*) Lee De Forest (*d*) Dennis Gabor.

5. Among many novels, Joseph Conrad also wrote two absorbing novels about revolutionaries in Europe, *The Secret Agent* (1907) and *Under Western Eyes* (1911). Where was he from?
(*a*) Russia (*b*) UK (*c*) USA (*d*) Poland.

6. Who was the first Prime Minister of Ireland who held the office from 1921 until his death in 1940?
(*a*) Douglas Hyde (*b*) Edward Carson
(*c*) James Craigavon (*d*) Sean Thomas O'Kelly.

7. Cupid was the Roman God of Love. What is he called in Greek mythology?
(*a*) Psyche (*b*) Eros (*c*) Satyr (*d*) Hercules.

8. Which game was introduced by YMCA instructor James Naismith in 1881 to keep his students occupied during winter break?
(*a*) Volleyball (*b*) Handball (*c*) Basketball (*d*) Baseball.

9. Which Asian country's name is derived from the Arabic for 'Fort'?
(*a*) Iraq (*b*) Iran (*c*) Syria (*d*) Kuwait.

10. Bubonic and pneumonic are two types of which deadly disease?
(*a*) Plague (*b*) Leprosy (*c*) Schizophrenia (*d*) Parkinson.

11. In the nursery rhyme, how many men did the 'Grand Old Duke of York' have?
(*a*) 1,000 (*b*) 5,000 (*c*) 10,000 (*d*) 15,000.

12. Among the following, which is the world's longest railway tunnel?
(*a*) Furka Base (Switzerland) (*b*) Apennine (Italy)
(*c*) Channel (England-France) (*d*) Seikan (Japan).

13. Which American city is known as the 'Big Apple'?
(*a*) Tucson (*b*) Denver (*c*) New York (*d*) Houston.

14. What do you mean by *bonsai* in Japanese?
(*a*) Japanese warriors (*b*) Cultivation of dwarf trees
(*c*) Archery (*d*) Tea ceremony.

15. Which is the first country to use a national flag?
(*a*) Denmark (*b*) Spain (*c*) France (*d*) Italy.

16. For which film did Michael Caine win the Academy Award for best performance by an actor in a supporting role in 1986?
(*a*) *Ordinary People* (*b*) *The Killing Fields*
(*c*) *The Last Emperor* (*d*) *Hannah and Her Sisters.*

17. Who commanded the first space flight to orbit the moon?
(*a*) John Young (*b*) James Lovell, Jr.
(*c*) Frank Borman (*d*) Yuri Gagarin.

18. The term 'Bible' comes from the kind of scroll paper available at the city of Byblos. Which tribe traded it all over Europe?
(*a*) Indians (*b*) Phoenicians (*c*) Chinese (*d*) Arabs.

19. In which month of 1945 was the Food and Agriculture Organization (FAO) established?
(*a*) October (*b*) August (*c*) June (*d*) April.

20. How do you define deprecate?
(*a*) Castigate (*b*) Indict (*c*) Elaborate (*d*) Disapprove.

QUIZ 61

1. Who discovered the element, holmium?
   (*a*) J.L. Soret (*b*) Karl Klaus
   (*c*) Humphry Davy (*d*) A. Crawford.
2. Where in Africa is Mt. Soira?
   (*a*) Tanzania (*b*) Nigeria (*c*) Eritrea (*d*) Uganda.
3. Which undersea explorer commanded US Navy submarine *Nautilus* during voyage under Arctic waters to the North Pole in 1958?
   (*a*) Don Walsh (*b*) William Beebe
   (*c*) William R. Anderson (*d*) Jacques Piccard.
4. Who won the 1980 Academy Award as best director for *Ordinary People*?
   (*a*) Woody Allen (*b*) Robert Redford
   (*c*) Warren Beatty (*d*) James L. Brooks.
5. In terms of estimated number, which is the third largest religion in the world?
   (*a*) Christianity (*b*) Buddhism (*c*) Islam (*d*) Hinduism.
6. Noor M. Hassanali, a lawyer, became the President of which country in 1987?
   (*a*) Trinidad and Tobago (*b*) Ghana
   (*c*) Ivory Coast (*d*) Honduras.
7. What was the name of Duke of Wellington's horse which carried him to victory in the Battle of Waterloo in 1815?
   (*a*) Marengo (*b*) Copenhagen (*c*) Shergar (*d*) Bucephalus.
8. What is the process of uniting parts of two plants to form a single plant called?
   (*a*) Rootstock (*b*) Hybrid (*c*) Grafting (*d*) Scion.
9. In Greek mythology, Graces were the daughters of which king?
   (*a*) Zeus (*b*) Solomon (*c*) Saul (*d*) David.

10. Who once called grayling, a game fish, 'the Flower of Fishes'?
(*a*) Saint Augustine (*b*) Saint Xavier
(*c*) Saint Joseph (*d*) Saint Ambrose.

11. Which two places does the Strait of Bonifacio separate?
(*a*) Italy and Sicily (*b*) Corsica and Sardinia
(*c*) Corsica and France (*d*) India and Sri Lanka.

12. Whose popular books for children are *Gremlins* (1943), and *James and the Giant Peach* (1961)?
(*a*) Roald Dahl (*b*) Walt Disney
(*c*) Hans C. Anderson (*d*) Jakob Grimm.

13. Which boxer was nick-named the *Manassa Mauler* by sports journalist Damon Runyon?
(*a*) Sonny Liston (*b*) Jack Dempsey
(*c*) Mike Tyson (*d*) Joe Louis.

14. What is the approximate number of people that died in the earthquake that occurred in Central China in 1927?
(*a*) 50,000 (*b*) 100,000 (*c*) 150,000 (*d*) 200,000.

15. Where did Gautam Buddha deliver his first sermon?
(*a*) Sanchi (*b*) Lumbini (*c*) Sarnath (*d*) Nalanda.

16. What name is given to the flower which retains its natural form and color indefinitely after it has been dried?
(*a*) Gomphrena (*b*) Pansy (*c*) Lotus (*d*) Immortelle.

17. Who invented the steam locomotive in 1804?
(*a*) James Nasmyth (*b*) Richard Trevithick
(*c*) John Fitch (*d*) Charles Parsons.

18. What is the moon?
(*a*) Constellation (*b*) Satellite (*c*) Star (*d*) Planet

19. When was World Health Organization (WHO) established?
(*a*) 1948 (*b*) 1947 (*c*) 1946 (*d*) 1945.

20. What do you mean by subterfuge?
(*a*) Sly (*b*) Pardon (*c*) Evasion (*d*) Shock.

QUIZ 62

1. Which was Ingrid Bergman's first film?
   (*a*) *Casablanca* (*b*) *Intermezzo*
   (*c*) *Gaslight* (*d*) *Spellbound*.
2. *Synoptic Gospels* are those that describe the life of Jesus, Matthew, Mark and Luke and have similarities of detail and arrangement. From which language does the word *synoptic* comes from meaning *see together*?
   (*a*) Latin (*b*) German (*c*) Greek (*d*) Sanskrit.
3. Where are the international headquarters of B'nai and B'rith, the oldest and largest international Jewish Service Organization?
   (*a*) Washington D.C. (*b*) Paris (*c*) London (*d*) Berlin.
4. In which country is the magnificent Buddhist temple 'Borobudur'?
   (*a*) Thailand (*b*) Sri Lanka (*c*) Nepal (*d*) Indonesia.
5. Who was the heavyweight boxing champion recognized both by the World Boxing Association (WBA) and World Boxing Council (WBC) between 1962 to 1964?
   (*a*) Sony Liston (*b*) Joe Fraizer
   (*c*) Gene Tunney (*d*) Evander Holyfield.
6. What is a 'bream'?
   (*a*) Bird (*b*) Dog (*c*) Wolf (*d*) Fish.
7. In which country was Gautam Buddha, also called Light of Asia, born?
   (*a*) India (*b*) Nepal (*c*) Thailand (*d*) Bhutan.
8. What was the occupation of Juan Belmonte?
   (*a*) Heavyweight boxer (*b*) Bull fighter
   (*c*) Motor car racer (*d*) Sprinter.

9. Which country's official language shqiperia means *The Land of the Eagle*?
(*a*) Albania (*b*) Bulgaria (*c*) Greece (*d*) Turkey.

10. On April 9, 1865, Confederate General Robert E. Lee surrendered his ragged army to General Ulysses S. Grant at Appomattox Court House. In which state?
(*a*) Virginia (*b*) Texas (*c*) Utah (*d*) Kansas.

11. What is the atomic number of americium?
(*a*) 65 (*b*) 75 (*c*) 85 (*d*) 95.

12. Which institution received the Nobel Peace Prize in 1977?
(*a*) International Red Cross (*b*) World Health Organization
(*c*) Amnesty International (*d*) Doctors San Borders.

13. Who wrote the autobiography called *The Fairy Tale of My Life*?
(*a*) Jonathan Swift (*b*) Hans Christian Anderson
(*c*) Victor Hugo (*d*) Lewis Caroll.

14. Angstrom is a unit of length used to measure very small distances. What is 1 angstrom equal to?
(*a*) 0.0000001 millimeter (*b*) 0.00001 millimeter
(*c*) 0.001 millimeter (*d*) 0.1 millimeter.

15. If a circular piece with a hole in the center is heated, what will happen to the size of the hole?
(*a*) Change its shape (*b*) Remain stable
(*c*) Increase (*d*) Decrease.

16. Excess of uric acid causes which disease?
(*a*) Heart problems (*b*) Gout
(*c*) Swelling of pancreas (*d*) Malfunctioning of liver.

17. What is the middle name of Robert S. McNamara who became US defense Secretary and also President of the World Bank?
(*a*) Simple (*b*) Strange (*c*) Simon (*d*) Saul.

18. The apogee of Zapotec Red Indian culture was attained between 300 AD and 600 AD. It had a certain colonial city as its crucial center. Which one?
(*a*) Zacatecas (*b*) Acapulco (*c*) Oaxaca (*d*) Orizaba.

19. Who wrote the book *Choice of Techniques*?
(*a*) Amartya K. Sen (*b*) Maurice Dobb
(*c*) F.W. Taussig (*d*) J.M. Clark.

20. What do you mean by humane?
(*a*) Congenial (*b*) Traits of human beings
(*c*) Bombastic (*d*) Kind.

QUIZ 63

1. Who won the 1999 US National Book Award for *Waiting*?
   (*a*) Ha Jin (*b*) Ward Just
   (*c*) Jean Strouse (*d*) Alex S. Jones.
2. Of the following music albums, which does Regina Carter own?
   (*a*) Blondes Have More Fun (*b*) Elegiac Cycle
   (*c*) Rhythms of the Heart (*d*) Breakfast in America.
3. According to studies, what percentage is the Arctic ice thinner than it was just 20 to 40 years ago?
   (*a*) 10 (*b*) 20 (*c*) 30 (*d*) 40.
4. What is a 'chirus'?
   (*a*) *Tibetan antelope* (*b*) *African deer*
   (*c*) *Australian platypus* (*d*) *Siberian tiger.*
5. Name the banker, who offered loan to Walt Disney when he ran $2 million over budget on *Snow white*?
   (*a*) Douglas Fairbanks (*b*) A.P. Giannini
   (*c*) D.W. Griffith (*d*) Daniel Kadlec.
6. Name the blood vessels supplying the heart.
   (*a*) Pulmonary arteries (*b*) Cardiac arteries
   (*c*) Coronary arteries (*d*) Aorta.
7. Who was the British Conservative party leader, largely responsible for Locarno Pact of 1925?
   (*a*) Austen Chamberlain (*b*) Neville Chamberlain
   (*c*) Ernest Bevin (*d*) Robert Clive.
8. Which US state is known as 'Pelican State'?
   (*a*) Iowa (*b*) Montana (*c*) Maine (*d*) Louisiana.
9. When did British Broadcasting Corporation (BBC) launch the world's first regular TV broadcasts?
   (*a*) 1930 (*b*) 1932 (*c*) 1934 (*d*) 1936.

10. Where was the Winter Olympic Games held in 1976?
(*a*) Grenoble, France (*b*) Sapporo, Japan
(*c*) Lake Placid, USA (*d*) Innsbruck, Austria.

11. By what name was the Asian country, Taiwan, formerly called?
(*a*) Cathay (*b*) Batavia
(*c*) Formosa (*d*) Dutch West Indies.

12. What is 'necrophobia'?
(*a*) Morbid fear of death or dead bodies
(*b*) Morbid fear of graves
(*c*) Morbid fear of night
(*d*) Morbid fear of jackals.

13. Who designed the world's first submarine?
(*a*) Robert Fulton (*b*) George Stephenson
(*c*) Rudolf Diesel (*d*) James Watt.

14. Which gas did Joseph Black isolate and term it as 'fixed air'?
(*a*) Carbon monoxide (*b*) Chlorine
(*c*) Oxygen (*d*) Carbon dioxide.

15. Where was the religion Zoroastrianism founded?
(*a*) Iraq (*b*) Iran (*c*) Japan (*d*) China

16. In which sea are the Balearic Islands situated?
(*a*) Adriatic Sea (*b*) Red Sea
(*c*) Mediterranean Sea (*d*) Black Sea.

17. In India, when did Samudra ascend the throne?
(*a*) 335 AD (*b*) 350 AD (*c*) 365 AD (*d*) 380 AD.

18. Apart from man, which primate has the most highly developed brain?
(*a*) Gorilla (*b*) Sloth (*c*) Orangutan (*d*) Chimpanzee.

19. Name the South American country, which defaulted on its Brady-bond interest payments.
(*a*) Brazil (*b*) Chile (*c*) Ecuador (*d*) Mexico.

20. What is the meaning of motley?
(*a*) Lustful (*b*) Multicoloured
(*c*) Wretched (*d*) Multiple.

QUIZ 64

1. Alpha particles are emitted in alpha-radioactivity; of which element are they the nuclei?
(*a*) Oxygen (*b*) Helium (*c*) Nitrogen (*d*) Hydrogen.
2. What is Portland Vase made of?
(*a*) Glass (*b*) Steel (*c*) Brass (*d*) Aluminum.
3. In ancient Greece and Rome, what colour was a symbol of power, worn by kings, magistrates and military commanders?
(*a*) Red (*b*) Blue (*c*) Green (*d*) Purple.
4. In World War I, troops from which Commonwealth captured Vimy Ridge, in April 1917?
(*a*) Canada (*b*) Australia (*c*) Nigeria (*d*) India.
5. In David Storey's novel *This Sporting Life*, what is the sport of the main character, Arthur Machin?
(*a*) Marathon (*b*) Javelin (*c*) Rugby (*d*) Football.
6. In 1972, Queen Margrethe of Denmark became the first female sovereign of her country for quite a number of years. How many?
(*a*) 500 (*b*) 600 (*c*) 700 (*d*) 800.
7. A tercentenary is an anniversary marking the passage of how many years?
(*a*) 200 (*b*) 300 (*c*) 400 (*d*) 500
8. Where did Charles I raise his standard in August 1642, at the outbreak of the First Civil War?
(*a*) London (*b*) Hastings (*c*) Dover (*d*) Nottingham.
9. How many sides has a decagon?
(*a*) Eight (*b*) Ten (*c*) Twelve (*d*) Fourteen.
10. For what were the Guarneri family famous?
(*a*) Violin-making (*b*) Piano-making
(*c*) Guitar-making (*d*) Drum-making.

11. How many milligrams of caffeine are there in an average cup of tea?
(*a*) Thirty (*b*) Fifty (*c*) Seventy (*d*) Ninety.

12. Boris Pasternak's *Doctor Zhivago* could not be published in Russia, but was published in another country in 1957. Name the country.
(*a*) Spain (*b*) Sweden (*c*) UK (*d*) Italy.

13. Which place is +12 hours from Greenwich Mean Time (GMT)?
(*a*) Thailand (*b*) Malaysia
(*c*) Japan (*d*) New Zealand.

14. Which Scandinavian country is known as 'The Land of Thousand Lakes'?
(*a*) Finland (*b*) Sweden (*c*) Norway (*d*) Denmark.

15. On which organ of the human body has the nuclear radiation least effect?
(*a*) Pancreas (*b*) Kidneys (*c*) Brain (*d*) Scortum.

16. *Tour de France* is which long-distance sporting event?
(*a*) Horse racing (*b*) Cycling
(*c*) Motor car racing (*d*) Motor cycle racing.

17. Who described the size and structure of the Milky Way galaxy?
(*a*) Albert Schweitzer (*b*) Victor Hess
(*c*) Harlow Shapley (*d*) Alois Alzheimer.

18. Who acts as a blind boy in *The Colour of Paradise*?
(*a*) Mohsen Ramizani (*b*) Majid Majidi
(*c*) Tom Cruise (*d*) Dustin Hoffman.

19. When was the World Bank's Special Programme of Assistance (SPA) for indebted low-income countries formed?
(*a*) June 1988 (*b*) April 1988
(*c*) February 1988 (*d*) December 1987.

20. If a metal is described as ductile, what is the meaning?
(*a*) Can be bended
(*b*) Can be shaped into different forms
(*c*) Cannot be bended
(*d*) Very rigid.

QUIZ 65

1. When was the African National Congress (ANC) founded in South Africa?
(*a*) 1908 (*b*) 1910 (*c*) 1912 (*d*) 1914.

2. In surgical terms, what do you call to the creation of an opening in an eardrum to relieve pressure and to permit drainage of fluid from an infected middle ear?
(*a*) Nephrectomy (*b*) Myringotomy
(*c*) Mastectomy (*d*) Cholecystectomy.

3. Which is the largest lake in Italy?
(*a*) Lake Constance (*b*) Lake District
(*c*) Lake Como (*d*) Lake Garda.

4. Among the following, which was not an original member of the League of Nations?
(*a*) Iraq (*b*) Iran (*c*) USA (*d*) Japan.

5. In which field did the Norwegian Marius Sophus Lie specialize?
(*a*) Chemistry (*b*) Physics
(*c*) Mathematics (*d*) Biology.

6. From which language has the name 'Christopher' originated?
(*a*) Hebrew (*b*) Greek (*c*) Celtic (*d*) Teutonic.

7. Who wrote the *The Great Gatsby* in 1925?
(*a*) Ernest Hemingway (*b*) William Faulkner
(*c*) F. Scott Fitzgerald (*d*) J.D. Salinger.

8. In opera, whose best-known works include *Rigoletto* (1851) and *Il Trovatore* (1853)?
(*a*) Gialcomo Meyerbeer (*b*) Gioacchino Rossini
(*c*) Richard Wagner (*d*) Giuseppe Verdi.

9. What is central Honshu called in Japanese?
(*a*) Chubu (*b*) Tohoku (*c*) Kanto (*d*) Chugoku.

10. In Roman mythology, Jupiter was King of the Gods and ruler of the universe. What was his other name?
(*a*) Juno (*b*) Jove (*c*) Zeus (*d*) Vulcan.

11. Lee Harvey Oswald shot John F. Kennedy on November 22, 1963; but who shot Lee Harvey Oswald?
(*a*) Jack Ruby (*b*) Earl Warren (*c*) J.D. Tippit (*d*) John Booth.

12. Which was the capital of England before 1000s and has a cathedral — 169 meters long — the longest in England?
(*a*) Plymouth (*b*) Salisbury (*c*) Winchester (*d*) Bath.

13. Who propounded in 1939 that DDT is a powerful insecticide?
(*a*) Werner Heisenberg (*b*) Albert Szent-Gyorgyi
(*c*) Willard Libby (*d*) Paul Muller.

14. Steve Jobs and another colleague developed the Apple II. Name the colleague.
(*a*) John Mauchly (*b*) Vannevar Bush
(*c*) Bill Gates (*d*) Steve Wozniak.

15. Which American President said "We are all Keynesians now"?
(*a*) John F. Kennedy (*b*) Richard Nixon
(*c*) Jimmy Carter (*d*) Bill Clinton.

16. Whom did Leon Spink defeat in 1978 in the World Heavyweight Boxing championship?
(*a*) Muhammad Ali (*b*) Joe Fraizer
(*c*) Mike Tyson (*d*) George Foreman.

17. What are plastics?
(*a*) Solvents (*b*) Salts (*c*) Polymers (*d*) Acids.

18. Who was the first President of the Chinese Republic?
(*a*) Zhao Yang (*b*) Sun Yat Sen
(*c*) Chiang Kai Shek (*d*) Mao Tse Tung.

19. Who was the first American to win the Nobel Prize in Economics in1970.
(*a*) James Tobin (*b*) Milton Friedman
(*c*) Paul Samuelson (*d*) George Stigler.

20. What do you mean by deploy?
(*a*) Spread troops systematically
(*b*) Encounter the enemy
(*c*) Trick the enemy
(*d*) Utilize with a certain objective.

QUIZ 66

1. Which is often considered by many experts to be the oldest city in Europe?
   (*a*) Moscow (*b*) Cadiz (*c*) Rome (*d*) Burgundy.
2. Can you name Erskine Caldwell's famous book, which featured his best-known character, Jeeter Lester and was adopted into a play in 1933 that ran for more than seven years on Broadway?
   (*a*) *The Sure Hand of God* (*b*) *Georgia Boy*
   (*c*) *God's Little Acre* (*d*) *Tobacco Road.*
3. Canaan dog is the native of which country?
   (*a*) Lebanon (*b*) Jordan (*c*) Israel (*d*) Syria.
4. Jose R. Capablanca was world chess champion between 1921 — 1927. Which country did he represent?
   (*a*) Cuba (*b*) Haiti (*c*) Panama (*d*) EL Salvador.
5. In which country is the Atacama Desert?
   (*a*) Chile (*b*) Canada (*c*) South Africa (*d*) Australia.
6. Name the planet between Uranus and Pluto.
   (*a*) Saturn (*b*) Neptune (*c*) Venus (*d*) Mercury.
7. In which month in 1982 did Spain become the 16th member of North Atlantic Treaty Organization (NATO)?
   (*a*) January (*b*) March (*c*) May (*d*) July.
8. Among the following countries, which produces the most petroleum in a year?
   (*a*) Iran (*b*) Saudi Arabia (*c*) USA (*d*) Russia.
9. When did Max Planck publish his quantum theory?
   (*a*) 1895 (*b*) 1900 (*c*) 1905 (*d*) 1910.
10. Name the term used in poetry whose sound suggests the sound it refers to.
    (*a*) Alliteration (*b*) Stanza (*c*) Onomatopoeia (*d*) Trochee.

11. How much was a 'groat' worth?
(*a*) Twopence (*b*) Fourpence
(*c*) Sixpence (*d*) Eightpence.

12. Which organ of the body is affected by Bright's disease?
(*a*) Lung (*b*) Heart (*c*) Pancreas (*d*) Kidney.

13. How many muscles are there in the trunk of an elephant?
(*a*) About 35,000 (*b*) About 40,000
(*c*) About 45,000 (*d*) About 50,000.

14. In the mid 1500s, what was the approximate population of England?
(*a*) 1 million (*b*) 2 million (*c*) 3 million (*d*) 4 million.

15. Of which state was V.P. Singh, a former Prime Minister of India, Chief Minister during the early 1980s?
(*a*) Uttar Pradesh (*b*) Bihar (*c*) Orissa (*d*) Gujarat.

16. In skiing, what is the impression made in the snow by a fallen skier called?
(*a*) Sitzmark (*b*) Stem (*c*) Snowplough (*d*) Schussing.

17. In 280 BC, King Pyrrhus of Epirus went to Italy and vanquished the Romans. This was called a Pyrrhic victory. Can you give its precise meaning?
(*a*) Victory against a superior power
(*b*) Victory attained by much bloodshed and large-scale massacre
(*c*) Victory against a puny power
(*d*) Victory in which the loses were almost tantamount to gain.

18. Alums utilized for purifying water are chemically :
(*a*) Hydrated nitrates (*b*) Double Chlorides
(*c*) Double sulfates (*d*) Sulfate of aluminum.

19. At what rate of interest does the World Bank provide loans to developing countries?
(*a*) 2.5% (*b*) 3.5% (*c*) 4.5% (*d*) 5.5%.

20. What do you mean by berserk?
(*a*) Violent and destructive (*b*) Dirty
(*c*) Strange (*d*) Disturbed.

QUIZ 67

1. When did Burundi become a member of the United Nations (UN)?
   (*a*) 1954 (*b*) 1958 (*c*) 1962 (*d*) 1966.
2. Who won the Olympic gold medal in the 100 meter run in 1980?
   (*a*) Jim Hines (*b*) Allan Wells
   (*c*) Hasely Crawford (*d*) Carl Lewis.
3. In which country is Timbuktu?
   (*a*) Mali (*b*) Malawi (*c*) Lesotho (*d*) Kenya.
4. What is a group of peacocks called?
   (*a*) Husk (*b*) Pride (*c*) Gaggle (*d*) Muster.
5. For which film did Whoopi Goldberg win the Academy Award for best performance by an actress in a supporting role in 1990?
   (*a*) *Ghost* (*b*) *Reversal of Fortune*
   (*c*) *Unforgiven* (*d*) *Misery*.
6. What is the study of flag history and symbolism called?
   (*a*) Numismatics (*b*) Vexillology
   (*c*) Philately (*d*) Ornithology.
7. Whose first novel was *This Side of Paradise* (1920)?
   (*a*) F. Scott Fitzgerald (*b*) D.H. Lawrence
   (*c*) William B. Yeats (*d*) Saul Bellow.
8. Among the following, which is the leading country in forest products?
   (*a*) Canada (*b*) India (*c*) China (*d*) USA.
9. Who founded the *Merovingian dynasty* (a series of rules of the same family), and adopted Christianity?
   (*a*) Charles Martel (*b*) Hugh Capet
   (*c*) Clovis (*d*) Herod.

10. Among the following, which is the world's longest motor-traffic tunnel?
(*a*) S.T. Gotthard Road (Switzerland) (*b*) Arlberg (Austria)
(*c*) Gran Sasso (Italy) (*d*) Ena (Japan).

11. Dabbling, porching, whistling and stifftail are all varieties of which bird?
(*a*) Peacock (*b*) Duck (*c*) Dove (*d*) Kingfisher.

12. After which inventor of the first digital calculator has a computer language been named?
(*a*) Albert A. Michelson (*b*) Hendrik Lorentz
(*c*) John Strutt (*d*) Blaise Pascal.

13. Which traditional Scottish drink, literally means, 'the drink which satisfies' in Gaelic?
(*a*) Drambuie (*b*) Gin (*c*) Screw driver (*d*) Whisky sour.

14. In which city was the German Republic established under the Constitution of 1911 before being finally overthrown in 1933?
(*a*) Cologne (*b*) Hamburg (*c*) Weimar (*d*) Berlin.

15. In the Hindu epic *Mahabharat*, who was Abhimanyu's mother?
(*a*) Draupadi (*b*) Subhadra (*c*) Kunti (*d*) Urmila.

16. What type of animals are those who are arboreal?
(*a*) Living on desert (*b*) Living on sea
(*c*) Living on trees (*d*) Living on land.

17. Which Asian capital city literally mean 'Red Hero' in the native language?
(*a*) Phnom Penh (*b*) Pyong Yang
(*c*) Bandar Seri Begwan (*d*) Ulan Bator.

18. What is gold paint made from?
(*a*) Palladium (*b*) Gold (*c*) Platinum (*d*) Copper.

19. Trygve Haavelmo received the Nobel Memorial Prize in Economics in 1989. From which Scandinavian country was he?
(*a*) Sweden (*b*) Norway (*c*) Finland (*d*) Denmark.

20. What is the meaning of marsupial?
(*a*) Pertaining to kangaroos (*b*) Pertaining to wolves
(*c*) Pertaining to bears (*d*) Pertaining to lions.

QUIZ 68

1. Who wrote the following books : *Soul on Ice* (1968) and *Soul on Fire* (1978)?
   (*a*) Eldridge Cleaver (*b*) Samuel Beckett
   (*c*) Ivo Andric (*d*) John Steinbeck.
2. Among the following, which is the leading coal-producing country in the world?
   (*a*) USA (*b*) China (*c*) Poland (*d*) India.
3. Which inventor developed the *wireless telegraph* (radio)?
   (*a*) Samuel Morse (*b*) Thomas A. Edison
   (*c*) Heinrich Hertz (*d*) Guglielmo Marconi.
4. The Tory Party first appeared in English politics in the late 1600s. What is the meaning of *Tory* in Irish?
   (*a*) Sailor (*b*) Solider (*c*) Goldsmith (*d*) Robber.
5. To which country does the Corregidor island belong?
   (*a*) Indonesia (*b*) Malaysia
   (*c*) Philippines (*d*) Papua New Guinea.
6. Who was Viceroy of India from 1899 to 1905 and later became Chancellor of Oxford University?
   (*a*) Lord Curzon (*b*) Henry Pelham
   (*c*) A. J. Balfour (*d*) Earl Russell.
7. When was the first Dalai Lama born in Central Tibet?
   (*a*) 1371 (*b*) 1381 (*c*) 1391 (*d*) 1401.
8. Who said of Beethoven, "Altogether he has an utterly untamed personality"?
   (*a*) Dante (*b*) Goethe (*c*) Mozart (*d*) Wagner.
9. Which US President won a Pulitzer Prize?
   (*a*) Harry S. Truman (*b*) Franklin D. Roosevelt
   (*c*) Dwight D. Eisenhower (*d*) John F. Kennedy.

10. Which vitamin prevents blood-clotting?
(*a*) Vitamin A (*b*) Vitamin C
(*c*) Vitamin D (*d*) Vitamin K.

11. How many toes did Charles VIII of France have on his right foot?
(*a*) Four (*b*) Five (*c*) Six (*d*) Seven.

12. In the binary system, what would 100 represent?
(*a*) Two (*b*) Four (*c*) Six (*d*) Eight.

13. How many times per minute does a canary's pulse beat?
(*a*) About 500 (*b*) About 1000
(*c*) About 1500 (*d*) About 2000.

14. Which channel between Albania and the heel of Italy joins the Adriatic and Ionian Seas?
(*a*) Strait of Otranto (*b*) Strait of Messina
(*c*) Strait of Bonifacio (*d*) Cook Strait.

15. What is a 'gazetteer'?
(*a*) A religious dictionary (*b*) An economics dictionary
(*c*) A geographical dictionary (*d*) A historical dictionary.

16. Who discovered the vaccine for cholera?
(*a*) J. Nicolle (*b*) Edward Jenner
(*c*) John E. Salk (*d*) Louis Pasteur.

17. Who was voted 'Sportswoman of the Decade' in November 1989 (1980-1989)?
(*a*) Florence Griffith Joyner (*b*) Martina Navratilova
(*c*) Chris Evert (*d*) Anne Murray.

18. Which of the following explodes on heating?
(*a*) Azides (*b*) Phosphides (*c*) Sulfates (*d*) Chlorides.

19. When was the Asian Development Bank (ADB) established?
(*a*) 1972 (*b*) 1968 (*c*) 1966 (*d*) 1963.

20. What is larceny?
(*a*) Intercourse (*b*) Suicide (*c*) Theft (*d*) Liar.

QUIZ 69

1. Where is Pitch Lake?
   (*a*) Trinidad (*b*) Kibrati (*c*) Western Samoa (*d*) Grenada.
2. What is a group of monkeys called?
   (*a*) School (*b*) Pride (*c*) Troop (*d*) Pack.
3. Who discovered logarithm in 1614?
   (*a*) Isaac Newton (*b*) John Napier
   (*c*) Johannes Kepler (*d*) Galileo
4. Who is the author of *Last Days of Pompeii*?
   (*a*) A.J. Cronin (*b*) Charles Reade
   (*c*) Hermann Rauschning (*d*) Lord Lytton.
5. When did Marie and Pierre Curie discover radium, used in treating cancer?
   (*a*) 1896 (*b*) 1898 (*c*) 1900 (*d*) 1902.
6. Franz Mesmer, an Austrian doctor, pioneered in the practice of hypnotism. He developed a theory, which was later named mesmerism and believed that a *mysterious* fluid penetrates all bodies. Where, in Austria, was he born?
   (*a*) Iznang (*b*) Vienna (*c*) Salzburg (*d*) Innsbruck.
7. Who painted *The Crucifixion of Saint Peter*?
   (*a*) Michelangelo (*b*) Leonardo da Vinci
   (*c*) Jacopo Bellini (*d*) Giotto.
8. In mining terms, what do you mean by worthless material mixed with the ore?
   (*a*) Adit (*b*) Dip (*c*) Gangue (*d*) Outcrop.
9. What is the monetary unit of Bahrain?
   (*a*) Koruna (*b*) Boliviano (*c*) Colon (*d*) Dinar.
10. Which disease is sometimes called, *hydrophobia*, which means *fear of water*?
    (*a*) Leprosy (*b*) Rabies (*c*) Schizophrenia (*d*) AIDS.

11. Rhode Island is state in the USA. What is its capital?
(*a*) Providence (*b*) Salem (*c*) Bismarck (*d*) Columbus.

12. Who is often regarded as 'Father of Nuclear Science' because of many contributions?
(*a*) Arthur H. Compton (*b*) Albert Einstein
(*c*) Enrico Fermi (*d*) Ernest Rutherford.

13. Which 'City of Water' is built on thirteen islands?
(*a*) Venice (*b*) Helsinki (*c*) Stockholm (*d*) Rotterdam.

14. 'Toxophily' is a love for which sport?
(*a*) Swimming (*b*) Archery (*c*) Fencing (*d*) Judo.

15. In which two European countries is the parliament called 'cortes'?
(*a*) Belgium and Holland (*b*) Austria and Switzerland
(*c*) France and Italy (*d*) Spain and Portugal.

16. Diamond is the hardest substance. Name the second hardest.
(*a*) Corundum (*b*) Platinum (*c*) Palladium (*d*) Ruby.

17. In 1918, from which country did the USA acquire Florida against cancellation of debts?
(*a*) Russia (*b*) Denmark (*c*) Spain (*d*) Portugal.

18. In November 1989, who was voted 'Sportsman of the Decade'?
(*a*) Carl Lewis (*b*) Boris Becker
(*c*) Michael Jordan (*d*) Diego Maradona.

19. Which of the following is not the work of E.H. Chamberlain?
(*a*) Economics of Welfare
(*b*) Theory of Monopolistic Competition
(*c*) Towards a More General Theory of Value
(*d*) The Economic Analysis of Labour Union Power.

20. What do you mean by onerous?
(*a*) Traveling (*b*) Burdensome
(*c*) Veritable (*d*) Probable.

QUIZ 70

1. Who explored coasts of Australia, New Guinea and New Britain?

(*a*) William Dampier (*b*) Charles Stuart
(*c*) William Jansz (*d*) Robert O. Burke.

2. Where is Mount Carmel?

(*a*) Lebanon (*b*) Israel (*c*) Jordan (*d*) Syria.

3. Which British Prime Minister wrote *One Nation*?

(*a*) Winston Churchill (*b*) Harold Wilson
(*c*) Edward Heath (*d*) Margaret Thatcher.

4. Where was Hercules, one of the greatest heroes of Greek mythology, born?

(*a*) Thebes (*b*) Troy (*c*) Babylon (*d*) Thermopylae.

5. Felix Houphouet-Boigny was the President of which country from 1960 to 1993?

(*a*) Ghana (*b*) Zambia (*c*) Cameroon (*d*) Ivory Coast.

6. What do you call an untamed horse in the USA?

(*a*) Bronco (*b*) Dam (*c*) Gelding (*d*) Mustang.

7. In grammar, what shows a change in meaning or in the relationship between one word and another word or group of words?

(*a*) Word order (*b*) Inflection
(*c*) Suprasegmentals (*d*) Conjugation.

8. Who painted *The Burial of Count Orgaz*?

(*a*) Van Gogh (*b*) Mary Ann Moses
(*c*) El Greco (*d*) James Whistler.

9. Who was elected pope in 1073?

(*a*) Gregory XIII (*b*) Gregory IX
(*c*) Gregory VII (*d*) Gregory I

10. What kind of drugs are 'diuretics'?
(*a*) They increase the formation of urine
(*b*) They induce you to sleep
(*c*) They augment the circulation of blood
(*d*) They result in mitigating the pain of rheumatoid arthritis.

11. Ninety-five per cent of a typical duralumin alloy is made up of which element?
(*a*) Copper (*b*) Magnesium (*c*) Manganese (*d*) Aluminum.

12. Scientists divide dinosaurs in two major groups. One is saurischians. What is the other?
(*a*) Brontosaurus (*b*) Ornithischians
(*c*) Iguanodon (*d*) Corythosaurus

13. Where do earliest dolls originate?
(*a*) China (*b*) Japan (*c*) Egypt (*d*) Ghana.

14. Who participated in the Battle of Gravelines?
(*a*) France and Spain (*b*) Spain and Portugal
(*c*) Spain and England (*d*) England and Portugal.

15. Who became the first black to receive a Ph.D. degree from Harvard University?
(*a*) Ralph Bunche (*b*) Martin Luther King Jr.
(*c*) Jesse Jackson (*d*) W.E.B. Du Bois.

16. At which degree is Fahrenheit and Centigrade the same?
(*a*) –20° (*b*) –40° (*c*) –80° (*d*) –100°

17. Which county's flag became official on Independence Day on August 17, 1945 where red stands for courage, and white for purity?
(*a*) Indonesia (*b*) Philippines (*c*) Malaysia (*d*) Thailand.

18. In which state of India was the 'kuchipudi' dance developed?
(*a*) Madhya Pradesh (*b*) Uttar Pradesh
(*c*) Andhra Pradesh (*d*) Himachal Pradesh.

19. What rate of interest does the IMF charge for providing additional concessional balance of payments assistance, under the structural adjustment facilities, to low-income countries?
(*a*) 0.5% (*b*) 1% (*c*) 1.5% (*d*) 2%.

20. What do you mean by oblique?
(*a*) Confused (*b*) Trendy (*c*) Topsy-turvy (*d*) Indirect.

QUIZ 71

1. Who settled on the Gulf of Mexico in 1500 BC, and soon developed the first civilization in the Western Hemisphere?
(*a*) Red Indians (*b*) Olmecs (*c*) British (*d*) Spanish.

2. Who became Prime Minister of Nepal after Kirti Nidhi Bista in 1979?
(*a*) Girija Prasad Koirala (*b*) Marich Man Singh Shrestha
(*c*) Surya Bahadur Thapa (*d*) Lokendra Bahadur Chand.

3. Alexander Solzhenitsyn returned to Russia in 1994. Which was the first city that he set his foot upon?
(*a*) Vladivostok (*b*) Moscow
(*c*) St. Petersburg (*d*) Ekaterinburg.

4. In Miss World 1999 title, Miss Martina Thorogood was placed second. What was her nationality?
(*a*) South Africa (*b*) Venezuela (*c*) Israel (*d*) USA.

5. Who was Sri Ramkrishna's disciple who subsequently became world famous as Swami Vivekananda?
(*a*) Girish Chandra Ghosh (*b*) Manilal Mallick
(*c*) Vijay Goswami (*d*) Narendranath.

6. In the 1960 Olympics in Rome, in which category in boxing did Muhmmad Ali (then, Cassius Clay) win the championship?
(*a*) Super Heavyweight (*b*) Light Heavyweight
(*c*) Middle Weight (*d*) Flyweight.

7. Which city in the Philippines is known as 'the City of Flowers'?
(*a*) Baguio (*b*) Manila (*c*) Quezon City (*d*) Banawe.

8. In ballet, how do you define a pose in which one leg is raised and bent either behind or in front of the dancer?
(*a*) Labanotation (*b*) Arabesque
(*c*) Attitude (*d*) Turnout.

9. Who was the first President of the Republic of Malawi?
(*a*) Idi Amin (*b*) Hastings K. Banda
(*c*) Robert Mugabe (*d*) Modibo Keita.

10. Basutoland was the colonial name of which country?
(*a*) Gabon (*b*) Liberia (*c*) Gambia (*d*) Lesotho.

11. Who wrote *Moby Dick*?
(*a*) Walt Whitman (*b*) Herman Melville
(*c*) Emily Dickinson (*d*) Henry James.

12. Who discovered the basic laws of hydrostatics?
(*a*) Archimedes (*b*) Aristarchus
(*c*) Aristotle (*d*) Socrates.

13. What is a female goat called?
(*a*) Calf (*b*) Ewe (*c*) Nanny (*d*) Cygnet.

14. What is hyptephobia?
(*a*) Fear of cats (*b*) Fear of being touched
(*c*) Fear of fire (*d*) Fear of insects.

15. Which country had the ancient name Albion?
(*a*) France (*b*) Spain (*c*) Portugal (*d*) England.

16. Which country produces the maximum amount of gold in the world?
(*a*) South Africa (*b*) Russia (*c*) Canada (*d*) USA.

17. Which Indonesian Island is called the 'Island of a Thousand Temples'?
(*a*) Borneo (*b*) Bali (*c*) Java (*d*) Sumatra.

18. Antibiotics fight disease and save and preserve life. Of the following which is not an antibiotic?
(*a*) Carbomycin (*b*) Neomycin
(*c*) Cyclohexane (*d*) Tetracycline.

19. Two founder members of the European Free Trade Association (EFTA) left it in 1972 to join the Europe Economic Community. One was Denmark; which was the other?
(*a*) UK (*b*) Belgium (*c*) Netherlands (*d*) France.

20. What is meaning of amorphous?
(*a*) Frustrating (*b*) Flowery (*c*) Shapeless (*d*) Indirect.

QUIZ 72

1. In which American state is the highest peak of North America, Mount McKinley, situated?
   (*a*) North Dakota (*b*) Alaska (*c*) Oregon (*d*) Minnesota.
2. The desert *poires belle helene* consists of ice cream, hot chocolate sauce and which other ingredient?
   (*a*) Pears (*b*) Mangoes (*c*) Oranges (*d*) Apples.
3. What kind of musical instrument is known by the Scottish Gaelic name 'clarsach'?
   (*a*) Guitar (*b*) Flute (*c*) Harp (*d*) Saxophone.
4. A member of the family *Alaudidae*, Woodsworth wrote a poem in its praise. Name it.
   (*a*) The nightingale (*b*) The parrot
   (*c*) The kingfisher (*d*) The skylark.
5. Occasionally known as mark gas or fire damp, what is the real chemical name?
   (*a*) Methane (*b*) Helium (*c*) Nitrogen (*d*) Oxygen.
6. Which King established the measurement of a yard?
   (*a*) Henry VI (*b*) Henry I (*c*) Edward III (*d*) Edward II.
7. In a game of croquet, how many hoops are employed?
   (*a*) Five (*b*) Six (*c*) Seven (*d*) Eight.
8. What kind of a person is a 'benedick'?
   (*a*) A childless couple (*b*) A divorced woman
   (*c*) A newly married man (*d*) An old man.
9. Whose famous painting is named *Arnolfini and his wife*?
   (*a*) Jan van Eyck (*b*) Leonardo Da Vinci
   (*c*) Van Gogh (*d*) Pablo Picasso.
10. In the 1930s, a besieging general boasted that he had four columns encircling a city and a fifth column working secretly within. Name this city.
    (*a*) Malaga (*b*) Madrid (*c*) Barcelona (*d*) Seville.

11. Which common garden flower was developed from the wild viola tricolor or heartsease?
(*a*) Poppy (*b*) Rose (*c*) Pansy (*d*) Lily.

12. In which city is the Chester Beatly Library located?
(*a*) Belfast (*b*) Cardiff (*c*) Glasgow (*d*) Dublin.

13. Toucans are native to South and Central America. What are they?
(*a*) Lions (*b*) Horses (*c*) Dogs (*d*) Birds.

14. Where in the body would you find cells called rods and cones?
(*a*) Retina (*b*) Brain (*c*) Liver (*d*) Pancreas.

15. In the early 1790s, L'Enfant, a French military engineer, drew up plans, which formed the basis of which North American City?
(*a*) New York (*b*) Toronto (*c*) Washington (*d*) Ottawa.

16. On which river is the Russian city Leningrad located?
(*a*) Volga (*b*) Neva (*c*) Elbe (*d*) Danube.

17. For which number does CD in Roman Numeral stand for?
(*a*) 300 (*b*) 400 (*c*) 500 (*d*) 600.

18. According to William Miller, when was the end of the world supposed to take place?
(*a*) 1833 (*b*) 1838 (*c*) 1843 (*d*) 1848.

19. When was the Organization of Petroleum Exporting Countries (OPEC) formed to control the production and pricing of crude oil?
(*a*) 1957 (*b*) 1960 (*c*) 1963 (*d*) 1966.

20. What is the meaning of the adjective hircine?
(*a*) Bearlike (*b*) Wolflike (*c*) Goatlike (*d*) Fishlike.

QUIZ 73

1. King Ferdinand V seized the kingdom of Navarre, completing the unification of what is now Spain. When did this occur?
   (*a*) 1502 (*b*) 1512 (*c*) 1522 (*d*) 1532.
2. What is a 'springbok'?
   (*a*) Antelope (*b*) Penguin (*c*) Tiger (*d*) Bear.
3. Who led the first European expedition to track the Mississippi River of North America to the Gulf of Mexico?
   (*a*) Christopher Columbus (*b*) John Cabot
   (*c*) Sieur de la Salle (*d*) Ericsson.
4. What was the nationality of Karl Marx?
   (*a*) Swiss (*b*) Russian (*c*) Pole (*d*) German.
5. Which of the following countries has the highest life expectancy at birth?
   (*a*) Sweden (*b*) USA (*c*) Japan (*d*) Germany.
6. Which is the longest river in Ireland?
   (*a*) Liffey (*b*) Shannon (*c*) Annalee (*d*) Moy.
7. Who succeeded Abraham Lincoln as President of USA after his assassination?
   (*a*) Ulysses Grant (*b*) Andrew Jackson
   (*c*) Zachary Taylor (*d*) Andrew Johnson.
8. When did the first crossword appear in a British newspaper, the *Daily Express*?
   (*a*) November 2, 1924 (*b*) December 2, 1924
   (*c*) January 2, 1925 (*d*) February 2, 1925.
9. Which city do Moslems regard as their third holiest city?
   (*a*) Medina (*b*) Jericho (*c*) Jerusalem (*d*) Mecca.
10. In which country is the Umfolozi park, which covers 48,000 ha, located?
    (*a*) Kenya (*b*) South Africa (*c*) Uganda (*d*) Ghana.

11. Which is the highest volcano in the world?
(*a*) Cotopaxi (*b*) Paricutin (*c*) Aconcagua (*d*) Stromboli.

12. From which language did the word 'bank' originate?
(*a*) Indian (*b*) French (*c*) Spanish (*d*) Italian.

13. Who is considered to be the 'Father of Geometry'?
(*a*) Pythagoras (*b*) Euclid (*c*) Aristotle (*d*) Archimedes.

14. What is astraphobia?
(*a*) Morbid fear of thunder and lightening
(*b*) Morbid fear of bees
(*c*) Morbid fear of traveling in airplanes
(*d*) Morbid fear of swimming.

15. What could be the age of a campfire girl?
(*a*) Between 10 and 14 (*b*) Between 12 and 16
(*c*) Between 14 and 20 (*d*) Between 12 and 20.

16. What is the currency of China?
(*a*) Kip (*b*) Won (*c*) Yuan (*d*) Yen

17. What are the *quinto*, *conga* and *tumbadora*?
(*a*) Saxophone (*b*) Trumpet (*c*) Guitar (*d*) Drum.

18. Who was awarded the Nobel Prize for Chemistry in 1901 for discovering the laws of chemical dynamics?
(*a*) Eduard Buchner of Germany
(*b*) Henri Moissan of France
(*c*) Alfred Werner of Switzerland
(*d*) Jacobus H. Van't Hoff of Holland.

19. Among the following economic models, which makes the assumption of constant saving-income ratio?
(*a*) Solow model (*b*) Harrod-Domar model
(*c*) Leontief model (*d*) Kaldor model.

20. What is the meaning of turbid?
(*a*) Muddy (*b*) Dysfunctional (*c*) Bombastic (*d*) Ill.

QUIZ 74

1. Who wrote Deerslayer (1841) and *The Last of the Mohicans* (1826)?
   (*a*) James F. Cooper (*b*) Oscar Wilde
   (*c*) Charles Dickens (*d*) Daniel Defoe.

2. Among the following, which is the leading cotton- growing country?
   (*a*) USA (*b*) China (*c*) India (*d*) Pakistan.

3. What is the study of extremely low temperatures called?
   (*a*) Eugenics (*b*) Photosynthesis
   (*c*) Pediatrics (*d*) Cryogenics.

4. Who landed in Cuba in 1492 and claimed the island for Spain?
   (*a*) Christopher Columbus (*b*) John Cabot
   (*c*) Leif Rescission (*d*) Amerigo Vespucci.

5. Stephen Hawking is one of the greatest living theoretical physicists. Name the ailment which he is suffering from.
   (*a*) Parkinson's disease (*b*) Alzhemier disease
   (*c*) Lou Gehrig's disease (*d*) Leprosy.

6. When did Queen Elizabeth I ascend the throne?
   (*a*) 1538 (*b*) 1558 (*c*) 1578 (*d*) 1598.

7. Which American President made the famous remark, "I am a Berliner."
   (*a*) John F. Kennedy (*b*) Richard Nixon
   (*c*) Ronald Regan (*d*) Dwight Eisenhower.

8. Who was described as the following : "He was the artist with whom virtually every other artist had to reckon, and there was scarcely a 20th century movement that he didn't inspire, contribute to or...beget"?
   (*a*) Van Gogh (*b*) Jackson Pollock
   (*c*) Miles Davis (*d*) Pablo Picasso

9. Which animals attract the most fleas?
(*a*) Mongoose (*b*) Dogs (*c*) Cats (*d*) Squirrels.

10. How wide is a hockey goal?
(*a*) 8 feet (*b*) 10 feet (*c*) 12 feet (*d*) 14 feet.

11. What odds are paid for a single number at roulette?
(*a*) 25 to 1 (*b*) 30 to 1
(*c*) 35 to 1 (*d*) 40 to 1.

12. What is the common name for *juglans regia*?
(*a*) Peanut (*b*) Walnut (*c*) Cashewnut (*d*) Groundnut.

13. In which city did the eight-year old Mozart compose his first symphony?
(*a*) Vienna (*b*) Berlin (*c*) Paris (*d*) London.

14. Travelling at the speed of light, how long would it take to reach the planet, Pluto?
(*a*) 6 hours (*b*) 8 hours (*c*) 10 hours (*d*) 12 hours.

15. What are the neighboring countries of Liechtenstein?
(*a*) Switzerland and Holland
(*b*) Austria and Czech Republic
(*c*) Germany and Slovakia
(*d*) Switzerland and Austria.

16. In which year was Burma separated from India?
(*a*) 1937 (*b*) 1938 (*c*) 1939 (*d*) 1940.

17. What is the scientific study and analysis of handwriting called?
(*a*) Numismatics (*b*) Ornithology
(*c*) Graphology (*d*) Scatology.

18. About 90 per cent of which metal is consumed by the world?
(*a*) Tin (*b*) Steel (*c*) Aluminum (*d*) Copper.

19. To which element did Marx attribute the capitalist crisis?
(*a*) Exploitation of labour
(*b*) Inflationary pressures
(*c*) High rate of wages
(*d*) Falling rate of profit.

20. Give a synonym for stymie.
(*a*) Void (*b*) Directionless (*c*) Thwart (*d*) Halt.

QUIZ 75

1. In which sport would you come across the term shell and crab?
(*a*) Archery (*b*) Rowing (*c*) Hang-gliding (*d*) Skiing.

2. The J-league is the national football league of which country?
(*a*) Japan (*b*) Jordan (*c*) Jamaica (*d*) South Korea.

3. Which Geek mythological figure was endowed by the gift of prophecy but was fated never to be believed?
(*a*) Cassandra (*b*) Mercury (*c*) Diana (*d*) Jocasta.

4. Which simple food preparation is named after the eighteenth century British Earl, John Montagu?
(*a*) Pizza (*b*) Sandwich (*c*) Noodle (*d*) Pasta.

5. How many colours are there on the squares of Rubik Cube?
(*a*) Ten (*b*) Eight (*c*) Six (*d*) Four.

6. Which of Dickens' novels was the first work of English fiction to be serialized in weekly parts?
(*a*) *Bleak House* (*b*) *Oliver Twist*
(*c*) *A Tale of Two Cities* (*d*) *Pickwick Papers*.

7. Which film in the James Bond series is named after Ian Fleming's retreat in Jamaica?
(*a*) *Golden Eye* (*b*) *Goldfinger*
(*c*) *Dr. No* (*d*) *The Man with the Golden Gun*.

8. In Roman numerals, which letter represents hundred?
(*a*) M (*b*) C (*c*) L (*d*) X.

9. Frontal, parietal and temporal are the divisions of which organ of the human body?
(*a*) Liver (*b*) Heart (*c*) Lung (*d*) Brain.

10. Among the following countries, which produces the most tobacco?
(*a*) India (*b*) USA (*c*) China (*d*) Brazil.

11. When did the first balloon ascent take place in Australia?
(*a*) 1838 (*b*) 1848 (*c*) 1858 (*d*) 1868.

12. Mineral fertilizers are the most widely used fertilizers. They supply three main elements; two of them are nitrogen and phosphorus. What is the third?
(*a*) Potassium (*b*) Gypsum (*c*) Compost (*d*) Manure.

13. What do you mean by *leis*?
(*a*) Diamond necklace (*b*) Flower necklace
(*c*) Pearl necklace (*d*) Gold necklace.

14. In which country is the Orsay Museum located?
(*a*) Italy (*b*) France (*c*) UK (*d*) USA.

15. Where was Napoleon born?
(*a*) Sicily (*b*) Crete (*c*) Sardinia (*d*) Corsica.

16. What is the capital of Papua New Guinea?
(*a*) Port Moresby (*b*) Suva (*c*) Apia (*d*) Hamilton.

17. Which part of the body is most likely to be affected by nuclear radiation first?
(*a*) Heart (*b*) Eyes (*c*) Bone marrow (*d*) Blood.

18. Which diluted acid is called synthetic vinegar?
(*a*) Nitric acid (*b*) Sulfuric acid
(*c*) Hydrochloric acid (*d*) Acetic acid.

19. Which British philosopher and economist is acknowledged as the 'Founder of Utilitarianism'?
(*a*) John Stuart Mill (*b*) Jeremy Bentham
(*c*) Adam Smith (*d*) David Ricardo.

20. Give a synonym for paroxysm.
(*a*) Fit (*b*) Tipsy (*c*) Anti-climax (*d*) Plunder.

QUIZ 76

1. Who were the 'Sadducees'?
   (*a*) Jews (*b*) Arabs (*c*) Egyptians (*d*) Syrians.
2. Where in Africa could you find the Ahagger Mountain?
   (*a*) Nigeria (*b*) Sudan (*c*) Algeria (*d*) Kenya.
3. Which city in the USA was the site of witchcraft trials in the 1690s?
   (*a*) Nashville (*b*) Little Rock (*c*) Santa Fe (*d*) Salem.
4. What was the pen name of Amantine-Aurore-Luciledupin, a French novelist of the 1800s?
   (*a*) George Sand (*b*) Saki
   (*c*) George Eliot (*d*) Mark Twain.
5. When was Emperor Haile Selassie I of Ethiopia overthrown after 58 years as that country's ruler?
   (*a*) 1970 (*b*) 1975 (*c*) 1980 (*d*) 1985.
6. What is a 'shad'?
   (*a*) Whale (*b*) Alligator (*c*) Fish (*d*) Bird.
7. The ship *Lady of the Lake* struck iceberg in North Atlantic killing 215 people. When did this happen?
   (*a*) 1823 (*b*) 1833 (*c*) 1843 (*d*) 1853.
8. In 604, who introduced Japan's first known written law, the Seventeen Article Constitution?
   (*a*) Suiko (*b*) Yomei (*c*) Shotoku (*d*) Yamada.
9. Snuff is a moist or dry powder made from the leaves of which plant?
   (*a*) Poppy (*b*) Tea (*c*) Tobacco (*d*) Banana.
10. Which Indian served as the first woman president of the United Nations General Assembly?
    (*a*) Vijayalakshmi Pandit (*b*) Indira Gandhi
    (*c*) Sheela Dixshit (*d*) Sarojini Naidu

11. In which city were the Declaration of the Independence and the Constitution of the USA both adopted?
(*a*) Boston (*b*) San Francisco
(*c*) Richmond (*d*) Philadelphia.

12. When did John D. Cockcroft and Ernest T.S. Walton built the first particle accelerator?
(*a*) 1930 (*b*) 1932 (*c*) 1934 (*d*) 1936.

13. Who said the following : (i) "A little learning is a dangerous thing" and (ii) "To err is human, to forgive divine"?
(*a*) William Shakespeare (*b*) Charles Dickens
(*c*) Alexander Pope (*d*) Benjamin Franklin.

14. Which country's Parliament is called Lok Sabha?
(*a*) India (*b*) Denmark (*c*) Germany (*d*) Norway.

15. Which African country's old name was Nyasaland?
(*a*) Mali (*b*) Malawi (*c*) Nigeria (*d*) Kenya.

16. Among the following, which is not a wonder of the ancient World?
(*a*) Hanging Gardens of Baylon
(*b*) Catacombs of Alexandria
(*c*) Temple of Diana at Epheus
(*d*) Light House at Alexandria

17. Who won the 1986 Wimbledon Tennis Men's Singles championship?
(*a*) Pat Cash (*b*) Stefen Edberg
(*c*) Boris Becker (*d*) Arthur Ashe.

18. What highly valued item do we get if gold is added to glass?
(*a*) Pearls (*b*) Diamonds (*c*) Gems (*d*) Rubies.

19. What is the reduction or elimination of inflation known as?
(*a*) Recession (*b*) Disinflation
(*c*) Stagflation (*d*) Deflation.

20. What is the antonym of obnoxious?
(*a*) Pleasant (*b*) Likeable (*c*) Flowery (*d*) Corpulent.

QUIZ 77

1. Which country governs the Shikoku Island?
(*a*) Japan (*b*) South Korea (*c*) China (*d*) Philippines.

2. Where was Thomas Carlyle born?
(*a*) Reading (*b*) Ecclefechan (*c*) Leeds (*d*) Brighton.

3. Which carcinogen or agent causes the oesophagus cancer?
(*a*) Alcohol (*b*) Asbestos (*c*) Benzene (*d*) Scalding tea.

4. Which French surgeon and biologist won the 1912 Nobel Prize in Medicine for his work in blood-vessel surgery and in transplanting organs and tissues?
(*a*) Charles R. Richet (*b*) Alexis Carrel
(*c*) Charles R.A. Laveran (*d*) Jacques Monod.

5. Castile and Aragon were two separate and powerful kingdoms of Spain. When were they united under the rule of Ferdinand and Isabella?
(*a*) 1499 (*b*) 1489 (*c*) 1479 (*d*) 1469.

6. Chad has two official languages. One is Arabic, what is the other?
(*a*) French (*b*) English (*c*) Spanish (*d*) German.

7. What does polymer chemistry deals with?
(*a*) Chemical substances that contain carbon-to-carbon bonds
(*b*) Chemical processes of living organisms
(*c*) Chemical substances that do not contain carbon-to-carbon bonds
(*d*) Plastics and other chainlike molecules formed by linking many smaller molecules.

8. Which of the following works does not belong to Geoffrey Chaucer?
(*a*) *The Canterbury Tales* (*b*) *The Book of the Duchess*
(*c*) *Lady of the Lake* (*d*) *The House of Fame.*

9. Which is the country that produces the most cheese?
(*a*) France (*b*) USA (*c*) Russia (*d*) Italy.

10. Who wrote *God Bless America*'?
(*a*) Irving Berlin (*b*) Paul Revere
(*c*) Mark Twain (*d*) Gore Vidal.

11. About how much larger is the sun than the earth?
(*a*) 230,000 times (*b*) 330,000 times
(*c*) 430,000 times (*d*) 530,000 times.

12. Which planet is called the 'evening star'?
(*a*) Mercury (*b*) Pluto (*c*) Uranus (*d*) Venus.

13. Which was the first peak over 8,000 meters to be climbed?
(*a*) Everest (*b*) K-2
(*c*) Annapurna — I (*d*) Kanchenjunga.

14. How many points are there in a compass?
(*a*) Twenty-eight (*b*) Thirty
(*c*) Thirty-two (*d*) Thirty-four.

15. From which country does the elkhound originate?
(*a*) Norway (*b*) Holland (*c*) France (*d*) Finland.

16. When was the Berlin Wall built?
(*a*) 1966 (*b*) 1961 (*c*) 1956 (*d*) 1951.

17. Rainer Warner Fassbinder, a renowned German film-maker, died at the age of thirty-six. Identify his film from the following :
(*a*) *David Holzman's Diary*
(*b*) *Life to the Scaffold*
(*c*) *The Moment of Truth*
(*d*) *The Marriage of Maria Braun.*

18. Which country won the World Cup football finals in 1962?
(*a*) Brazil (*b*) Italy (*c*) Holland (*d*) Argentina.

19. Who is usually regarded as the 'Father of Modern Management'?
(*a*) Herbert Simon (*b*) Jacob Viner
(*c*) Heavy Fayol (*d*) James D. Mooney.

20. What is the opposite of retribution?
(*a*) Pardon (*b*) Punishment
(*c*) Improvement (*d*) Emancipation.

QUIZ 78

1. Who wrote *The Elegant Universe*?
   (*a*) Brian Greene (*b*) Edward Witten
   (*c*) John Schwarz (*d*) Joel Scherk.
2. Who said the following : "If I'm going to be a symbol of something, I'd rather have it sex than some other things...."
   (*a*) Paul Newmann (*b*) Elizabeth Taylor
   (*c*) Marilyn Monroe (*d*) Sophia Loren.
3. Which is the largest city in Europe?
   (*a*) Istanbul (*b*) Paris (*c*) London (*d*) Moscow.
4. What is clarinet, a musical instrument, usually made of?
   (*a*) Wood (*b*) Brass (*c*) Glass (*d*) Lead.
5. Who was the youngest Prime Minister in the history of Canada?
   (*a*) Brian Mulroney (*b*) Charles J. Clark
   (*c*) Pierre Tradeau (*d*) Lester Pearson.
6. In computer term, what do you call a group of bits that act as a single unit of information, such as a letter or numeral?
   (*a*) Input (*b*) Bit (*c*) Byte (*d*) Modem.
7. What types of birds are classified as *gymnogyps californianus* and *vultur gryphus*?
   (*a*) Condors (*b*) Vultures (*c*) Eagles (*d*) Owls.
8. When did the Cairo metro, the first underground railway in Africa, open?
   (*a*) 1981 (*b*) 1983 (*c*) 1985 (*d*) 1987.
9. Which is the most heavily populated state in USA?
   (*a*) New York (*b*) California (*c*) Texas (*d*) Florida.
10. Among the following, which country produces the most uranium?
    (*a*) USA (*b*) Russia (*c*) Canada (*d*) Australia.

11. When did the allied occupation of Japan end?
(*a*) 1950 (*b*) 1952 (*c*) 1954 (*d*) 1956.

12. When was Winston Churchill born?
(*a*) November 30, 1874 (*b*) October 30, 1874
(*c*) September 30, 1874 (*d*) August 30, 1874.

13. In opera, what do you call an elaborate vocal solo that usually expresses a character's feelings?
(*a*) Verismo (*b*) Singspeil (*c*) Leitmotif (*d*) Aria.

14. Where did *solitarie*, a board game, originate?
(*a*) Germany (*b*) France (*c*) Spain (*d*) Italy.

15. Anyone who has an IQ of over 140 is called a genius. What should be the IQ of a normal intelligent person ?
(*a*) 115 (*b*) 100 (*c*) 85 (*d*) 75.

16. Who was the first recipient of the Nobel Prize in Literature in 1901?
(*a*) Rudyard Kipling (*b*) Romain Rolland
(*c*) Giosue Carducci (*d*) Rene Fa. Sully-Prudhomme.

17. What is the growth rate of hair on a normal human head?
(*a*) 1" in 4-6 weeks (*b*) 4" every month
(*c*) 5" every month (*d*) 2" every two weeks.

18. Which island nation has one of the world's biggest phosphate deposits, where it is said that the mining activity may be reducing its size?
(*a*) Philippines (*b*) Mauritius (*c*) Maldives (*d*) Nauru.

19. Of the following which is an economic flow?
(*a*) Inhabitants of a country
(*b*) Current account of a household in a bank
(*c*) Demand for machinery
(*d*) Gross capital stock.

20. What is the opposite of suave?
(*a*) Lax (*b*) Rough (*c*) Soothing (*d*) Vapid.

QUIZ 79

1. Who was the US Open champion in men's single tennis between 1985 — 1987?
(*a*) Jimmy Conors (*b*) John McEnroe
(*c*) Ivan Lendl (*d*) Bjorn Borg.

2. Who is the first Ph.D. in Nepal?
(*a*) Dr. Yadav Prasad Pant (*b*) Dr. Mohan Man Saiju
(*c*) Dr. Dilli Raman Regmi (*d*) Dr. Badri Prasad Shrestha.

3. Sabines were members of which ancient tribe?
(*a*) German (*b*) English (*c*) French (*d*) Italian.

4. Which is the leading salmon-fishing country in the world?
(*a*) USA (*b*) Japan (*c*) Norway (*d*) Canada.

5. In terms of population, Mexico City is the largest city in the world. Which is the second largest?
(*a*) New York (*b*) Seoul (*c*) London (*d*) Tokyo.

6. When was the planet Neptune discovered?
(*a*) 1826 (*b*) 1836 (*c*) 1846 (*d*) 1856.

7. Who wrote *Pericles* and *The Merry Wives of Windsor*?
(*a*) Charles Dickens (*b*) William Shakespeare
(*c*) Alexander Dumas (*d*) Thomas Hardy.

8. Shar-pei is a breed of dog that originated in a certain country in about 200 BC. Name the country.
(*a*) Germany (*b*) Mexico (*c*) China (*d*) India.

9. Which is the leading country in the world in terms of merchant fleets?
(*a*) Liberia (*b*) Greece (*c*) USA (*d*) Norway.

10. Which is the third largest country in South America?
(*a*) Venezuela (*b*) Argentina
(*c*) Colombia (*d*) Peru.

11. Who coined the following "Early to bed and early to rise, makes a man healthy, wealthy and wise"?
(*a*) Paul Revere (*b*) Berjamin Franklin
(*c*) Thomas Jefferson (*d*) James Buchan.

12. In which of Shakespeare's play is a 'dog' mentioned?
(*a*) *Two Gentlemen of Verona* (*b*) *As You Like It*
(*c*) *Merchant of Venice* (*d*) *Macbeth*.

13. Coffee was first grown in which country?
(*a*) Brazil (*b*) Mali (*c*) Ethiopia (*d*) Paraguay.

14. What would 50°C be in the Fahrenheit?
(*a*) 140° (*b*) 122° (*c*) 90° (*d*) 75°.

15. China, Russia, USA and UK have the power of veto in the United Nations. Name the other country, which has it.
(*a*) France (*b*) Germany (*c*) Italy (*d*) Japan.

16. What disease are you referring to when you talk of myocardial infarction?
(*a*) Paralysis (*b*) Malaria
(*c*) Chest pain (*d*) Heart attack.

17. Where in the body are Betz cells?
(*a*) The brain (*b*) The kidney
(*c*) The lung (*d*) The heart.

18. On which planet is the highest known mountain in our solar system?
(*a*) Earth (*b*) Jupiter (*c*) Venus (*d*) Mars.

19. What is the first level of needs in Maslow's needed hierarchy?
(*a*) Esteem needs (*b*) Physiological needs
(*c*) Security needs (*d*) Social needs.

20. What is the opposite meaning of tantamount?
(*a*) Estimated (*b*) Forgetful
(*c*) Unequal (*d*) Bombastic.

QUIZ 80

1. In which of the following countries did the Industrial Revolution first commence?
   (*a*) Japan (*b*) England (*c*) France (*d*) Germany.
2. What is a 'catmaran'?
   (*a*) A boat (*b*) A car (*c*) An airplane (*d*) A bicycle.
3. Where is cathedral 'To Pinu' located?
   (*a*) Dublin, Ireland (*b*) Geraldton, Australia
   (*c*) Reims, France (*d*) Gozo, Malta.
4. When did captain Matthew Webb become the first man to swim the English Channel crossing from England to France in 21 hours 45 minutes?
   (*a*) 1865 (*b*) 1870 (*c*) 1875 (*d*) 1880.
5. Who owns the Chatham Islands?
   (*a*) Australia (*b*) New Zealand
   (*c*) Indonesia (*d*) Tonga.
6. Who is generally considered to have been the first major black American writer of fiction?
   (*a*) Charles Waddell Chesnutt (*b*) James Baldwin
   (*c*) Ralph Bunche (*d*) William W. Brown.
7. When did Chile acquire independence from Spain?
   (*a*) 1808 (*b*) 1818 (*c*) 1828 (*d*) 1838.
8. What is a 'nutria'?
   (*a*) Cow (*b*) Cat (*c*) Dog (*d*) Rodent.
9. When was the first 'Model T' Ford can put on the market?
   (*a*) 1912 (*b*) 1910 (*c*) 1908 (*d*) 1906.
10. When was Anwar el-Sadat, President of Egypt, assassinated?
    (*a*) 1980 (*b*) 1981 (*c*) 1982 (*d*) 1983.

11. Who wrote *Critique of Pure Reason, Critique of Practical Reason* and *Critique of Judgement*?
(*a*) Immanuel Kant (*b*) David Hume
(*c*) John Milton (*d*) Oliver Goldsmith.

12. What are sarus, demoiselle and sandhill types of?
(*a*) Swan (*b*) Crane (*c*) Ostrich (*d*) Emu.

13. Who invented game theory?
(*a*) J. Presper Eckert (*b*) John Mauchly
(*c*) Albert Einstein (*d*) John Von Neumann.

14. Whom did Germany defeat in Davis Cup finals in 1993?
(*a*) France (*b*) USA (*c*) Australia (*d*) UK.

15. Who is the patron saint of France?
(*a*) Saint Olaf II Richardson (*b*) Saint Denis
(*c*) Saint Augustine (*d*) Saint Xavier.

16. The first to start a joint stock company to trade with India were the :
(*a*) Dutch (*b*) Danish (*c*) French (*d*) Portuguese.

17. What does the first degree BAO stands for?
(*a*) Bachelor of Ornithology
(*b*) Bachelor of Oneology
(*c*) Bachelor of Obstetrics
(*d*) Bachelor of Opthamology.

18. When did F.W. De Klerk and Nelson Mandela jointly win the Nobel Prize for Peace?
(*a*) 1990 (*b*) 1991 (*c*) 1992 (*d*) 1993.

19. Who said, "Keynes' thinking moved the world...as profoundly as Adam Smith's *Wealth of Nations* did in his time"?
(*a*) Alan Greenspan (*b*) Arthur Burns
(*c*) Walter Hellor (*d*) Paul Samuelson.

20. What is the opposite of tribulation?
(*a*) Feast (*b*) Fame (*c*) Happiness (*d*) Fear.

QUIZ 81

1. Who built the Red Fort in Delhi, India?
(*a*) Babar (*b*) Shah Jahan (*c*) Humayun (*d*) Akbar.

2. Who defeated Muhammad Ali in World Heavyweight Boxing champion in 1971?
(*a*) Joe Fraizer (*b*) Ken Norton
(*c*) George Foreman (*d*) Sonny Liston.

3. Which country ranks seventh in the world in area?
(*a*) Brazil (*b*) Canada (*c*) India (*d*) Indonesia.

4. Who developed the quick-freezing process of preserving food in the 1920s?
(*a*) Clarence Birdseye (*b*) Jonas Salk
(*c*) Richard Arkwright (*d*) James Hargreaves.

5. Which of the following is not a halogen family of elements?
(*a*) Bromine (*b*) Astatine (*c*) Chlorine (*d*) Sulfur.

6. Iraq is an Arab country at the head of the Persian Gulf in southwestern Asia. Six countries border it; five of them are Turkey, Iran, Kuwait, Saudi Arabia and Jordan. Name the sixth.
(*a*) Afghanistan (*b*) Lebanon (*c*) Russia (*d*) Syria.

7. In which European country is parliament called the Oireachtas?
(*a*) Austria (*b*) Ireland (*c*) Germany (*d*) France.

8. Among the following, which is the leading iron ore mining country?
(*a*) Russia (*b*) USA (*c*) Canada (*d*) India.

9. Which volcano means 'white woman' in the Aztec language?
(*a*) Ixtacihuatl (*b*) Cotopaxi
(*c*) Aconcagua (*d*) Mauna Loa.

10. How did Yuri Gagrin, the first human to travel in space, die?
(*a*) Suicide (*b*) Hear-attack
(*c*) Car crash (*d*) Airplane crash.

11. Who published his first scientific masterpiece in 1632 entitled *Dialogue Concerning the Two Chief World Systems*?
(*a*) Isaac Newton (*b*) Galileo Galilei
(*c*) Nicolaus Copernicus (*d*) Cosimo de Medici.

12. When did Indira Gandhi marry Feroze Gandhi?
(*a*) 1940 (*b*) 1941 (*c*) 1942 (*d*) 1943.

13. When was Richard Wagrer's opera *Lohengrin* based on a medieval German legend first performed?
(*a*) 1846 (*b*) 1850 (*c*) 1854 (*d*) 1858.

14. What is the official language of Ghana?
(*a*) English (*b*) French (*c*) German (*d*) Spanish.

15. What is the smallest member of the ape family?
(*a*) Monkey (*b*) Sloth (*c*) Orangutan (*d*) Gibbon.

16. Which strait connects the Mediterranean Sea and the Atlantic Ocean?
(*a*) Strait of Gibraltar (*b*) Bosporus Strait
(*c*) Strait of Bonifacio (*d*) Strait of Messina.

17. Which is the third largest city in Egypt?
(*a*) Alexandria (*b*) Giza (*c*) Tanta (*d*) Isna.

18. Where was the famous Portland Vase probably made?
(*a*) Paris (*b*) Athens (*c*) Rome (*d*) London.

19. What do you mean by subsistence production?
(*a*) Low levels of production
(*b*) Exports tantamount to imports
(*c*) Production of necessities for life
(*d*) Production for self-consumption only.

20. What is the opposite of relegate?
(*a*) Dismiss (*b*) Promote (*c*) Disperse (*d*) Authorize.

QUIZ 82

1. Which is the world's oldest railway station?
   (*a*) Delhi (*b*) Liverpool (*c*) Vladivostok (*d*) Tokyo.

2. The days and nights are the longest in which planet in our solar system?
   (*a*) Pluto (*b*) Mercury (*c*) Mars (*d*) Venus.

3. In which year did the first manned space flight take place?
   (*a*) 1965 (*b*) 1963 (*c*) 1961 (*d*) 1959.

4. Who is the author of *Small is Beautiful*, which advocates the use of technology in tune with the environment?
   (*a*) E.F. Schumacer (*b*) I.M.D. Little
   (*c*) Kenneth Arrow (*d*) Jacob Viner.

5. In a wrestling match, how many referees are there?
   (*a*) 1 (*b*) 2 (*c*) 3 (*d*) 4.

6. Among animals, which is the most common mating system?
   (*a*) Polygyny (*b*) Monogamy (*c*) Polygamy (*d*) Polyandry.

7. Quince is a type of attractive shrub or small tree that is closely related to which tree?
   (*a*) Apple (*b*) Mango (*c*) Orange (*d*) Strawberry.

8. Expand the middle initial of Ronald W. Regan
   (*a*) Whitcomb (*b*) Wilbur (*c*) White (*d*) Wilson.

9. Who founded Carmelites whose official name is Order of Our Lady of Mount Carmel?
   (*a*) St. Benedict (*b*) St. Berthold
   (*c*) St. Dominic (*d*) St. Francis.

10. This rifle was a long-range hunting rifle popular during the 1870s and 1880s and could be fired by lightly touching one trigger after pulling the other. Name it.
    (*a*) The Flintlock rifle (*b*) The Colt revolving rifle
    (*c*) The Sharps buffalo rifle (*d*) The M16 A2 rifle.

11. When did rioting occur in South Africa following the murder of Chris Hani, leader of the communist party?
(*a*) 1993 (*b*) 1988 (*c*) 1983 (*d*) 1978.

12. Stephen Roche won the Tour de France race in 1987 and also the tour of Italy that same year. What is his nationality?
(*a*) British (*b*) American
(*c*) Irish (*d*) Canadian.

13. It has been indicated that Rome was founded by the twin brothers Romulus and Remus in 753 BC. Which animal tended these twins?
(*a*) Lion (*b*) Bear (*c*) Jackal (*d*) Wolf.

14. How many kopecks make a rouble?
(*a*) 100 (*b*) 75 (*c*) 50 (*d*) 25.

15. In which city in 1431 did the English burn Joan of Arc at the stake?
(*a*) Paris (*b*) Rouen (*c*) Lyons (*d*) Nice.

16. Which of the periods did Age of Reason, a period of European history, cover?
(*a*) Late 1400s to the late 1500s
(*b*) Late 1500s to the late 1600s
(*c*) Late 1600s to the late 1700s
(*d*) Late 1700s to the late 1800s.

17. RSPCA is the oldest animal protection society in the world. What do the initials stand for?
(*a*) Royal Society for the Prevention of Cruelty to Animals
(*b*) Royal Society for the Protection of Cruelty to Animals
(*c*) Rapid Society for the Prevention of Cruelty to Animals
(*d*) Rapid Society for the Protection of Cruelty to Animals.

18. Bleaching powder is used in an array of activities, some of which are mentioned below. Which is the false one?
(*a*) For making chloroform
(*b*) For decolourizing sugar
(*c*) For bleaching paper pulp
(*d*) For sterilizing water.

19. What are purchases made by the French Embassy in Nepa part of?

(*a*) Net factor earnings from abroad

(*b*) Domestic consumption expenditure

(*c*) Transfer payments

(*d*) Exports from Nepal to France.

20. Give a synonym for stringent.

(*a*) Unstable (*b*) Lonely (*c*) Sociable (*d*) Rash.

QUIZ 83

1. Which state of USA is nicknamed 'Aloha state'?
   (*a*) Alaska (*b*) Alabama (*c*) Hawaii (*d*) New Mexico.
2. Before climbing mountains, what job did Sir Edmund Hillary hold?
   (*a*) Sailor (*b*) Bee-Keeper (*c*) Civil servant (*d*) Diplomat.
3. Hay fever and asthma belong to the group of :
   (*a*) Allergies (*b*) Deficiency diseases
   (*c*) Hormonical diseases (*d*) Degenerative diseases.
4. What is the use of tachometer?
   (*a*) To measure the strength of direct current
   (*b*) To measure temperature
   (*c*) To determine the speeds of airplanes and motor boats
   (*d*) To measure blood pressure.
5. What is a 'margay'?
   (*a*) Ass (*b*) Dog (*c*) Cow (*d*) Wildcat.
6. Mendelevium is an artificially created radioactive element whose chemical symbol is Md, and its atomic number is 101. How many known isotopes does it have?
   (*a*) 11 (*b*) 13 (*c*) 15 (*d*) 17.
7. Who wrote an orchestral overture, *A Mid-Summer Night's Dream* based on William Shakespeare's play?
   (*a*) Carl Zelter (*b*) Moses Mendelssohn
   (*c*) Felix Mendelssohn (*d*) William Faulkner.
8. What is the monetary unit of Ethiopia?
   (*a*) Birr (*b*) Cedi (*c*) Pound (*d*) Colon.
9. What was Hudson's Bay Company famous for?
   (*a*) Automobiles (*b*) Passenger ship service
   (*c*) Diamonds (*d*) Fur trade.

10. What was the *Anschluss*?
(*a*) Union of Germany and Poland in 1937
(*b*) Union of Germany and Austria in 1938
(*c*) Union of Germany and Czechoslovakia in 1939
(*d*) Union of Germany and Hungary in 1940.

11. Who founded International Red Cross?
(*a*) William Booth (*b*) Hermann Gmeiner
(*c*) Henri Durant (*d*) Leonard Cheshire.

12. Who created the fictional character 'Jeeves'?
(*a*) John Buchan (*b*) P.G. Woodehouse
(*c*) James Hilton (*d*) H.G. Wells.

13. Who stated the following, "Government of the people by the people, for the people, shall not perish from the earth"?
(*a*) John F. Kennedy (*b*) Franklin Roosevelt
(*c*) Abraham Lincoln (*d*) George Washington.

14. Who is known as 'the Weathervane'?
(*a*) Jiang Zemin (*b*) Bill Clinton (*c*) Tony Blair (*d*) Ha Jin.

15. Who succeeded Jenny Shiley as Prime Minister of New Zealand?
(*a*) Mike Moore (*b*) Helen Clark
(*c*) Winston Peters (*d*) Peter Davis.

16. The 1906 Olympic games was not recognized by International Olympic Committee. Where was it held?
(*a*) St. Louis (*b*) Paris (*c*) London (*d*) Athens.

17. Where is the headquarters of International Maritime Organization (IMO)?
(*a*) Montreal (*b*) Vienna (*c*) Geneva (*d*) London.

18. Name the highest peak of South America and its location.
(*a*) Yerupaja, Peru (*b*) Aconcagua, Argentina
(*c*) Illimoni, Bolivia (*d*) Chimborazo, Ecuador.

19. Net national product (NNP) at factor cost is
(*a*) Always more than the gross national product
(*b*) Less than national income
(*c*) Equal to national income
(*d*) More than national income.

20. Give a synonym for turpitude.
(*a*) Depravity (*b*) Evil (*c*) Tardy (*d*) Bulky.

QUIZ 84

1. Who is the author of the short stories, *The Snows of Kilimanjaro*?
   (*a*) Ernest Hemmingway (*b*) Leo Tolostoy
   (*c*) William Hanna (*d*) Somerset Maugham.
2. In winter Olympics, in skiing, a certain woman athlete captured the gold medal in 500 meters (1964), 1000 meters (1964), 1,500 meters (1960 and 1964), and 3,000 meters (1960 and 1964). Can you name her?
   (*a*) Helga Haase (*b*) Lydia Skoblikova
   (*c*) Carolina Geijssen (*d*) Kaija Mustonen.
3. Who discovered Peru in 1532?
   (*a*) Francisco Pizprro (*b*) Alonso de Pineda
   (*c*) Vicente Y Pinzon (*d*) Francis Drake.
4. When did Kublai Khan make Peking his capital?
   (*a*) 1287 (*b*) 1277 (*c*) 1267 (*d*) 1257.
5. Who made the statue of Zeus (Jupiter) at Olympia, which is considered to be one of the Seven Wonders of the World?
   (*a*) Mercury (*b*) Chares (*c*) Sostratos (*d*) Phidias.
6. Which battle was the turning point of the Japanese advance in World War II?
   (*a*) Battle of Iwo Jima (*b*) Battle of Midway
   (*c*) Battle of Tarawa (*d*) Battle of Saipan.
7. Where is the deepest point in the Indian Ocean?
   (*a*) Ob' Trench (*b*) Java Trench
   (*c*) Vema Trench (*d*) Diamasstina Trench.
8. What is the name of the volcano that erupted in Colombia on November 13, 1985 that killed nearly 23,000 people?
   (*a*) Mt. Nevado del Ruiz (*b*) Mt. Santa Maria
   (*c*) Mt. Papandayan (*d*) Mt. Saint Helena.

9. Who assassinated President of USA, William McKinley, in 1901?
(*a*) Charles J. Guiteau (*b*) John Wilkes Booth
(*c*) Leon Czolgosz (*d*) Gavrilo Princip.

10. Which country's flag is simply and completely green?
(*a*) Swaziland (*b*) Iran (*c*) Malawi (*d*) Libya.

11. Who was the Prime Minister of Canada during World War I?
(*a*) John J.C. Abbott (*b*) Robert L. Borden
(*c*) Arthur Meighen (*d*) Wilfrid Laurier.

12. Which country is 5¾ hours ahead of Greenwich Mean Time (GMT).
(*a*) India (*b*) Pakistan (*c*) Bangladesh (*d*) Nepal.

13. Between which two Scandinavian countries does the Gulf of Bothnia lie?
(*a*) Denmark and Norway (*b*) Norway and Sweden
(*c*) Finland and Sweden (*d*) Denmark and Finland.

14. Who won the Nobel Prize in Literature and Medicine, respectively, in 1999?
(*a*) Gunter Grass and Gunter Blobel
(*b*) Camilo Jose Cela and Susumu Tonegawa
(*c*) Ivo Andrick and Daniel Bovet
(*d*) Saul Bellow and Max Theiler.

15. In December 1999, a donor meeting on East Timor was held in Tokyo. What was the approximate amount of aid that was pledged by the donors?
(*a*) US$ 200 million (*b*) US$ 440 million
(*c*) US$ 520 million (*d*) US$ 700 million.

16. When was Benito Mussolini and his mistress executed?
(*a*) May 15, 1945 (*b*) April 28, 1945
(*c*) April 15, 1945 (*d*) March 28, 1945.

17. The Sumerians worshipped anthropomorphic gods representing natural forces. Who was Anu?
(*a*) God of Water (*b*) God of Fire
(*c*) God of Hell (*d*) God of Heaven.

18. Thc glass bulb of electric bulbs becomes black due to the deposition of vapor from the :
(*a*) Joint in the glass (*b*) Glass of the bulb
(*c*) Metal filament (*d*) Gas in the bulb.

19. In which American university does the Indian economist, Professor Jagdish Bhagwati teach?
(*a*) Princeton University (*b*) Columbia University
(*c*) Yale University (*d*) Harvard University.

20. What do you mean by plausible?
(*a*) Seemingly reasonable (*b*) Factual
(*c*) Honest (*d*) Probable.

QUIZ 85

1. Who won the United States Open Golf in 1989?
   (*a*) Hale Irwin (*b*) Curtis Strange
   (*c*) Ray Floyd (*d*) Andy North.
2. Name the headquarters of Rolpa, a remote district in Nepal?
   (*a*) Liwang (*b*) Tulsipur (*c*) Dunja (*d*) Musikot.
3. Whom did President Jimmy Carter appoint as Secretary of State in 1977?
   (*a*) Dean Rusk (*b*) Edmund S. Muskie
   (*c*) Cyrus R. Vance (*d*) Dean G. Acheson.
4. Who was the Premier of China between 1980-1988?
   (*a*) Hua Guofeng (*b*) Zhao Ziyong
   (*c*) Li Peng (*d*) Hu Yaobang.
5. How many Oscar Awards did the film Titanic win in 1998?
   (*a*) 11 (*b*) 10 (*c*) 9 (*d*) 8.
6. River Jordan outflows into which Sea?
   (*a*) Red Sea (*b*) Tyrrhenian Sea
   (*c*) Caspian Sea (*d*) Dead Sea.
7. To which country does the island of Ascension on the Atlantic Ocean belong?
   (*a*) USA (*b*) Canada (*c*) UK (*d*) France.
8. On November 13, 1970, a cyclone killed 300,000 people in a particular Asian country. Name the country.
   (*a*) India (*b*) China
   (*c*) Bangladesh (*d*) Philippines.
9. Who was the Indian economist who became the first Asian to be awarded the Nobel Memorial Prize in Economics?
   (*a*) Jagdish Bhagwati (*b*) Man Mohan Singh
   (*c*) T.N. Srinivasan (*d*) Amartya K. Sen.

10. Which motion picture won the Oscar Award in 1937?
(*a*) *Captain Courageous* (*b*) *Life of Emile Zola*
(*c*) *The Good Earth* (*d*) *In Old Chicago.*

11. When did the first jumbo jet, the Boeing 747, enter airline service?
(*a*) 1966 (*b*) 1970 (*c*) 1974 (*d*) 1978.

12. In 1936, aviator R.D. Swain recorded a height of 15,223 meters. Which country did he represent?
(*a*) UK (*b*) USA (*c*) Canada (*d*) Australia.

13. Which country's official languages are Pashto and Dari?
(*a*) Pakistan (*b*) Iran (*c*) Iraq (*d*) Afghanistan.

14. How many African colonies gained Independence between 1950 and 1980?
(*a*) 37 (*b*) 42 (*c*) 47 (*d*) 52.

15. Who were the 'vandals'?
(*a*) German Tribe (*b*) Danish Tribe
(*c*) Roman Tribe (*d*) Greek Tribe.

16. Which is the largest country in Africa?
(*a*) Nigeria (*b*) Sudan (*c*) Algeria (*d*) Egypt

17. In plays such as The Basis Training of Pavlo Hummel and Sticks and Bones, who portrayed the disillusionment of the soldiers in the Vietnam War?
(*a*) Toni Morisson (*b*) Alice Walker
(*c*) Arthur Miller (*d*) David Rabe.

18. Of the following elements, which has a relatively stable nucleus (center of the atom)?
(*a*) Radium (*b*) Iron (*c*) Hydrogen (*d*) Uranium.

19. Among the various determinants of the growth of national income, in which sector is Adam Smith accorded foremost place?
(*a*) Technology (*b*) Natural resources
(*c*) Division of labour (*d*) Capital.

20. What is the opposite of redolent?
(*a*) Flowery (*b*) Removed
(*c*) Irregular (*d*) Malodorous.

QUIZ 86

1. Who wrote *Moll Flanders*?
   (*a*) Thomas Hardy (*b*) Daniel Defog
   (*c*) Jonathan Swift (*d*) Walter Scott
2. Name the group of people who were emancipated in Britain in 1829.
   (*a*) Protestants (*b*) Lutherans
   (*c*) Roman Catholics (*d*) Moslems.
3. Who was Centaur?
   (*a*) Half man and half jackal
   (*b*) Half man and half elephant
   (*c*) Half man and half lion
   (*d*) Half man and half horse.
4. Who founded Moscow's Church of St. Basil the blessed?
   (*a*) Ivan the Terrible (*b*) Peter the Great
   (*c*) Alexander I (*d*) Nicholas II.
5. The term 'Concentration Camp' was first coined in which war?
   (*a*) Russia — Japanese War (*b*) Boer War
   (*c*) World War I (*d*) World War II.
6. The second 'Dog Watch' covers what period of time at sea?
   (*a*) 2 pm to 4 pm (*b*) 4 pm to 6 pm
   (*c*) 6 pm to 8 pm (*d*) 8 pm to 10 pm.
7. Who preceded Field Marshall Paul Von Hindenburg as President of the Weimar Republic?
   (*a*) Adolf Hitler (*b*) Friedrich Ebert
   (*c*) Herman Goring (*d*) Karl Doenitz.
8. Name the musician who was born in Vienna in 1797 and died there at the age of 31.
   (*a*) Josias Priest (*b*) Handel
   (*c*) Franz Peter Schubert (*d*) Alphonse Daudet.

9. In March 1966, the monument of Horatio Nelson was blown up. Where?
(*a*) London (*b*) Manchester (*c*) Birmingham (*d*) Dublin.

10. Which city in South America is dominated by a mountiain called Sugar Loaf?
(*a*) Valparaiso (*b*) Rio de Janeiro (*c*) Caracas (*d*) Bogota.

11. In which religion do people follow two celebrations, namely, the Great Festival and the Lesser Festival?
(*a*) Islam (*b*) Buddhism (*c*) Hinduism (*d*) Judaism.

12. Who directed the films *Juliet of the Spirits* (1965) and *The City of Women* (1979)?
(*a*) Federico Fellini (*b*) W.C. Fields
(*c*) Robert Wise (*d*) Robert Benton.

13. *Pesapallo* is a form of baseball played in which country?
(*a*) France (*b*) Germany (*c*) Spain (*d*) Finland.

14. Among the following, which is a fish of coral reefs?
(*a*) Sea mullet (*b*) Haddock (*c*) Neon goby (*d*) Clown loach.

15. Which flower is known as *antirrhinum majus*?
(*a*) Cornflower (*b*) Snapdragon
(*c*) Morning glory (*d*) Hollyhock.

16. In which country are taipans, most dangerous snakes, found?
(*a*) Brazil (*b*) USA (*c*) Zambia (*d*) Australia.

17. Name the person who won gold medal in discus throw in four consecutive Olympic games, namely, 1956, 1960, 1964 and 1968?
(*a*) Al Oerter (*b*) Ludvik Danek
(*c*) Sim Iness (*d*) Adolfo Consolini.

18. Which of the following is not synthetic rubber?
(*a*) Polyethylene (*b*) Neoprene
(*c*) Buna-N rubber (*d*) Buna-S rubber

19. Which sector did Ricardo reiterate the most in the context of economic growth?
(*a*) Irrigation (*b*) Education (*c*) Industry (*d*) Agriculture.

20. What is the meaning of gruesome?
(*a*) Repugnant (*b*) Itching (*c*) Terrible (*d*) Revengeful.

QUIZ 87

1. Sulgrave Manor in Engalnd was the ancestral home of an American President. Which one?
   (*a*) John F. Kennedy (*b*) Abraham Lincoln
   (*c*) Thomas Jefferson (*d*) George Washington.
2. There are three primary colours in pigments. Red and yellow are two of them. What is the third?
   (*a*) Blue (*b*) Black (*c*) White (*d*) Purple.
3. In cookery, what vegetable is included in the dish 'egg florentine'?
   (*a*) Brinjal (*b*) Radish (*c*) Spinach (*d*) Onion.
4. A talbot is occasionally noted in heraldic designs. What was it?
   (*a*) A cat (*b*) A dog (*c*) A beer (*d*) A lion.
5. Jacopo Peri composed the earliest operas. Which is the Italian city where they were first performed?
   (*a*) Venice (*b*) Turin (*c*) Florence (*d*) Rome.
6. Which popular sport patented in 1874 by Major Walter Wingfield was originally called 'sphairistike'?
   (*a*) Lawn Tennis (*b*) Table Tennis
   (*c*) Badminton (*d*) Snooker.
7. By what name is the Anatolia in ancient Turkey better known?
   (*a*) Caledonia (*b*) Mesopotamia
   (*c*) Phoenicia (*d*) Asia Minor.
8. The parliament of which country, first convened in 930 AD, is called the *Althing*?
   (*a*) Finland (*b*) Iceland (*c*) Norway (*d*) Sweden.
9. Which island state in the West Indies is named after the Portuguese for 'Bearded'?
   (*a*) Barbados (*b*) Bahamas
   (*c*) Grenada (*d*) Trinidad and Tobago.

10. Which astronomer classified the galaxies into spiral. elliptical and irregular types?

(*a*) Carl Sagan (*b*) Edwin Hubble
(*c*) Isaac Asimov (*d*) Stephen Hawking.

11. In Africa, where would you find the Tibseti Mountains?

(*a*) Cameroon (*b*) Burundi (*c*) Chad (*d*) Lesotho

12. Who completed the statue of 'George Washington'?

(*a*) Frederic Remington (*b*) Auguste Rodin
(*c*) William Rimmer (*d*) Horatio Greenough.

13. What do you mean by Melanesia?

(*a*) Black islands (*b*) Tiny islands
(*c*) Large islands (*d*) Many islands.

14. Peter was a leading apostle of Jesus Christ and was a leader of the early Christian community. Where was he born?

(*a*) Jerusalem (*b*) Antioch
(*c*) Bethsaidia (*d*) Capernaum.

15. Petitgrain is a yellowish oil made from the leaves, twigs and fruit of which tree?

(*a*) Mango (*b*) Orange (*c*) Pear (*d*) Banana.

16. Under what name did Benjamin Franklin write *Poor Richard's Almanac*?

(*a*) Richard Saunders (*b*) Richard Stone
(*c*) Richard Sorge (*d*) Richard Smith.

17. Among the following cheese, which is produced in Italy?

(*a*) Edam (*b*) Munster (*c*) Gruyere (*d*) Parmesan.

18. Which is the use of sodium cyanide?

(*a*) Creation of fires (*b*) Cleaning of silver
(*c*) Extraction of gold (*d*) Purification of acids.

19. Who first formulated the hypothesis regarding development with unlimited supplies of labour?

(*a*) John Fei (*b*) W.A. Lewis
(*c*) P.T. Bauer (*d*) J. Schumpeter.

20. What do you mean by gamester?

(*a*) Thief (*b*) Quack (*c*) Athlete (*d*) Gambler.

QUIZ 88

1. In association with what is the term Q-value used?
   (*a*) Solar energy (*b*) Nuclear energy
   (*c*) Thermal energy (*d*) Electrical energy.

2. Where does the word 'good bye' derived from?
   (*a*) 'Peace be with you' (*b*) 'See you again'
   (*c*) 'God be with you' (*d*) 'Take care of your health.'

3. Name the first month of the year in the old Roman Calendar.
   (*a*) January (*b*) March (*c*) May (*d*) July.

4. Where is the Demerara River?
   (*a*) Guyana (*b*) Venezuela
   (*c*) Lesotho (*d*) Gabon.

5. What is the colour of two flags that should be flown if a ship enters into a British port carrying a patient with an infectious disease?
   (*a*) Green (*b*) Purple (*c*) White (*d*) Yellow.

6. Which game is played on a board or table with numbered cups, instead of pockets?
   (*a*) Snooker (*b*) Billiards (*c*) Bagatelle (*d*) Pool.

7. Which sportswear and equipment did Dassler found in the 1920s?
   (*a*) Nike (*b*) Adidas (*c*) Raebok (*d*) Levi.

8. In ancient Gaul, which city did the Romans call 'Lutetia'?
   (*a*) Paris (*b*) Burgundy (*c*) Nice (*d*) Lyons.

9. Where does bile juice get stored in the human body before flowing into the intestine?
   (*a*) Heart (*b*) Liver (*c*) Gall Bladder (*d*) Kidney.

10. *Eider* and *mallard* are species of which animal?
    (*a*) Cats (*b*) Bears (*c*) Penguins (*d*) Ducks.

11. What was the old name of Jakarta, the capital of Indonesia?
(*a*) Batavia (*b*) Bandung (*c*) Buitenzorg (*d*) Surabaya.

12. When was Bohemian religious reformer, John Has, burned at the stake?
(*a*) 1405 (*b*) 1415 (*c*) 1425 (*d*) 1435.

13. Which is the largest city in Australasia?
(*a*) Auckland (*b*) Melbourne (*c*) Sydney (*d*) Brisbane.

14. Which country produces the most coffee?
(*a*) Brazil (*b*) Colombia (*c*) Indonesia (*d*) Mexico.

15. Who wrote *On the Revolution of the Heavenly Spheres*?
(*a*) Aaron Copland (*b*) Galileo Galilei
(*c*) Johannes Kepler (*d*) Nicolaus Copernicus.

16. Which 20th century figure best suits the following description : "He is obsessed with the idea that some day it may be possible to write a message on a pad at one's desk or beside and have it instantaneously transmitted to address anywhere on earth"?
(*a*) Haile Selassie (*b*) Owen Young
(*c*) Andrew Grove (*d*) Harry S. Truman.

17. In UK, where are the Sperrin Mountains located?
(*a*) Wales (*b*) England
(*c*) Northern Ireland (*d*) Scotland.

18. What are lead chromate and zinc chromate used as?
(*a*) Pigments (*b*) Lakes (*c*) Lacquers (*d*) Mordants.

19. With which of the following kinds of dualism is H. Myint associated?
(*a*) Social dualism (*b*) Financial dualism
(*c*) Geographical dualism (*d*) Technological dualism.

20. What is the meaning of ruminate?
(*a*) Incline (*b*) Rue (*c*) Remember (*d*) Ponder.

QUIZ 89

1. Who is often called the 'Father of Economics'?
   (*a*) John M. Keynes (*b*) Adam Smith
   (*c*) David Ricardo (*d*) Paul Samuelson.
2. *Eohippus* and *Mesohippus* are phases in the evolution of which animal?
   (*a*) Cow (*b*) Lion (*c*) Horse (*d*) Bear.
3. Over which organ of the body do the adrenal glands lie?
   (*a*) Liver (*b*) Pancreas (*c*) Heart (*d*) Kidney.
4. What is a 'bittern'?
   (*a*) Bird (*b*) Fish (*c*) Donkey (*d*) Bear.
5. Pinchbeck is an alloy of zinc and what else?
   (*a*) Copper (*b*) Silver (*c*) Aluminum (*d*) Gold.
6. What is the 'Hans der Kunst' in Munich?
   (*a*) A zoo (*b*) An art gallery
   (*c*) A national library (*d*) A church.
7. In India, which state government gives away an annual prestigious award in the name of Lata Mangeshkar?
   (*a*) Maharastra (*b*) Gujarat
   (*c*) Karnatak (*d*) Madhya Pradesh.
8. The historical film titled *Ivan the Terrible* by Russian Sergei Einstein was at first banned on the grounds that it was a satire on which Russian leader?
   (*a*) Lenin (*b*) Khruschev (*c*) Stalin (*d*) Brezhnev.
9. Which African country was founded in 1821 as a haven for freed American slaves by the American Colonization Society?
   (*a*) Lesotho (*b*) Uganda (*c*) Liberia (*d*) Chad.
10. Which US boxer became the first man to win world titles at five officially recognized weights?
    (*a*) Sugar Ray Leonard (*b*) Mike Tyson
    (*c*) Muhammad Ali (*d*) George Foreman.

11. Which country has the fastest train?
(*a*) Japan (*b*) France (*c*) Germany (*d*) India.

12. When did reggae, a type of popular music, develop in Jamaica?
(*a*) 1950s (*b*) 1960s (*c*) 1970s (*d*) 1980s.

13. In which country is River Shannon located?
(*a*) UK (*b*) Canada (*c*) Australia (*d*) Ireland.

14. In Romania, what do you mean by 'tzuica'?
(*a*) Whisky (*b*) Gin (*c*) Brandy (*d*) Vodka.

15. Which protein substance is obtained by boiling bones or other animal parts?
(*a*) Gelatin (*b*) Glycerin (*c*) Gelusil (*d*) Protoplasm.

16. Who became Prime Minister of Australia after John Gray Gorton in 1971?
(*a*) William McMahon (*b*) Bob Hawke
(*c*) Gough Whitlam (*d*) Malcolm Fraser.

17. In New York Stock Exchange, share prices dropped rapidly on October 24, 1929. What is this day known as?
(*a*) Black Monday (*b*) Black Tuesday
(*c*) Black Wednesday (*d*) Black Thursday.

18. *Grimm's Fairy Tales* is a famous collection of German folk tales. Two brothers, namely Wilhelm Grimm and whom, collected most of them?
(*a*) Helmut (*b*) Jakob (*c*) Walter (*d*) Matthias.

19. The Incremental Capital-Output ratio (ICOR) refers to the
(*a*) Relationship between investment that is financed by the citizens of a country and the income enjoyed by them
(*b*) Marginal productivity of capital
(*c*) Ratio of investment to change in output
(*d*) Ratio of capital stock to change in output.

20. What do you mean by checkered?
(*a*) Marked by fluctuations of fortune
(*b*) Vivid description
(*c*) Failure occasionally
(*d*) Perversity.

QUIZ 90

1. Who inspired the Organization of Latin American Solidarity (OLAS)?
   (*a*) Fidel Castro (*b*) Salvador Allendae
   (*c*) Juan Peron (*d*) Simon Bolivar.
2. In which South American city was the German battleship scuttled off on December 7, 1939?
   (*a*) Caracas (*b*) Rio de Janiero
   (*c*) Buenos Aires (*d*) Montevideo.
3. In which year did Tycho Brahe noticed a nova in the constellation of Cassiopeia?
   (*a*) 1552 (*b*) 1572 (*c*) 1592 (*d*) 1612.
4. In Izaak Walton's The *Compleat Angler*, we find Piscator; Auceps and Venator, Piscator and Auceps refer to a fisherman and a fowler, respectively. To whom does Venator refer?
   (*a*) Hunter (*b*) Butcher (*c*) Goldsmith (*d*) Printer.
5. In 1848, what did Marx and Angels publish?
   (*a*) *Das Capital*
   (*b*) *German Ideology, XIth Thesis of Feuerback*
   (*c*) *Communist Manifesto*
   (*d*) *Wealth of Nations*.
6. In which county is the official country residence of the Prime Minister of UK?
   (*a*) Berkshire (*b*) Buckinghamshire
   (*c*) Wiltshire (*d*) Leicestershire.
7. "He will be looked upon by posterity as a brave, bad man." Of whom was this said?
   (*a*) William Gladstone (*b*) Benjamin Disraeli
   (*c*) Stanley Baldwin (*d*) Oliver Cromwell.
8. Who was the husband of Corretta Scott?
   (*a*) Muhammad Ali (*b*) Ralph Bunche
   (*c*) Martin Luther King Jr. (*d*) Booker Washington.

9. Who worked with Alfred Binet in formulating the first scales for measuring intelligence?
(*a*) Ernest Shepherd (*b*) Vachel Lindsay
(*c*) Theodore Simon (*d*) Carl Jung.

10. What is the capital of the American state, Montana?
(*a*) Helena (*b*) Carson City (*c*) Bismarck (*d*) St. Paul.

11. Which African city was the seat of the French government in exile during World War II?
(*a*) Tunis (*b*) Rabat (*c*) Algiers (*d*) Tripoli.

12. In which organ of the human body would you find a cluster of cells, which produce insulin?
(*a*) Pancreas (*b*) Liver (*c*) Heart (*d*) Intestine.

13. Which Australian city is named after a British astronomer and colonial administrator?
(*a*) Darwin (*b*) Brisbane (*c*) Melbourne (*d*) Sydney.

14. Who developed the electric self-starter in cars in 1911?
(*a*) Malcolm Loughead (*b*) Lee De Forest
(*c*) Frank Whittle (*d*) Charles Kettering.

15. Who owns the Ionian Islands?
(*a*) Turkey (*b*) Cyprus (*c*) Greece (*d*) Albania.

16. When did Iraq invade Kuwait?
(*a*) 1989 (*b*) 1990 (*c*) 1991 (*d*) 1992.

17. Who was the President of Ireland between 1959-1973?
(*a*) Eamon de Valera (*b*) Douglas Hyde
(*c*) Patrick Hillery (*d*) Mary Robinson.

18. Which of the following acids is present in our stomach?
(*a*) Formic acid (*b*) Nitric acid
(*c*) Hydrochloric acid (*d*) Sulfuric acid.

19. Who is the author of the seminal work *Asian Drama : An Inquiry into the Causes* of Poverty of Nations?
(*a*) S. Chakravarty (*b*) Gunnar Mydral
(*c*) Bertil Ohlin (*d*) L. Euler.

20. What is the opposite of flatant?
(*a*) Indirect (*b*) Blatant (*c*) Pushy (*d*) Quick.

QUIZ 91

1. How many cents are there in an American nickel?
   (*a*) One (*b*) Five (*c*) Ten (*d*) Twenty-five.
2. In the manufacture of rubber, the raw rubber is often heated with a certain substance and this process is called vulcanization. Identify the substance.
   (*a*) Sulfur (*b*) Potassium (*c*) Phosphorus (*d*) Mercury.
3. Movement of the earth round the sun is called :
   (*a*) Rotation (*b*) Circulation (*c*) Spinning (*d*) Revolution.
4. The spacecraft *Voyager* relayed magnificent pictures of which planet in August 1981?
   (*a*) Uranus (*b*) Jupiter (*c*) Venus (*d*) Saturn.
5. The 'Tragic Muse' referred to a great actress as painted by Sir Joshua Reynolds. Which one?
   (*a*) Sophia Loren (*b*) Marilyn Monroe
   (*c*) Sarah Siddons (*d*) Elizabeth Taylor.
6. What kind of a mammal is a 'pipistrelle'?
   (*a*) Whale (*b*) Bat (*c*) Platypus (*d*) Man.
7. Which South African city, founded in 1886, is the richest gold-mining region?
   (*a*) Johannesburg (*b*) Cape Town
   (*c*) Durban (*d*) Port Elizabeth.
8. What wartime phrase for a subversive operation was popularized by General Emilo Mola during the Spanish Civil War in 1937?
   (*a*) Second Column (*b*) Third Column
   (*c*) Fourth Column (*d*) Fifth Column.
9. By what common name do we know the reddish variety of the mineral corundum?
   (*a*) Diamond (*b*) Pearl (*c*) Ruby (*d*) Gem.

10. Of what breed of dog is Snoopy in the Comic strip P*eanuts?*
(*a*) German shepherd (*b*) Beagle (*c*) Bull dog (*d*) Grey hound.

11. Which twelfth century ruler and founder of the Honenstaufens dynasty added the title of 'Holy' to the name of the Roman Empire?
(*a*) Charles the Great (*b*) Frederick I
(*c*) Henry I (*d*) John Lackland.

12. In which of Dickens' novel does the hero work for a time as a schoolmaster at Dothebys Hall?
(*a*) *Nicholas Nickleby* (*b*) *David Copperfield*
(*c*) *Oliver Twist* (*d*) *Great Expectations.*

13. What is the exact area of Nepal?
(*a*) 148,291 sq. km (*b*) 140,000 sq. km
(*c*) 146,225 sq. km (*d*) 147,181 sq. km.

14. Djibouti was a colony of which country?
(*a*) UK (*b*) Spain (*c*) France (*d*) Portugal.

15. What is the capital of Dominica?
(*a*) Roseau (*b*) Santo Domingo (*c*) Tegucigalpa (*d*) Managua.

16. Where is the Secretariat of Association of South East Asian Nations (ASEAN)?
(*a*) Kuala Lumpur (*b*) Jakarta (*c*) Manila (*d*) Singapore.

17. Of which countries are the currencies, lek, lev and leu, respectively?
(*a*) Turkey, Greece and Albania
(*b*) Bulgaria, Turkey and Greece
(*c*) Romania, Slovenia and Bulgaria
(*d*) Albania, Bulgaria and Romania.

18. When did Josef Stalin become dictator of Soviet Union?
(*a*) 1927 (*b*) 1928 (*c*) 1929 (*d*) 1930.

19. If the elasticity of foreign demand for the country's exports is unity, the supply curve of foreign exchange will be :
(*a*) Vertical
(*b*) Horizontal
(*c*) Positively sloping from left to right
(*d*) Backward bending.

20. What do you mean by facade?
(*a*) Difficulty (*b*) Front (*c*) Serious (*d*) Outlook.

QUIZ 92

1. The painter brothers Hubert and Jan Van Eyck are famous for the altarpiece in which cathedral?
   (*a*) St. Bavon, Ghent
   (*b*) St. Basil, Moscow
   (*c*) The Roman Catholic Church
   (*d*) The Bible Church of Christ.

2. *Kent bigarreau* and *morello* are varieties of which fruit?
   (*a*) Oranges (*b*) Peaches (*c*) Cherries (*d*) Bananas.

3. In 1855, who discovered and named the Victoria Falls on the Zambezi?
   (*a*) Henry Stanley (*b*) David Livingstone
   (*c*) John Davis (*d*) William Scoresby.

4. Name the more common name of the tree *salix babylonica*.
   (*a*) Bamboo (*b*) Coconut (*c*) Pine (*d*) Weeping willow.

5. The brilliant blue coloring of which sea inspired Dr. C.V. Raman to work on the scattering of light and eventually discover the Raman effect?
   (*a*) Adriatic Sea (*b*) Mediterranean Sea
   (*c*) North Sea (*d*) Caspian Sea.

6. If all were alive, how many great-grand parents could you have at most?
   (*a*) Twenty-four (*b*) Twenty (*c*) Sixteen (*d*) Twelve.

7. What is the heaviest known substance?
   (*a*) Osmium (*b*) Tungsten (*c*) Gold (*d*) Platinum.

8. Which American City is called 'Music City'?
   (*a*) Tucson, Arizona (*b*) Nashville, Tennessee
   (*c*) St. Paul, Minnesota (*d*) San Jose, California.

9. With what is spangy played?
   (*a*) Rods (*b*) Stones (*c*) Sticks (*d*) Marbles.

10. When does Bermuda's lease to the US runs out?
(*a*) 2019 (*b*) 2029 (*c*) 2039 (*d*) 2049.

11. In which river did the pied piper drown the rats of Hamelin?
(*a*) Danube (*b*) Seine (*c*) Neva (*d*) Weser.

12. What is the maximum number of clubs allowed in a competition in golf?
(*a*) Sixteen (*b*) Fourteen (*c*) Twelve (*d*) Ten.

13. Which Russian writer was condemned to death, reprieved at the last minute and sent to Siberia for 10 years?
(*a*) Fyodor Dostoevsky (*b*) Alexander Solzhenitsyn
(*c*) Leo Tolstoy (*d*) Boris Pasternak.

14. What is the diameter of an average stroke of lightning?
(*a*) 6 inches (*b*) 10 inches (*c*) 14 inches (*d*) 18 inches.

15. What is pogonophobia the fear of?
(*a*) Beards (*b*) Heights (*c*) Cats (*d*) Crowds.

16. Which planet was going to be named George by its discoverer Herschel?
(*a*) Pluto (*b*) Neptune (*c*) Uranus (*d*) Mercury.

17. In which year did Thomas Edison win a Nobel Prize?
(*a*) 1910 (*b*) 1915 (*c*) 1920 (*d*) 1925.

18. Which country was known as Siam?
(*a*) Burma (*b*) Vietnam (*c*) Laos (*d*) Thailand.

19. When was the International Fund for Agriculture Development (IFAD) established?
(*a*) 1977 (*b*) 1974 (*c*) 1971 (*d*) 1968.

20. What do you mean by *cul de sac*?
(*a*) Isolated place (*b*) Hut (*c*) Love nest (*d*) Blind alley.

QUIZ 93

1. The quarter day called Lady Day falls on which date?
   (*a*) March 15 (*b*) March 25
   (*c*) April 15 (*d*) April 25.

2. A herbivorous animal eats plants. What does a nucivorous animal eat?
   (*a*) Nuts (*b*) Raisin (*c*) Flesh (*d*) Rice.

3. Perchloro ethylene is a fluid commonly used in which process?
   (*a*) Dish-washing (*b*) Sweeping
   (*c*) Dry-cleaning (*d*) Wine-making.

4. The bummalo is a small fish. How is it known after is has been dried and salted?
   (*a*) Peking Duck (*b*) Bombay Duck
   (*c*) Tokyo Duck (*d*) Singapore Duck.

5. The *dragoon*, the *antwerp*, the *tumbler* and the *horseman* are all types of what?
   (*a*) Swallow (*b*) Nightingale (*c*) Crow (*d*) Pigeon.

6. Forty-four is the country code of which country?
   (*a*) UK (*b*) France (*c*) Japan (*d*) China.

7. Where did ice hockey originate?
   (*a*) Russia (*b*) USA (*c*) Canada (*d*) Sweden.

8. Approximately, where is the visual center of the brain?
   (*a*) At the front (*b*) At the back
   (*c*) At the right side (*d*) At the left side.

9. Who said, "To cease smoking is the easiest thing I ever did : I ought to know because I've done it a thousand times"?
   (*a*) Daniel Defoe (*b*) Charles Dickens
   (*c*) Thomas Hardy (*d*) Mark Twain.

10. Who wrote the novel *Sailor Billy Budd*?
(*a*) Aldous Huxley (*b*) Henry Green
(*c*) Herman Melville (*d*) Emily Bronte.

11. What is an 'emmet'?
(*a*) Caterpillar (*b*) Grasshopper (*c*) Cricket (*d*) Ant.

12. In which year were all the three Apollo 11 astronauts born?
(*a*) 1928 (*b*) 1930 (*c*) 1932 (*d*) 1934.

13. Which was the Beatles' first hit record?
(*a*) 'Love me Do' (*b*) 'Come Together'
(*c*) 'Ticket to Ride' (*d*) 'Yellow Submarine'.

14. How long does it take bacteria to reach danger level in cooked food left in a temperature of 70° F?
(*a*) 4 hours (*b*) 3 hours (*c*) 2 hours (*d*) 1 hour.

15. The Archimedean Screw is mechanically limited to raise water to a maximum of how many feet?
(*a*) Two (*b*) Three (*c*) Four (*d*) Five.

16. Who invented neon lights in 1911?
(*a*) Samuel Morse (*b*) Thomas Edison
(*c*) Michael Faraday (*d*) Georges Claude.

17. Which Shakespearean-based opera did Verdi always mean to write, but never quite get round to?
(*a*) *King Lear* (*b*) *Hamlet*
(*c*) *Macbeth* (*d*) *Julius Caesar*.

18. At which sport was Boris Onishchenko found to be cheating at the Olympic games?
(*a*) Javelin (*b*) Long jump (*c*) Fencing (*d*) Shot put.

19. When does the liquidity trap condition occurs?
(*a*) Very high rate of interest (*b*) High rate of interest
(*c*) Low rate of interest (*d*) Very low rate of interest.

20. What do you mean by lurid?
(*a*) Animal – like (*b*) Sexy (*c*) Sensational (*d*) Dirty.

QUIZ 94

1. In music, the bass viol is occasionally known by its Italian name — viola de gamba. What is the English translation of the word 'gamba'?
   (*a*) Toe (*b*) Leg (*c*) Shoulder (*d*) Finger.
2. Which English City did the Romans call Venta Belgarum?
   (*a*) Bradford (*b*) Manchester
   (*c*) Winchester (*d*) Birmingham.
3. In cookery, the word *lyonnaise* means that a certain vegetable is utilized in a dish. Which one?
   (*a*) Potato (*b*) Onion (*c*) Lady finger (*d*) Garlic.
4. In Dickens' novel, what kind of firm was Dombey and Son?
   (*a*) Steel (*b*) Shipping (*c*) Chemical (*d*) Business.
5. What is a 'cottonmouth'?
   (*a*) Alligator (*b*) Fish (*c*) Dog (*d*) Snake.
6. In written English, which letter of the alphabet is most frequently utilized?
   (*a*) o (*b*) i (*c*) e (*d*) a.
7. The Canadian-US frontier passes though all the great lakes except one. Name this lake.
   (*a*) Lake Michigan (*b*) Lake Superior
   (*c*) Lake Erie (*d*) Lake Como.
8. According to Apuleius, who was the beautiful maiden beloved by the god Cupid?
   (*a*) Helen (*b*) Psyche (*c*) Diana (*d*) Janaki
9. What are karakul, texel and romney marsh types of?
   (*a*) Owls (*b*) Dogs (*c*) Leopards (*d*) Sheep.
10. About what percentage of fat children grow up to be fat adults?
    (*a*) 55 – 65 per cent (*b*) 65 – 75 per cent
    (*c*) 75 – 85 per cent (*d*) 85 – 95 per cent.

11. In the ancient world, approximately, how long was a cubit?
(*a*) 6 inches (*b*) 12 inches
(*c*) 18 inches (*d*) 24 inches.

12. Which race invented the mariner's compass?
(*a*) Indians (*b*) Chinese (*c*) Egyptians (*d*) Greeks.

13. In which Italian City would you find Michelangelo's David?
(*a*) Florence (*b*) Turn (*c*) Milan (*d*) Venice.

14. How many sides has a dodecagon?
(*a*) Six (*b*) Eight (*c*) Ten (*d*) Twelve.

15. Who wrote the play *An Inspector Calls*?
(*a*) William Faulkner (*b*) Oliver Goldsmith
(*c*) J.B. Priestly (*d*) Jane Austin.

16. The rock group Thompson Twins, comprise of three persons. Two of them are Tom Bailey and Alannah Currie, name the third.
(*a*) Phil Collins (*b*) Joe Leeway
(*c*) Barry Gibb (*d*) Boy George.

17. What is the US military academy called?
(*a*) East point (*b*) West point
(*c*) North point (*d*) South point.

18. Bulls and Bears are two of the three animals associated with the Stock Exchange. Name the third.
(*a*) Cows (*b*) Lions (*c*) Stags (*d*) Dogs.

19. What do you mean by Conversion cost?
(*a*) Cost of transforming direct materials into finished products
(*b*) Cost of labour
(*c*) Total cost of running business
(*d*) Cost of materials and labour.

20. What is the opposite of restive?
(*a*) Continual (*b*) Smart
(*c*) Recalcitrant (*d*) Obedient.

QUIZ 95

1. For how long did Alexander the Great rule?
   (*a*) 10 years (*b*) 12 years (*c*) 14 years (*d*) 18 years.
2. Approximately what percentage of women are colour blind?
   (*a*) Less than 1 per cent
   (*b*) More than 1 per cent but less than 2 per cent
   (*c*) More than 2 per cent but less than 3 per cent
   (*d*) More than 3 per cent but less than 4 per cent.
3. How many years of marriage does a ruby anniversary celebrate?
   (*a*) Sixty (*b*) Fifty (*c*) Forty (*d*) Thirty.
4. How many times greater is the earth's surface gravity than that of the moon?
   (*a*) Four (*b*) Six (*c*) Eight (*d*) Ten.
5. Which acid cannot be kept in a glass container?
   (*a*) Sulfuric acid (*b*) Hydrochloric acid
   (*c*) Nitric acid (*d*) Hydrofluoric acid.
6. Which instrument can play the highest note?
   (*a*) The violin (*b*) The flute
   (*c*) The cornet (*d*) The xylophone.
7. Which insect has the best eyesight?
   (*a*) Mosquito (*b*) Grasshopper
   (*c*) Housefly (*d*) Dragonfly.
8. Approximately, how far above the earth is the stratosphere?
   (*a*) 4 miles (*b*) 6 miles (*c*) 8 miles (*d*) 10 miles.
9. In which African country is the Mountains of the Moon?
   (*a*) Uganda (*b*) Kenya (*c*) Tanzania (*d*) Sudan.
10. What is a 'jumbuck'?
    (*a*) Wolf (*b*) Dog (*c*) Sheep (*d*) Cow.

11. In which year did William Shakespeare die?
(*a*) 1616 (*b*) 1621 (*c*) 1626 (*d*) 1631.

12. Which zone in Nepal has the maximum representation in the Lower House?
(*a*) Seti (*b*) Karnali (*c*) Mechi (*d*) Bagmati.

13. What was the name of Gautam Buddha's son?
(*a*) Sahdeb (*b*) Rahul (*c*) Nakul (*d*) Gopal.

14. Name the African capital city, also called El Djezair?
(*a*) Rabat (*b*) Tripoli (*c*) Algiers (*d*) Cairo.

15. Icosahedron is a solid with how many plane sides?
(*a*) 24 (*b*) 20 (*c*) 16 (*d*) 12.

16. Which US President died on July 4, 1826 exactly 50 years after the adoption of the Declaration of Independence?
(*a*) George Washington (*b*) John Adams
(*c*) Thomas Jefferson (*d*) James Monroe.

17. Which bone in the human body is called 'femur'?
(*a*) The thighbone (*b*) The hipbone
(*c*) The compact one (*d*) The cancellous bone.

18. Which city in the world has the maximum number of females as compared to males?
(*a*) Tokyo (*b*) London (*c*) Prague (*d*) Helsinki.

19. When was the Organization of Economic Co-operation and Development (OECD) established?
(*a*) 1961 (*b*) 1956 (*c*) 1951 (*d*) 1946.

20. What is the opposite of limbo?
(*a*) Horrible plan (*b*) Paradise
(*c*) Sickness (*d*) Hospitable.

QUIZ 96

1. What type of animal is the 'vmi-vmi'?
(*a*) Small pig (*b*) Small dog
(*c*) Small cat (*d*) Small jackal.

2. How long does it take a pint of milk to lose half of its vitamin B when left in bright sunlight?
(*a*) 1 hour (*b*) 2 hours (*c*) 3 hours (*d*) 4 hours.

3. From which animals does 'cony fur' come?
(*a*) Sables (*b*) Beavers (*c*) Bears (*d*) Rabbits.

4. Which metal has the atomic number of 30?
(*a*) Zinc (*b*) Tin (*c*) Aluminum (*d*) Silver.

5. Which vegetable comes in globe and Jerusalem varieties?
(*a*) Spinach (*b*) Potato (*c*) Artichoke (*d*) Brinjal.

6. Which European country produces the most wine?
(*a*) France (*b*) Italy (*c*) Spain (*d*) Portugal.

7. About what percentage of white people have rhesus-positive blood?
(*a*) 65 per cent (*b*) 75 per cent
(*c*) 85 per cent (*d*) 95 per cent.

8. How many players take part in a game of Solo?
(*a*) Four (*b*) Six (*c*) Eight (*d*) Ten.

9. How old does a horse have to be before it is classified as 'aged'?
(*a*) Four years (*b*) Seven years
(*c*) Ten years (*d*) Thirteen years.

10. Which writer was a military champion, a convicted murderer and in receipt of a royal pension?
(*a*) Thomas Hardy (*b*) D.H. Lawrence
(*c*) E. M. Forester (*d*) Ben Johnson.

11. Which is the 'City of Dreaming Spires'?
(*a*) Nice, France (*b*) Barcelona, Spain
(*c*) Oxford, England (*d*) Turin, Italy.

12. After the Amazon River, which is the longest river of South America?
(*a*) Parana River (*b*) Maipo River
(*c*) Chico River (*d*) Salado River.

13. What is a male swan called?
(*a*) Cygnet (*b*) Cob (*c*) Drake (*d*) Filly.

14. In which country did the dramatic genre *commedia dell'arte* originate?
(*a*) France (*b*) Spain (*c*) Germany (*d*) Italy.

15. What is mythomania?
(*a*) Abnormal tendency to tell lies
(*b*) Stealing habit
(*c*) Playing with fire
(*d*) Fear of open spaces

16. Which famous mountain was earlier known as Peak XV?
(*a*) Mount Blanc (*b*) Mount Kilimanjaro
(*c*) Mount Everest (*d*) Mount Cotopaxi.

17. *What You Will* is another title of which Shakespearean play?
(*a*) *As You Like It* (*b*) *Twelfth Night*
(*c*) *Hamlet* (*d*) *Macbeth.*

18. Where is the 'Ocean of Storms'?
(*a*) Mercury (*b*) Mars (*c*) Venus (*d*) Moon.

19. Where are the headquarters of the United Nations Fund for Population Activities (UNFPA) located?
(*a*) Montreal (*b*) Vienna (*c*) New York (*d*) Brussels.

20. What do you mean by gimcrack?
(*a*) Cheap (*b*) Nonsense (*c*) Foul (*d*) Inciting mob.

QUIZ 97

1. Mary Anning first found a fossil of the great fish-like dinosaur known as the Ichthyosaurus in 1811. How old was she at that time?
(*a*) 12 years (*b*) 14 years (*c*) 16 years (*d*) 18 years.

2. From which country does the Doberman Pinscher originate?
(*a*) China (*b*) Germany (*c*) France (*d*) Russia.

3. How many quires make a ream?
(*a*) Ten (*b*) Fifteen (*c*) Twenty (*d*) Twenty-five.

4. How many more bones in the human arm are there than in a human leg?
(*a*) Zero (*b*) One (*c*) Two (*d*) Three.

5. Davy Crockett, the American legend, wore an early pioneer style of hat made from the fur of which animal?
(*a*) Beaver (*b*) Otter (*c*) Sable (*d*) Raccoon.

6. Who beat Scotland 7 — 0 in the 1954 Soccer World Cup?
(*a*) Brazil (*b*) Italy (*c*) Uruguay (*d*) Argentina.

7. Which drink did Bach enjoy so much that he wrote a cantata for it?
(*a*) Coffee (*b*) Tea (*c*) Coca-cola (*d*) Wine.

8. In which city was Martin Luther King assassinated?
(*a*) Memphis (*b*) Little Rock (*c*) Trenton (*d*) Salem.

9. When was the Panama Canal opened?
(*a*) 1910 (*b*) 1914 (*c*) 1918 (*d*) 1922.

10. Trachoma is an infection of what?
(*a*) Ear (*b*) Nose (*c*) Throat (*d*) Eye.

11. Who was the last King of Egypt who ruled from 1936 to 1952?
(*a*) King Farouk (*b*) King Faisal
(*c*) King Ibn Saud (*d*) King Hussein.

12. Mount Korciusko (2,228m) is the highest peak of which continent?
(*a*) South America (*b*) Africa
(*c*) North America (*d*) Australia.

13. Name the youngest man ever to win the Nobel Prize.
(*a*) Albert Einstein (*b*) Thomas Edison
(*c*) W. L. Bragg (*d*) Paul Samuelson.

14. Which republic in Central Africa was once known as Bechuanaland?
(*a*) Botswana (*b*) Mali (*c*) Ghana (*d*) Chad.

15. *Mikado* was a title for the Emperor of which country?
(*a*) Korea (*b*) Japan (*c*) China (*d*) Thailand.

16. What was the ancient name of Tunisia?
(*a*) Mesopotamia (*b*) Casablanca
(*c*) Babylon (*d*) Carthage.

17. Which planet did French astronomer Urbain Jean Leverrier discover?
(*a*) Mars (*b*) Uranus (*c*) Neptune (*d*) Pluto.

18. In which country did the *fandango* dance originate?
(*a*) Spain (*b*) Mexico (*c*) Brazil (*d*) Portugal.

19. Who has defined money as "that by delivery of which debt contracts and price contracts are discharged, and in the shape of which general purchasing power is held"?
(*a*) Milton Friedman (*b*) Thomas Sargent
(*c*) James Tobin (*d*) John M. Keynes.

20. What is the meaning of chaos?
(*a*) Clever (*b*) Confusion
(*c*) Claustrophobic (*d*) Coma.

QUIZ 98

1. Which animal family does the ibex belong to?
(*a*) Goats (*b*) Horses (*c*) Cows (*d*) Elephants
2. Where is the oldest university in the world?
(*a*) China (*b*) Morocco (*c*) UK (*d*) USA
3. How did Van Gogh die?
(*a*) Assassinated (*b*) Horse accident
(*c*) Malaria (*d*) Suicide.
4. Who wrote the poem *Maud*?
(*a*) Alfred Tennyson (*b*) Henry Longfellow
(*c*) John Keats (*d*) Robert Browning.
5. Who invented the adding machine?
(*a*) Lord Byron (*b*) Michael Faraday
(*c*) Alfred Nobel (*d*) Charles Babbage.
6. How many teeth does a mature male horse have?
(*a*) Thirty-eight (*b*) Forty
(*c*) Forty two (*d*) Forty four.
7. For every ten attempted suicides, on average, how many are successful?
(*a*) One (*b*) Two (*c*) Three (*d*) Four.
8. Of what are brusells, wilton and axminster types?
(*a*) Garments (*b*) Silk (*c*) Carpets (*d*) Wool.
9. If a hole in golf were 251 yards long, what par would it be?
(*a*) Two (*b*) Four (*c*) Six (*d*) Eight.
10. How many symphonies did Hayden compose?
(*a*) 124 (*b*) 114 (*c*) 104 (*d*) 94.
11. What was the capital of USA from 1790 to 1800?
(*a*) Chicago (*b*) Washington
(*c*) San Francisco (*d*) Philadelphia.

12. Which sea is joined to the Mediterranean Sea by the Suez Canal?
(*a*) Red Sea (*b*) Black Sea
(*c*) North Sea (*d*) Caspian Sea.

13. Vitellin is a protein found in which dairy product?
(*a*) Cheese (*b*) Butter (*c*) Egg (*d*) Yogurt.

14. What are the grassy plains in Argentina called?
(*a*) Prairie (*b*) Savannah (*c*) Steppe (*d*) Pampas.

15. In which African country can you find the Table Mountains?
(*a*) Lesotho (*b*) South Africa (*c*) Zambia (*d*) Nigeria.

16. Where is the 'Leaning Tower' situated in Italy?
(*a*) Pisa (*b*) Genoa (*c*) Padua (*d*) Venice.

17. Which country has the native name of 'Magyarorszag'?
(*a*) Albania (*b*) Bulgaria (*c*) Hungary (*d*) Romania.

18. Which is the smallest bone in the human body?
(*a*) Thigh bone (*b*) Hip bone
(*c*) Stirrup bone (*d*) Compact bone.

19. In a partnership firm, what can be the maximum number of partners?
(*a*) 20 (*b*) 15 (*c*) 10 (*d*) 5.

20. What is the meaning of mantic?
(*a*) Insane (*b*) Having prophetic powers
(*c*) Murderer (*d*) English cloak.

QUIZ 99

1. How many months were there in the old Roman year?
(*a*) Eight (*b*) Nine (*c*) Ten (*d*) Eleven.

2. What colour is cochineal?
(*a*) Black (*b*) Red (*c*) Yellow (*d*) Blue.

3. Approximately how many calories would you burn if you knitted a jumper for 1 hour?
(*a*) Sixty-eight (*b*) Seventy-eight
(*c*) Eighty-eight (*d*) Ninety-eight.

4. What is the principal ingredient of sauerkraut?
(*a*) Cabbage (*b*) Brinjal (*c*) Radish (*d*) Onion.

5. Which creature lives in a holt?
(*a*) Beaver (*b*) Sable (*c*) Mongoose (*d*) Otter.

6. In which South American country is the Altiplano?
(*a*) Uruguay (*b*) Brazil (*c*) Bolivia (*d*) Venezuela.

7. What is the highest allowable percentage of alcohol in table wine?
(*a*) Ten (*b*) Fourteen (*c*) Eighteen (*d*) Twenty-two.

8. Which is the heaviest : lead, gold, mercury or platinum?
(*a*) Lead (*b*) Gold (*c*) Mercury (*d*) Platinum.

9. How many bones are there in the human skull (excluding the ears)?
(*a*) Twenty-two (*b*) Twenty-four
(*c*) Twenty-six (*d*) Twenty-eight.

10. UK has produced only one 'charity' stamp. In which year was it issued?
(*a*) 1985 (*b*) 1980 (*c*) 1975 (*d*) 1970.

11. Which civilization succeeded the Toltecs in Mexico?
(*a*) Incas (*b*) Aztecs (*c*) Zapotec (*d*) Mohican.

12. How is Jenny Lind popularly known as?
(*a*) Swiss Nightingale (*b*) Danish Nightingale
(*c*) Swedish Nightingale (*d*) Finnish Nightingale.

13. The 'Vulgate' is which language version of the Bible?
(*a*) German (*b*) Sanskrit (*c*) French (*d*) Latin.

14. Which King founded Eton College in 1440?
(*a*) Henry VI (*b*) Henry VIII (*c*) Charles I (*d*) Charles II.

15. Where is the Headquarters of the French Foreign Legion?
(*a*) Sidi-bel-Abbes (*b*) Aubagne
(*c*) Nice (*d*) Burgundy.

16. After which battle, did Brutus commit suicide?
(*a*) Battle of Pharsalia (*b*) First Battle of Philippi
(*c*) Second Battle of Philippi (*d*) Battle of Actium.

17. The Julian Calendar was introduced in 46 BC. It was also known as 'The Year of Confusion', because there were more than 365 days. How many?
(*a*) 430 days (*b*) 455 days (*c*) 480 days (*d*) 505 days.

18. From which century is the Paston Letters?
(*a*) 13th century (*b*) 14th century
(*c*) 15th century (*d*) 16th century.

19. Which country in the world has the highest per capita income?
(*a*) France (*b*) Japan (*c*) Sweden (*d*) Switzerland.

20. What is the meaning of morphology?
(*a*) Study of form and structure of words
(*b*) Study of medicine
(*c*) Study of oratory
(*d*) Study of insects.

QUIZ 100

1. Over how many days is the decathlon held?
(*a*) One (*b*) Two (*c*) Three (*d*) Four.

2. What type of animal is 'samoyed'?
(*a*) Dog (*b*) Cat (*c*) Goat (*d*) Deer.

3. Approximately, what is the total capacity of the human lungs?
(*a*) 9 liters (*b*) 7 liters (*c*) 5 liters (*d*) 3 liters.

4. What was the code name of the Israeli raid on Entebbe airport to free the hostages?
(*a*) Albatross (*b*) Thunderbolt
(*c*) Barbarossa (*d*) Desert Calm.

5. What birds do Japanese fishermen use to help them catch fish?
(*a*) Kingfisher (*b*) Sparrow (*c*) Hawk (*d*) Cormorant.

6. Name the country that started a first scheduled passenger air service.
(*a*) Holland (*b*) France (*c*) Denmark (*d*) Austria.

7. By what is the great Ape Pongo Pygmaeus commonly known?
(*a*) Gorilla (*b*) Sloth
(*c*) Orang-outang (*d*) Chimpanzee.

8. Name the famous biologist who served as a medical officer on board the *HMS Rattlesmake.*
(*a*) Alexander Fleming (*b*) Thomas Henry Huxley
(*c*) Charles Darwin (*d*) Ronald Ross.

9. Marzipan is made of which ingredients?
(*a*) Sugar and Cashew nuts (*b*) Sugar and peanuts
(*c*) Sugar and raisin (*d*) Sugar and almonds.

10. Name the reluctant American vice-presidential candidate who was referred to as "the contrariest Missouri mule I've ever dealt with"?
(*a*) Harry S. Truman (*b*) Hubert Humphrey
(*c*) Spiro T. Agnew (*d*) Gerald Ford.

11. Which bird incited Wordsworth to question whether it could be called a bird. 'or but a wandering voice'?
(*a*) Nightingale (*b*) Robin (*c*) Parrot (*d*) Cuckoo.

12. Simon, called Peter, and his brother were both disciples of Jesus. What was his brother's name?
(*a*) Judas (*b*) Mark (*c*) Andrew (*d*) Luke.

13. The traditional Scottish kelp industry was based on which type of plant?
(*a*) Cactus (*b*) Seaweed (*c*) Grass (*d*) Bamboo.

14. What kind of a creative is 'vendace'?
(*a*) Mouse (*b*) Dog (*c*) Cat (*d*) Fish.

15. Machine parts get jammed in winter. It is due to :
(*a*) Decrease in the viscosity of the lubricant
(*b*) Increase in the viscosity of the lubricant
(*c*) Decrease in the surface tension of the lubricant
(*d*) Increase in the surface tension of the lubricant.

16. Who created the group *The Burghers of Calais*?
(*a*) Auguste Rodin (*b*) Pabolo Picaso
(*c*) William Shakespeare (*d*) Alexander Dumas.

17. What is the popular name of the flower trapaeolum?
(*a*) Lotus (*b*) Chrysanthemum
(*c*) Gomphrena (*d*) Nasturtium.

18. The American philanthropist, Andrew Carnegie, contributed more than 1 million US dollar to build the Peace Palace. Where?
(*a*) Berne (*b*) Paris (*c*) The Hague (*d*) Rome.

19. Of the following, which is not a member of South Asian Association for Regional Cooperation?
(*a*) Bhutan (*b*) Myanamar (*c*) Nepal (*d*) Maldives.

20. What is the opposite of trepidation?
(*a*) Calmness (*b*) Tardy (*c*) Self-assured (*d*) Brave.

QUIZ 101

1. When did Australia become a member of the Baseball Federation of Asia?
   (*a*) 1968 (*b*) 1969 (*c*) 1970 (*d*) 1971.
2. In which country do people eat the most beef?
   (*a*) Argentina (*b*) Australia (*c*) USA (*d*) Japan.
3. Approximately, how many people died in Beijing area struck by a major earthquake in 1976?
   (*a*) 100,000 (*b*) 150,000 (*c*) 200,000 (*d*) 250,000.
4. Name the small country in Europe, which has an area of 464 square kms. and where the monetary units are French franc and Spanish peseta.
   (*a*) Malta (*b*) Luxembourg (*c*) Andorra (*d*) Monaco.
5. Whose arrow killed Achilles?
   (*a*) Agamemnon (*b*) Paris (*c*) Hector (*d*) Lycomedes.
6. Who was the first US Vice-President?
   (*a*) John Adams (*b*) Thomas Jefferson
   (*c*) James Monroe (*d*) Benjamin Franklin.
7. What was the University at Nalanda, Bihar famous for?
   (*a*) Studies in Jainism (*b*) Studies in Vaishnavism
   (*c*) Studies in Buddhism (*d*) Studies in witchcraft.
8. What is the national emblem of Pakistan?
   (*a*) Lily (*b*) Crescent (*c*) Eagle (*d*) Kangaroo.
9. Forest of Arden is believed to be the setting of which of Shakespeare's play?
   (*a*) *Othello* (*b*) *Twelfth Night*
   (*c*) *Macbeth* (*d*) *As you like it.*
10. Who was the Prime Minister of Australia between 1972–1975?
    (*a*) John McEwen (*b*) Harold E. Holt
    (*c*) Gough Whitlam (*d*) Malcolm Fraser.

11. Roughly, how many extant species of bird have been recorded?
(*a*) 7,600 (*b*) 8,600 (*c*) 9,600 (*d*) 10,600.

12. How long does it take a healthy heart to pump a gallon of blood if a normal person is running for a bus?
(*a*) 5 seconds (*b*) 10 seconds
(*c*) 15 seconds (*d*) 20 seconds.

13. In which year did Toscanini make his first recording?
(*a*) 1916 (*b*) 1918 (*c*) 1920 (*d*) 1922.

14. In which sport did Karen Briggs win World and European titles in 1982?
(*a*) Chess (*b*) Weightlifting
(*c*) High Jump (*d*) Judo.

15. What do you call a female fox or a quarrelsome woman?
(*a*) Vixen (*b*) Bunny (*c*) Cob (*d*) Cygnet.

16. Name the Greek philosopher who was the tutor of Alexander the Great?
(*a*) Homer (*b*) Aristotle (*c*) Archimedes (*d*) Socrates.

17. When did the six colonies of Australia become states in the federal Commonwealth of Australia?
(*a*) 1931 (*b*) 1921 (*c*) 1911 (*d*) 1901.

18. Beryl is the principal ore of which of the following metal?
(*a*) Boron (*b*) Magnesium (*c*) Beryllium (*d*) Lithium.

19. Who first put forward the phrase 'a temporary abode of purchasing power' while elucidating the concept of money?
(*a*) Milton Friedman (*b*) Irving Fisher
(*c*) Jacob Viner (*d*) John M. Keynes.

20. What is the meaning of gainsay?
(*a*) Profit (*b*) Deny (*c*) Hate (*d*) Embrace.

QUIZ 102

1. Who was the world's first female Prime Minister?
(*a*) Indira Gandhi (*b*) Golda Meir
(*c*) Sirimavo Bandarnaike (*d*) Benajir Bhutto.

2. In 1969, which pop singer released his album, *Man of Words, Man of Music*?
(*a*) Eric Clapton (*b*) Meat Loaf
(*c*) Phil Collins (*d*) David Bowie.

3. From the following, identity the two countries bordered by the Black Sea.
(*a*) Romania and Turkey (*b*) Iran and Russia
(*c*) Moldova and Rumania (*d*) Hungary and Bulgaria.

4. Madurai was the capital of which ancient Indian dynasty?
(*a*) Pallava (*b*) Pandya (*c*) Chola (*d*) Gupta.

5. In which present-day country is Philippi, where Brutus was defeated in 43 BC?
(*a*) Turkey (*b*) Italy (*c*) France (*d*) Greece.

6. Whom did Muhammad Ali defeat in 1967 to be recognized as champion by the World Boxing Association (WBA)?
(*a*) Sonny Liston (*b*) Henry Cooper
(*c*) Ernie Terrell (*d*) Joe Fraizer.

7. What are the following kinds of : Empire and Stayman?
(*a*) Apples (*b*) Peaches (*c*) Mangoes (*d*) Strawberries.

8. When did Neil Armstrong land on the moon?
(*a*) 1966 (*b*) 1969 (*c*) 1972 (*d*) 1975.

9. What is the queen of instruments in Western music?
(*a*) Piano (*b*) Trumpet (*c*) Violin (*d*) Flute.

10. If in France, you asked for *pamplemousse*, what would you get?
(*a*) Orange (*b*) Lemon (*c*) Strawberry (*d*) Grapefruit.

11. Who was the father of John the Baptist according to the New Testament?
(*a*) David (*b*) Zacharias (*c*) Solomon (*d*) Moses.

12. Who was the president of the USA when Hawaii became a state?
(*a*) Dwight D. Eisenhower (*b*) Harry S. Truman
(*c*) John F. Kennedy (*d*) Lyndon B. Johnson.

13. Keats wrote of a nightingale and Poe wrote of a raven; of which bird did Shelley write in his famous poem?
(*a*) Kingfisher (*b*) Skylark (*c*) Sparrow (*d*) Swallow.

14. What is the name of the Italian city that stands on the River Po and was once capital of the Kingdom of Italy?
(*a*) Venice (*b*) Genoa (*c*) Turin (*d*) Milan.

15. Which planet has the satellite Nereid?
(*a*) Saturn (*b*) Jupiter (*c*) Uranus (*d*) Neptune.

16. What is a viviparous creature?
(*a*) One that lays eggs
(*b*) One that gives birth to live young
(*c*) One that flies
(*d*) One that has jaws.

17. When Yoritomo died in 1199, his sons were pushed aside by his widow Masako's family, which was :
(*a*) Hojo (*b*) Tanaka (*c*) Fujiwara (*d*) Minamoto.

18. Soap forms lather (foam) with difficulty when the water is :
(*a*) Fresh (*b*) Chlorinated (*c*) Hard (*d*) Soft.

19. What is production a function of?
(*a*) Prices (*b*) Inputs (*c*) Costs (*d*) Profits.

20. What do you mean by caterwaul?
(*a*) Write (*b*) Howl (*c*) Honour (*d*) Display.

QUIZ 103

1. Which is Bolivia's official capital?
(*a*) La Paz (*b*) Sucre (*c*) Cochabamba (*d*) Potosi.

2. When did Portugal and Spain sign a treaty fixing areas of rule in South America?
(*a*) 1770 (*b*) 1760 (*c*) 1750 (*d*) 1740.

3. Who became head of state of Bulgaria in 1962?
(*a*) Todor Zhivkov (*b*) Georgi Dimitrov
(*c*) Vulko Chervenkov (*d*) Zhelyu Zhelev.

4. Between two parts of which country does the Gulf of Martaban lie?
(*a*) India (*b*) Australia (*c*) Thailand (*d*) Myanmar.

5. What is an 'affenpinscher'?
(*a*) Dog (*b*) Cat (*c*) Sheep (*d*) Wolf.

6. Of the following, who is a poet?
(*a*) James Baldwin (*b*) Robert Duncan
(*c*) Harper Lee (*d*) Leon Uris.

7. Kwanza is the monetary unit of which African country?
(*a*) Algeria (*b*) Libya (*c*) Angola (*d*) Nigeria.

8. The generals of Octavius Caesar (Augustus), namely, Agrippa and Tiberius, won victories in Pannonia. To which modern day country is this a part of?
(*a*) Austria (*b*) Hungary (*c*) Germany (*d*) Italy.

9. Where is the Lut desert?
(*a*) Pakistan (*b*) Iraq (*c*) Jordan (*d*) Iran.

10. Where was Czar Nicholas II and his family members executed by the Bolsheviks?
(*a*) Vladivostok (*b*) Ekaterinburg
(*c*) Kiev (*d*) Minsk.

11. What is the national flower of Japan?
(*a*) Pansy (*b*) Gomphrena
(*c*) Lotus (*d*) Chrysanthemum.

12. Who won the Nobel Prize in Physics in 1930?
(*a*) C.V. Raman (*b*) Paul A.M Dirac
(*c*) Owen W. Richardson (*d*) James Franck.

13. To which South American country does Juan Fernandez Islands belong?
(*a*) Peru (*b*) Venezuela (*c*) Chile (*d*) Brazil.

14. Who arranged the Inaugural ball for John F. Kennedy after he was elected 35th President of USA?
(*a*) Bob Hope (*b*) Frank Sinarta
(*c*) Robert Frost (*d*) Robert Kennedy.

15. Which is the oldest daily newspaper in Asia?
(*a*) The Statesman (in Hindi)
(*b*) The Gorkhapatra (in Nepali)
(*c*) The Yomuri Shimbun (in Japanese)
(*d*) The Bombay Samachar (in Gujrati).

16. Where was the first Winter Olympic games held in 1924?
(*a*) St. Mortiz, Switzerland (*b*) Lake Placid, USA
(*c*) Oslo, Norway (*d*) Chamonix, France.

17. King Chandragupta signed a treaty with this Greek to obtain full control over Alexander's Indian possessions. Who was this Greek?
(*a*) Menander (*b*) Ptolemy III
(*c*) Seleukos (*d*) Megasthenes.

18. Alumna is a compound, which composes of aluminum and what?
(*a*) Oxygen (*b*) Hydrogen (*c*) Nitrogen (*d*) Helium.

19. What is the shape of the average fixed cost (AFC) curve?
(*a*) Rectangular hyperbola
(*b*) Sloping down towards the right
(*c*) Vertical
(*d*) U-shaped.

20. What is the meaning of scathing?
(*a*) Direct (*b*) Dangerous (*c*) Tardy (*d*) Scornful.

QUIZ 104

1. In which continent is the Magellan Strait located?
(*a*) Europe (*b*) Asia (*c*) Africa (*d*) South America.

2. What is a 'midge'?
(*a*) Fly (*b*) Grasshopper (*c*) Caterpillar (*d*) Cockroach.

3. In which Italian city is the Catholic University of the Sacred Heart located?
(*a*) Turin (*b*) Rome (*c*) Milan (*d*) Venice.

4. In Mongolian term, what is a 'yurt'?
(*a*) Clothing (*b*) Tent (*c*) Wild animal (*d*) Woman.

5. Which is the oldest UN organization?
(*a*) ILO (*b*) UNESCO (*c*) UNICEF (*d*) FAO.

6. Among the following, which country produces the most sugarcane?
(*a*) China (*b*) Cuba (*c*) India (*d*) Brazil.

7. Who wrote *An Essay Concerning Human Understanding*?
(*a*) Francis Hutchison (*b*) John Locke
(*c*) Thomas Reid (*d*) David Hume.

8. Whose work is described as the following : "It has found important new techniques in picture-making and story telling.... It is not afraid to say the same thing twice if twice telling reveals a fourfold truth.... It is a work of art created by grown people for grown people"?
(*a*) Orson Welles' *Citizen Kane*
(*b*) F. Scott Fitzgerald's *The Great Catsby*
(*c*) Charles Dicken's *A Tale of Two Cities*
(*d*) Alexander Dumas' *The Count of Monte Cristo.*

9. Which US President was named 'Old Hickory' because of his toughness?
(*a*) Thomas Jefferson (*b*) Andrew Jackson
(*c*) Abraham Lincoln (*d*) Harry Truman.

10. The freezer in a refrigerator is situated in the uppermost section so that :

(*a*) Motor is not tampered

(*b*) Heat acquired from environment is less

(*c*) The complete chamber of the refrigerator is cooled rapidly

(*d*) Heat acquired from environment is more.

11. What do you mean by *mestizos*?

(*a*) American Indians who fought against white men

(*b*) Spanish who settled in South America

(*c*) A name given to explorers of South America

(*d*) Descendents of Spanish settlers who married Indians in South America.

12. Who built the first laser?

(*a*) Enrico Fermi (*b*) Theodore H. Maiman

(*c*) Otto Hahn (*d*) George Zweig.

13. What is a 'sampan'?

(*a*) Boat (*b*) Fish (*c*) Snake (*d*) Flower.

14. Selwyn Range is a series of low mountains. Where is it?

(*a*) Chile (*b*) Australia (*c*) Tanzania (*d*) Kenya.

15. Where was the world football cup match held in 1954?

(*a*) Paris (*b*) Madrid (*c*) Munich (*d*) Berne.

16. Who was Michel Fokine?

(*a*) French lead guitarist (*b*) German pop singer

(*c*) Russian ballet dancer (*d*) British drummer.

17. The earliest surviving example of stone masonry of the Old Kingdom is a step pyramid built by Imhotep, the architect Prime Minister of which famous pharaoh?

(*a*) Tutankhamen (*b*) Thutmose I

(*c*) Akhenaton (*d*) Djoser.

18. Gunshots are made of lead metal with a little bit of arsenic to increase what?

(*a*) Weight of fire (*b*) Brittleness of lead

(*c*) Range of fire (*d*) Power of fire.

19. Of the following items, which is invisible in the balance of payments?
(*a*) Foreign travel (*b*) Export of goods
(*c*) Foreign investment (*d*) Government expenditure abroad.

20. What is the meaning of crotchets?
(*a*) Part of underpants (*b*) Knives
(*c*) Hook-like devices (*d*) Support systems.

QUIZ 105

1. When did President Ferdinand Marcos of the Philippines resign from office and fled the country?
   (*a*) February 25, 1986 (*b*) February 25, 1987
   (*c*) March 25, 1986 (*d*) March 25, 1987.
2. When was British Labor Party Founded?
   (*a*) 1896 (*b*) 1898 (*c*) 1900 (*d*) 1902.
3. Who wrote *A Vindication of the Rights of Woman* (1792)?
   (*a*) Sarah M. Grimke (*b*) Mary Wollstonecraft
   (*c*) Eleanor Farjeon (*d*) Helen Frankenthaler.
4. Mount Haltia is 1,324 metres above sea level. In which Scandinavian country is it located?
   (*a*) Denmark (*b*) Norway (*c*) Sweden (*d*) Finland.
5. What are 'chimaeras' and 'rays'?
   (*a*) Fishes (*b*) Owls (*c*) Bears (*d*) Cats.
6. Which shark is considered one of the best species of game fish among all the sharks?
   (*a*) Basking shark (*b*) Bull shark
   (*c*) Mako shark (*d*) Nurse shark.
7. When did George Orwell complete *1984*?
   (*a*) 1947 (*b*) 1949 (*c*) 1951 (*d*) 1953.
8. Singapore has four official languages. Three are Chinese, English and Malay. What is the fourth?
   (*a*) Hindi (*b*) Tagalo (*c*) Japanese (*d*) Tamil.
9. Who built and piloted the first successful four-engine airplane in 1913?
   (*a*) Igor Sikorsky (*b*) Wilbur Wright
   (*c*) Charles Lindenbergh (*d*) Orville Wright.

10. Which American poet called Chicago the *City of the Big Shoulders*?
(*a*) Upton Sinclair (*b*) Amy Lowell
(*c*) Carl Sandburg (*d*) Robert Frost.

11. What is the monetary unit of Haiti?
(*a*) Gourde (*b*) Quetzal (*c*) Pound (*d*) Dollar.

12. What is the capital of Moldova?
(*a*) Baku (*b*) Kiev (*c*) Tashkent (*d*) Chisinau.

13. Where was the Ancient Order of Sikatuna established in 1951?
(*a*) Malaysia (*b*) Philippines (*c*) Indonesia (*d*) Thailand.

14. What was the occupation of Charles Dicken's father?
(*a*) Novelist (*b*) Politician (*c*) Clerk (*d*) Scientist.

15. *Taxus Wallichiana* is a type of confier tree found abundantly in Nepal. Which cancer is it supposed to mitigate?
(*a*) Lung (*b*) Skin (*c*) Blood (*d*) Breast.

16. Which city stands on the confluence of the Blue and the White Nile?
(*a*) Amman (*b*) Khartoum (*c*) Baghdad (*d*) Cairo.

17. Who overthrew the Sishunaga dynasty to found the first non-Kshatriya dynasty at Magadha?
(*a*) Kanishka (*b*) Mahapadmananda
(*c*) Dhanananda (*d*) Chandragupta.

18. Of the following, which is not an application of acetic acid?
(*a*) In making waterproofing fabrics
(*b*) In making soap
(*c*) In making dyes
(*d*) In making acetone.

19. What is the budget-line also known as?
(*a*) Consumption possibility line (*b*) Isoquant
(*c*) Indifference curve (*d*) Iso-utility curve.

20. What is the meaning of kleptocrat?
(*a*) Taxman
(*b*) Belonging to the class of compulsive thieves
(*c*) Ringleader of a robber's gang
(*d*) A rule by priests.

QUIZ 106

1. In 1920, who published *Hugh Selwyn Mauberley*?
   (*a*) James J. Joyce (*b*) William Yeats
   (*c*) Ezra L. Pound (*d*) Robert Frost.
2. Who lives in 'Aras an Uachtarian'?
   (*a*) President of France (*b*) President of Ireland
   (*c*) Chancellor of Germany (*d*) Prime Minister of Italy.
3. In which country do 'Dyaks' live?
   (*a*) Malaysia (*b*) Chile (*c*) South Africa (*d*) Australia.
4. Where does River Don Empty?
   (*a*) Sea of Marmara (*b*) Aegean Sea
   (*c*) Caspian Sea (*d*) Sea of Azov.
5. Which period is called the Golden Age of Spanish drama?
   (*a*) Mid-1500's to late 1600's
   (*b*) Early 1700's to late 1800's
   (*c*) Mid-1500's to mid-1600's
   (*d*) Early 1700's to late 1800's.
6. Who is often called the 'Founder of Modern Drama'?
   (*a*) Henry Arthur Jones (*b*) Anton Chekhov
   (*c*) Henrik Ibsen (*d*) James M. Barrie.
7. Who was called *faqih*?
   (*a*) Otto Bismarck (*b*) Ayatollah Khomeini
   (*c*) Francisco Franco (*d*) Benito Mussolini.
8. Where is Mount Damavond?
   (*a*) Jordan (*b*) Egypt (*c*) Syria (*d*) Iran.
9. Which country's flag was adopted in 1991 where the Arab inscription on the white stripe means 'God is Great'?
   (*a*) Iran (*b*) Saudi Arabia
   (*c*) Iraq (*d*) Kuwait.

10. What does the Bessemer process produce?
(*a*) Iron (*b*) Steel (*c*) Platinum (*d*) Copper.

11. When did the UK issue the Balfour Declaration expressing its support for a Jewish homeland in Palestine?
(*a*) 1917 (*b*) 1919 (*c*) 1921 (*d*) 1923.

12. What is a 'quandong'?
(*a*) Animal (*b*) Bird (*c*) Tree (*d*) Insect.

13. Ambassador of Japan, M. Kojima, on behalf of the Emperor, conferred 'Grand Cordon of the Order of the Rising Sun' on November 25, 1999 to Beni Bahadur Karki. Who were the other two Nepalese dignitaries to receive this medal in June 1978?
(*a*) Krishna Raj Arjyal and Dr. Yadav Prasad Pant
(*b*) Dr. Yadav Prasad Pant and Dr. Badri Prasad Shrestha
(*c*) Krishna Raj Arjyal and Dr. Bharat Prasad Dhital
(*d*) Bharat Rajbhandari and Prakash Chandra Thakur.

14. Which is the second largest state in India?
(*a*) Madhya Pradesh (*b*) Rajasthan
(*c*) Orissa (*d*) Tamil Nadu.

15. Who founded *Sinn Fein*?
(*a*) Jerry Adams (*b*) Arthur Griffith
(*c*) Michael Collins (*d*) Eamon de Valera.

16. Who owns the Gilbert Islands?
(*a*) New Zealand (*b*) Kirbati
(*c*) Papua New Guinea (*d*) Fiji.

17. Name the orator who incited the city states to the danger put forward by Philip of Macedonia, who threatened to disconnect their trade routes to the Black Sea?
(*a*) Epictetus (*b*) Cleisthenes
(*c*) Socrates (*d*) Demosthenes.

18. Of the following, which is utilized as a thickener in paints and lipstick?
(*a*) Ethyl chloride (*b*) Soap
(*c*) Bentonite (*d*) Calcium carbonate.

19. Who first formulated the 'Law of Comparative Costs'?
(*a*) Karl Marx (*b*) Alfred Marshall
(*c*) Adam Smith (*d*) David Ricardo.

20. What do you mean by proselytize?
(*a*) Pamper (*b*) Transform (*c*) Covert (*d*) Garner.

QUIZ 107

1. What do you say to 'please' in German?
(*a*) Bitte (*b*) Dort (*c*) Jawohl (*d*) Schwarz.

2. What is the study of glider flight called?
(*a*) Aerodynamics (*b*) Aerodonetics
(*c*) Dynamics (*d*) Statics.

3. When did India regain control of Goa from the Portuguese?
(*a*) 1957 (*b*) 1961 (*c*) 1965 (*d*) 1969.

4. What are *comet, lionhead* and *fantail*?
(*a*) Stars (*b*) Plants (*c*) Fishes (*d*) Cats.

5. What is a 'goldenrod'?
(*a*) Flower (*b*) Fish (*c*) Bird (*d*) Tree.

6. Whose orchestral work includes the following : 'Morning'; 'Anitra's Dance'; and 'In the Hall of the Mountain King'?
(*a*) Henrik Ibsen (*b*) Nina Hagerup
(*c*) Rikard Nordraak (*d*) Edvard Greig.

7. In Northern Egypt, more than 1 million people died in a major earthquake. When did it occur?
(*a*) 1201 (*b*) 1211 (*c*) 1221 (*d*) 1231.

8. Gerhard Domagk, a German doctor, identified the therapeutic ability of the chemical *prontosil rubrum,* the first of the sulfa drugs and showed that this drug effectively destroyed streptococcic bacteria which causes a wide variety of infections, including sore throat, scarlet fever, and impetigo. For this discovery, Domagk won the Nobel Prize in Medicine. When?
(*a*) 1943 (*b*) 1941 (*c*) 1939 (*d*) 1937.

9. Whose first novel was *Poor Folk* dealing with psychological study?
(*a*) Leo Tolstoy (*b*) Fyodor Dostoevsky
(*c*) Alexander Solzhenitsyn (*d*) Boris Pasternak.

10. In the medieval periods, which place was known as the 'Unknown Southern Land'?
(*a*) Argentina (*b*) Chile (*c*) New Zealand (*d*) Australia.

11. Who were the 'Druids'?
(*a*) Politicians (*b*) Judges (*c*) Economists (*d*) Scientists.

12. Whom did Mileva Marie marry?
(*a*) Albert Einstein (*b*) Adam Smith
(*c*) Care Jung (*d*) H.G. Wells.

13. What is a 'karakul'?
(*a*) Cow (*b*) Kangaroo (*c*) Sheep (*d*) Bear.

14. Which of the following fairies live in England?
(*a*) Pixies (*b*) Goblins (*c*) Nixes (*d*) Elves.

15. Who won the Academy Award for the best performance by an actress in a supporting role in 1965?
(*a*) Shirley Jones (*b*) Lila Kedrova
(*c*) Patty Duke (*d*) Shelley Winters.

16. What is the other name for the flower goldfields?
(*a*) *Papaver californicum* (*b*) *Lasthenia chrysostoma*
(*c*) *Gravillea punicea* (*d*) *Lewisia pygmee.*

17. The Dome of the Rock is a paragon of the cultural nerve of Arab conquerors to propound Islamic superiority over Christianity and Judaism. Where is this mosque, which is constructed on the site of a Jewish temple?
(*a*) Beirut (*b*) Tehran (*c*) Jerusalem (*d*) Damascus.

18. What is a chemical compound of sodium sulfate and water called?
(*a*) Epsom salt (*b*) Glauber's salt
(*c*) Hydrogen sulfide (*d*) Sodium chloride.

19. The economic set-up after 1955 in Nepal corresponded closest to :
(*a*) Mixed economy (*b*) Socialism
(*c*) Capitalism (*d*) Communism.

20. What do you mean by scatology?
(*a*) Eye defect (*b*) Insomnia
(*c*) Interest in excrement (*d*) Dislike of radio.

QUIZ 108

1. Who wrote the only book *Notes on the State of Virginia*?
   (*a*) Thomas Jefferson (*b*) George Washington
   (*c*) Abraham Lincoln (*d*) James Garfield.

2. What is a 'Siberian husky'?
   (*a*) Horse (*b*) Bear (*c*) Wolf (*d*) Dog.

3. Who was the first film director to win Academy Awards for four films?
   (*a*) Frank Capra (*b*) John Ford
   (*c*) David Lean (*d*) Billly Wilder.

4. Where is Duarte Peak located?
   (*a*) Dominica (*b*) Dominican Republic
   (*c*) Haiti (*d*) Honduras.

5. Who is considered to be the greatest French romantic composer?
   (*a*) Auguste Rodin (*b*) Victor Hugo
   (*c*) Hector Berlioz (*d*) Georges Bizel.

6. Which city in Italy became famous as the birthplace of the Renaissance?
   (*a*) Turin (*b*) Venice (*c*) Milan (*d*) Florence.

7. What is the real determinant of the size of the market in a country?
   (*a*) Its geographical area (*b*) Population size
   (*c*) Income of the population (*d*) Government's income.

8. Who are the 'Hasidim'?
   (*a*) Jews maintaining the highest standard of religions observance and moral action
   (*b*) Jews who survived the Holocaust
   (*c*) Jews migrating to Israel
   (*d*) Persecuted Jews in Russia.

9. Name the country that invented playing cards and whiskey.
(*a*) India (*b*) Germany (*c*) Britain (*d*) China.

10. When is a baby called premature?
(*a*) Born before the 37th week (*b*) Born before the 36th week
(*c*) Born before the 35th week (*d*) Born before the 34th week.

11. Where was the right of the woman to vote first introduced?
(*a*) Sweden (*b*) USA (*c*) Japan (*d*) UK.

12. Miss Marple, the detective, appears in whose books?
(*a*) E. Gardner (*b*) Leon Uris
(*c*) Agatha Christie (*d*) Henry Green.

13. Who was the British Prime Minister when Pakistan became independent?
(*a*) Clement Attlee (*b*) Harold Wilson
(*c*) Edward Heath (*d*) Winston Churchill.

14. According to the Prophet, how many times should his followers read the *namaz*?
(*a*) Three (*b*) Four (*c*) Five (*d*) Six.

15. Bachstroke swimming was first introduced in which country?
(*a*) UK (*b*) France (*c*) Egypt (*d*) Kenya.

16. In Hindu mythology, among her five husbands, whom did Draupadi rely upon most for the fulfillment of her wishes?
(*a*) Yudhisthira (*b*) Bhima (*c*) Arjun (*d*) Nahakul.

17. The Flavian amphitheatre, the Colosseum, built between 72AD and 81AD is supposed to be one of the greatest masterpieces of Roman architecture. Who conceived it?
(*a*) Marcus Aurelius (*b*) Justinian (*c*) Trajan (*d*) Vespasian.

18. In which instrument can hard water be softened?
(*a*) An ion exchanger (*b*) An earthenware pot
(*c*) A chromatograph (*d*) A calorimeter.

19. Which economist had little formal education and began to work at a tender age of fourteen in the money market?
(*a*) Thomas Malthus (*b*) J.B. Say
(*c*) David Ricardo (*d*) J. S. Mill.

20. What is the meaning of meatspace?
(*a*) Wooden shelf (*b*) Physical world
(*c*) Direction (*d*) Twin bed.

QUIZ 109

1. Where is the Gibson desert?
   (*a*) China (*b*) Ethiopia (*c*) Iran (*d*) Australia.

2. Gothic art is the name given to the art of the later Middle Ages, especially from when to when?
   (*a*) Mid – 1100s to 1400 (*b*) Mid – 1000s to 1300
   (*c*) Mid – 1200s to 1500 (*d*) Mid – 1300s to 1600.

3. Who was the evangelist whose early work in the USA and UK for the 'Youth for Christ Crusades' led him and his colleagues to conduct a large scale evangelistic campaign in Los Angeles in 1949?
   (*a*) Norman Vincent Peale (*b*) Robert Schuller
   (*c*) Billy Graham (*d*) Dale Carnegie.

4. The *Vouli* is the parliament of which country?
   (*a*) Turkey (*b*) Greece (*c*) Austria (*d*) Hungary.

5. What is a 'bazar'?
   (*a*) A market place (*b*) An overcoat
   (*c*) A suit (*d*) A garden.

6. In West Indies, which island did Christopher Columbus name Concepcion?
   (*a*) St. Vincent (*b*) Jamaica (*c*) St. Lucia (*d*) Grenada.

7. What is *odontaspis arenarius*?
   (*a*) Whale (*b*) Crocodile (*c*) Shark (*d*) Gorilla.

8. Griffin was a strange creature of Greek mythology. What was it like?
   (*a*) Head of an elephant and body of a man
   (*b*) Head and wings of an eagle and the body of a lion
   (*c*) Head of a jackal and body of a horse
   (*d*) Head of a lion and body of a man.

9. Hugo Grotius, a lawyer, theologian, statesman and poet is considered the 'Father of International Law' and wrote *On the Law of War and Peace* (1625). In which country was he born?
(*a*) Netherlands (*b*) Hungary
(*c*) Switzerland (*d*) Germany.

10. Who wrote *Child is the Father of Man*?
(*a*) Pope (*b*) Tennyson (*c*) Milton (*d*) Wordsworth.

11. Which planet has its length of day and the tilt of its axis almost identical to those of the earth?
(*a*) Pluto (*b*) Mars (*c*) Mercury (*d*) Jupiter.

12. When is International Children's Day celebrated?
(*a*) 30th November (*b*) 22nd November
(*c*) 14th November (*d*) 6th November.

13. Which of the following do not lay eggs?
(*a*) Bats (*b*) Pigeons (*c*) Ants (*d*) Frogs.

14. With which sport is Michael Ferriera associated?
(*a*) Badminton (*b*) Volleyball (*c*) Golf (*d*) Billiards.

15. How does a yellow flower appear in red light?
(*a*) Black (*b*) Yellow (*c*) Purple (*d*) Green.

16. In which city did Lal Bahadur Shastri, former Prime Minister of India, die of a heart attack?
(*a*) Frankfurt (*b*) Tashkent (*c*) Karachi (*d*) Bombay.

17. Who was the rebel general who established his Han domain in the Wei Valley?
(*a*) Hsiang Yu (*b*) Wu Ti (*c*) Liu Pang (*d*) Shih Huang.

18. Which of the following is a chemical change?
(*a*) Dissolution (*b*) Evaporation
(*c*) Oxidation (*d*) Condensation.

19. When is total utility maximum?
(*a*) Average utility is maximum
(*b*) Marginal utility is equivalent to average utility
(*c*) Marginal utility is maximum
(*d*) Marginal utility is zero.

20. What do you mean by bruschetta?
(*a*) Toast (*b*) Bicycle (*c*) Fainting (*d*) Story.

QUIZ 110

1. What is polio's other name?
   (*a*) Infantile paralysis (*b*) Down's syndrome
   (*c*) Parkinson's disease (*d*) Schizophrenia.
2. When did Japanese troops invade Manchuria?
   (*a*) 1927 (*b*) 1931 (*c*) 1935 (*d*) 1939.
3. Who said these words : "We had no funds, no technology, just the desire to stand and face powerful competitors"?
   (*a*) Ed Reingold (*b*) Eiji Toyoda
   (*c*) Soichiro Honda (*d*) Takeo Fujisawa.
4. Who wrote the book *Breaking the Ties*?
   (*a*) Soseki Natsume (*b*) Salman Rushdie
   (*c*) Nhat Linh (*d*) Pramoldya Ananta Toer.
5. In 1999, in which African country did a global team uncover fossilized jaws believed to be 230 million years old-possibly the oldest dinosaur bones ever found?
   (*a*) Chad (*b*) Gambia (*c*) Mozambique (*d*) Madagascar.
6. Name the alpinist whose body was found after nearly 75 years after disappearing into the mists on the world's highest mountain?
   (*a*) George Mallory (*b*) John Hunt
   (*c*) Edmund Hillary (*d*) Junko Tabei.
7. From which bank in Indonesia was US$ 80 million mysteriously transferred to an account operated by a senior ruling-party official?
   (*a*) Tamara Bank (*b*) Bank Bira
   (*c*) Bank Bali (*d*) Bank Duta.
8. Who was the brilliant engineer and top designer at Mercedes — Benz who was also a Hilter's crony?
   (*a*) Herman Goring (*b*) Ferdinand Porsche
   (*c*) Rudolf Hess (*d*) Martin Bormann.

9. In which country was Louis B. Mayer, the film maker, born?
(*a*) Hungary (*b*) France (*c*) Poland (*d*) Byelorussia.

10. Where in California did A.P. Giannini, the banker, die in June 1949?
(*a*) Los Angeles (*b*) San Jose (*c*) Riverside (*d*) San Mateo.

11. When did the Wright Brothers (Wilbur and Orville) obtain a contract to manufacture planes for US Army?
(*a*) 1904 (*b*) 1906 (*c*) 1908 (*d*) 1910.

12. What nationality is the pop group 'Les Nubians'?
(*a*) Canada (*b*) France (*c*) Germany (*d*) Spain.

13. When was the first sex-change operation performed on a patient named George Jorgenson, latter known as Christine Jorgenson?
(*a*) 1942 (*b*) 1947 (*c*) 1952 (*d*) 1957.

14. Which was the first artificial satellite to orbit around Earth?
(*a*) Sputnik (*b*) Vostok (*c*) Gemini (*d*) Soyuz.

15. When did the first supersonic commercial airplane, the Concorde, go into service?
(*a*) 1973 (*b*) 1976 (*c*) 1979 (*d*) 1982.

16. In 1997, Scottish researchers cloned a sheep from cells of an adult ewe. What was the name of the sheep?
(*a*) Dolly (*b*) Samantha (*c*) Lolita (*d*) Sherry.

17. From Lahore, where did the successor of Qutbuddin Aibak as Sultan shift the capital city?
(*a*) Calcutta (*b*) Patna (*c*) Dacca (*d*) Delhi.

18. When did the Battle of Saloms take place?
(*a*) 490 BC (*b*) 480 BC (*c*) 470 BC (*d*) 460 BC

19. When did John M. Keynes publish his seminal work *The General Theory of Employment, Interest and Money*?
(*a*) 1944 (*b*) 1940 (*c*) 1936 (*d*) 1932.

20. What do you mean by raffish?
(*a*) Vulgar (*b*) Fancy (*c*) Kind (*d*) Unstable.

QUIZ 111

1. Which country launched the first satellite?
   (*a*) Russia (*b*) France (*c*) USA (*d*) UK.
2. Who developed superheterodyne circuit, the receiver-amplifier at the center of radios and televisions?
   (*a*) John A. Fleming (*b*) Edwin Armstrong
   (*c*) Guglielmo Marconi (*d*) Lee De Forest.
3. Who did Franklin D. Roosevelt blast in the 1932 presidential election for running a deficit, and promised he would balance the budget if elected?
   (*a*) Woodrow Wilson (*b*) Theodore Roosevelt
   (*c*) Herbert Hoover (*d*) James Garfield.
4. Who formed commonsense principles of child learning that helped shape the baby-boom generation?
   (*a*) Carl Jung (*b*) Alfred Kinsey
   (*c*) Benjamin Spock (*d*) B.F. Skinner.
5. Whose work forms the basis of modern chemotherapy?
   (*a*) Ernest Rutherford (*b*) Fredrick Hopkins
   (*c*) Thomas H. Morgan (*d*) Paul Ehrlich.
6. When was lobotomy first used in the treatment of mental illness?
   (*a*) 1931 (*b*) 1935 (*c*) 1939 (*d*) 1943.
7. Who wrote *A Brief History of Time*?
   (*a*) Stephen Hawking (*b*) Richard Feynman
   (*c*) Albert Einstein (*d*) Thomas A. Edison.
8. In 1984, who were the two doctors to discover the virus that causes AIDs?
   (*a*) J. Michael Bishop and Harold E. Varmus
   (*b*) Michael S. Brown and Joseph L. Goldstein
   (*c*) Barbara McClintock and Stanley Cohen
   (*d*) Luc Montagnier and Robert Gallo.

9. Who divided scores on Binet's test by the subject's age to arrive at his or her IQ?
(*a*) Michael Young (*b*) Nicholas Lemann
(*c*) Lewis Terman (*d*) Francis Galton.

10. When did Japan annex Korea?
(*a*) 1910 (*b*) 1912 (*c*) 1914 (*d*) 1916.

11. What was the population of India in 1900?
(*a*) 210 million (*b*) 238 million
(*c*) 266 million (*d*) 294 million.

12. Who said the following words : "Confrontation or condemnation; I don't think it works. The only practical way is to be a genuine friend"?
(*a*) Satya Sai Baba (*b*) Rev Sun Myung Moon
(*c*) Ngo Van Chieu (*d*) Dalai Lama.

13. With which work did Rabindranath Tagore win a Nobel Prize in Literature?
(*a*) *Hungry Stones* (*b*) *Gitanjali* (*c*) *Lipika* (*d*) *Bisarjan.*

14. Who owns the album *Tusk* that was released in 1979?
(*a*) Fleetwood Mac (*b*) Pink Floyd (*c*) Exile (*d*) Rod Stewart.

15. To which nationality does the film *Rosetta* belong?
(*a*) French (*b*) Italian (*c*) Belgian (*d*) Spanish.

16. Who was the District Judge who ruled that Bill Gates' Microsoft abused its monopoly power?
(*a*) Thomas P. Jackson (*b*) Edwin L. Nelson
(*c*) Richard M. Bilby (*d*) Henry Woods.

17. Which country was referred to as 'Tamraparni' in the rock edicts of Ashoka, the great Mauryan king?
(*a*) Persia (*b*) Thailand (*c*) Sri Lanka (*d*) Nepal

18. What is added to keep tobacco moist?
(*a*) Gums (*b*) Polyhydric alcohols
(*c*) Vegetable oil (*d*) Glucose sugar.

19. Who is the author of *The Trade Cycle*?
(*a*) A.K. Sen (*b*) Jan Tinbergen
(*c*) Maurice Dobb (*d*) R.C. Matthews.

20. What do you mean by dyspraxia?
(*a*) Speaking difficulty (*b*) Yellow-flowered plant
(*c*) Brain disorder (*d*) Axiom.

QUIZ 112

1. Who was the former chancellor of Germany who admitted that during his tenure he had used secret bank accounts that allegedly contained hundreds of thousands of dollars to finance party campaigns?
   (*a*) Willy Brandt (*b*) Konrad Adenauer
   (*c*) Helmut Schimdt (*d*) Helmut Kohl.
2. Who crated the child wizard Harry Potter?
   (*a*) J. K. Rowling (*b*) Vince McMahon
   (*c*) Laetitia Casta (*d*) Alfred Hitchcock.
3. Name the panda cub that was born at the San Diego Zoo in 1999?
   (*a*) Hua Mei (*b*) Wang Chi
   (*c*) Huang Peng (*d*) Li Zong.
4. Name the two major political parties of USA.
   (*a*) Labour and Republican (*b*) Conservative and Democrat
   (*c*) Democrat and Republican (*d*) Labour and Conservative.
5. In American politics, with who is the term 'shuttle diplomacy' associated?
   (*a*) Cyrus Vance (*b*) Henry Kissinger
   (*c*) Alexander Haig (*d*) Ronald Baker.
6. What was the former name of Zimbabwe?
   (*a*) Nyasaland (*b*) Ivory Gold Coast
   (*c*) South Rhodesia (*d*) Bechuanaland.
7. In which country was paper money invented?
   (*a*) Greece (*b*) Italy (*c*) India (*d*) China.
8. Who was the second man to set foot on the moon?
   (*a*) Edwin Aldrin (*b*) Neil Armstrong
   (*c*) Michael Collins (*d*) John Glenn.

9. What are the two major languages of People's Democratic Republic of Laos?
(*a*) Lao and English (*b*) English and French
(*c*) Lao and French (*d*) Lao and Thai.

10. What is the inland sea surrounded by Turkey and Eastern Europe called?
(*a*) Caspian Sea (*b*) Black Sea
(*c*) North Sea (*d*) Aegean Sea.

11. In which country are crickets (a kind of insects) set to fight?
(*a*) China (*b*) Thailand (*c*) Spain (*d*) Philippines.

12. Name the bird known as 'Bird of Minerva'?
(*a*) Eagle (*b*) Bat (*c*) Crow (*d*) Owl.

13. What is androphobia?
(*a*) Morbid fear of men
(*b*) Morbid fear of women
(*c*) Morbid fear of old-aged persons
(*d*) Morbid fear of children.

14. In which US State is the district, Crater of the moon, located?
(*a*) Iowa (*b*) Idaho (*c*) Montana (*d*) Wyoming.

15. In which city in France did General Dwight Eisenhower receive the unconditional surrender of Germany in 1945?
(*a*) Nice (*b*) Lyon (*c*) Rheims (*d*) Paris.

16. Which Canadian province in 1605 was first settled by the French as Acadia?
(*a*) Ontario (*b*) Alberta (*c*) Manitoba (*d*) Nova Scotia.

17. When was Jesus Christ crucified?
(*a*) 29 AD (*b*) 32 AD (*c*) 35 AD (*d*) 38 AD.

18. What is cellophane — used as a plastic wrapper — made from?
(*a*) Petroleum (*b*) Cellulose (*c*) Gum (*d*) Phenol.

19. What is one thing in terms of the alternative given up known as?
(*a*) Actual cost (*b*) Opportunity cost
(*c*) Consumption cost (*d*) Production cost.

20. What do you mean by chuddies?
(*a*) Shoes (*b*) Wild boors (*c*) Cotton cloth (*d*) Underpants.

QUIZ 113

1. Who was Sigmund Freud's famous daughter who became a famous analyst in her own right, specializing in children?
(*a*) Anna (*b*) Rebecca (*c*) Mary (*d*) Jane.

2. When was the first successful launch of a liquid-fueled rocket conducted?
(*a*) 1922 (*b*) 1926 (*c*) 1930 (*d*) 1934.

3. Who published *The Common Sense Book of Baby and Child Care*?
(*a*) Benjamin Spock (*b*) Elizabeth Hurlock
(*c*) Maria Montessori (*d*) Alfred Binet.

4. Name the world's first test-tube baby.
(*a*) Yetsuko Kishiba (*b*) Janet Fonda
(*c*) Louise Brown (*d*) Jackie Hawn.

5. When did Mao Zedong die?
(*a*) 1973 (*b*) 1974 (*c*) 1975 (*d*) 1976.

6. According to Time Magazine, which was the best cinema of 1999?
(*a*) *Tempting Heart* (*b*) *The Straight Story*
(*c*) *The Matrix* (*d*) *All About My Mother.*

7. Which construction company did German Chancellor Gerhard Schroder bailout in 1999 to save jobs?
(*a*) Saacke (*b*) Erisman & Cie
(*c*) Philipp Holzmann (*d*) Seip Antriebstechnik.

8. Both the IMF and the World Bank have revealed a plan to cancel the debts of the world's poorest countries. How much is this plan worth in US dollars?
(*a*) $ 17 billion (*b*) $ 23 billion
(*c*) $ 29 billion (*d*) $ 35 billion.

9. Who said the following : "I will build a car for the great multitude...so low in price that no man will be unable to own one."?
(*a*) Henry Ford (*b*) Eiji Toyoda
(*c*) Lee Iacocca (*d*) Walter P. Chrysler.

10. Which American tribe worshipped the deity Quetzalcoatl ('plumed serpent')?
(*a*) The Mohicans (*b*) The Incas (*c*) The Siouxs (*d*) The Toltecs.

11. Which mathematician developed the binomial theorem?
(*a*) Stephen Hawking (*b*) John von Newmann
(*c*) Isaac Newton (*d*) Marcel Grossman.

12. In which country world you find the Oeta Mountains?
(*a*) Turkey (*b*) Cyprus (*c*) Greece (*d*) Albania.

13. Which planet has the longest day?
(*a*) Earth (*b*) Venus (*c*) Mars (*d*) Jupiter.

14. Douglas Wilder became the first black Gvernor of which US state?
(*a*) Idaho (*b*) Montana (*c*) Virginia (*d*) Wyoming

15. What is orography?
(*a*) Physical geography of mountains
(*b*) Physical geography of ocean
(*c*) Physical geography of land
(*d*) Physical geography of sky.

16. Which islands, from 1798 to mid — 1945, were known as the Dutch East Indies?
(*a*) Philippines (*b*) Malaysia
(*c*) Papua New Guinea (*d*) Indonesia.

17. Name the last dynasty to rule China, also called the Ch'ing Dynasty.
(*a*) Manchu Dynasty (*b*) Shang Dynasty
(*c*) Qin Dynasty (*d*) Song Dynasty.

18. Which metal is alloyed with tin to produce bronze?
(*a*) Zinc (*b*) Copper (*c*) Aluminum (*d*) Iron.

19. In the short term, what happens to average fixed cost when the output of a firm augments?
(*a*) Fist decreases and then soars (*b*) Remains stable
(*c*) Falls (*d*) Rises.

20. What do you mean by eyeteeth?
(*a*) Small holes in dresses (*b*) Fork
(*c*) Wisdom teeth (*d*) Upper canines

QUIZ 114

1. When did US endocrinologists Gregory Pincus, John Rock and C.R. Garcia develop the birth-control pill?
(*a*) 1948 (*b*) 1950 (*c*) 1952 (*d*) 1954.

2. Where was Elisabeth Kubler-Ross, a psychiatrist, who published *On Death and Dying,* born?
(*a*) Austria (*b*) Germany (*c*) Switzerland (*d*) Poland.

3. Name Dr. Christian Barnard's patient on whom the first successful human heart transplant was performed.
(*a*) Regina Bruno (*b*) Louis Washkansky
(*c*) Dawn Funk (*d*) Joan Faulkner.

4. When did USA ban DDT because of its adverse effects on the environment?
(*a*) 1964 (*b*) 1968 (*c*) 1972 (*d*) 1976.

5. Who is the author of *Video Night in Kathmandu*?
(*a*) Pico Iyer (*b*) Hannah Beech
(*c*) M. Ando (*d*) Boris Lisanovich.

6. Who is the actor of the film *My Intimate Enemy*?
(*a*) Fernando Lujan (*b*) Ted Hughes
(*c*) Sylvia Chang (*d*) Klaus Kinski.

7. Which car has been referred to as Hitler's project?
(*a*) 1934 Citroen 7CV (*b*) 1937 Chrysler Airflow
(*c*) Volkswagen Beetle (*d*) Willys Jeep.

8. Who made the following remarks : "Hoover Dam put us in a prime position as being big-time, real thinkers. We bet our shirts on it"?
(*a*) Bill Waste (*b*) Stephen Bechtel
(*c*) John McCone (*d*) George J. Church.

9. This drug launched in 1988 by Eli Lilly, works by blocking serotonin rather than allowing it to be released from the brain. Can you name it?
(*a*) Valium (*b*) Risperidol (*c*) Clozapine (*d*) Prozac.

10. With which religion is 'Tripitika' associated?
(*a*) Hinduism (*b*) Buddhism (*c*) Islam (*d*) Christianity.

11. What was Surinam formerly known as?
(*a*) Dutch Guyana (*b*) French Guyana
(*c*) British Guyana (*d*) American Samoa.

12. What is bromatology?
(*a*) Study of elements (*b*) Study of plants
(*c*) Study of food and diet (*d*) Study of animals.

13. Name the country that used toothbrush in 1498 for the first time.
(*a*) China (*b*) Egypt (*c*) UK (*d*) France.

14. The 25th Wedding anniversary is called a Silver wedding. Which wedding anniversary is associated with paper?
(*a*) The twentieth (*b*) The tenth (*c*) The fifth (*d*) The first.

15. To which country did navigator, Christopher Columbus belong?
(*a*) Portugal (*b*) Spain (*c*) France (*d*) Italy.

16. *Igbo* is a tribe belonging to which African country?
(*a*) Kenya (*b*) Nigeria (*c*) Tanzania (*d*) Rwanda.

17. Under which Russian leader was Afghanistan invaded?
(*a*) Brezhnev (*b*) Chernenko
(*c*) Gorbachev (*d*) Andropov.

18. In which of the following is acetone, a sweet-smelling solvent, used?
(*a*) Sweet-smelling erasers (*b*) Vanilla
(*c*) Nail-polishes (*d*) Face cream.

19. In the short term, total costs are dichotomized into fixed costs and variable costs. Identify the variable cost from the following.
(*a*) Rent payments on buildings
(*b*) Interest payment on past borrowing
(*c*) Cost of machinery
(*d*) Cost of raw materials

20. What do you mean by prodigious?
(*a*) Gigantic (*b*) Mundane
(*c*) Wasteful (*d*) Adroit.

QUIZ 115

1. Who published *Silent Spring*?
   (*a*) Rachel Carson (*b*) Jonas Salk
   (*c*) C.R. Garcia (*d*) Willard Libby.
2. When was valium, a sleeping drug, introduced?
   (*a*) 1960 (*b*) 1963 (*c*) 1966 (*d*) 1969.
3. What was the name of the communication satellite that was first launched in 1962?
   (*a*) Titan (*b*) Challenger (*c*) Atlantis (*d*) Telestar.
4. When did Mohandas Gandhi lead Salt March protesting British rule in India?
   (*a*) 1920 (*b*) 1925 (*c*) 1930 (*d*) 1935.
5. Who is the screenwriter and also the author of the classic talk of Hollywood, *What Makes Sammy Run*?
   (*a*) Jack Warner (*b*) Adolph Zukor
   (*c*) George Lucas (*d*) Budd Schulberg.
6. What medicine is the brand name for acetaminophen?
   (*a*) Tylenol (*b*) Lozapin (*c*) Loxapac (*d*) Plaquenil.
7. Who uttered the following remarks : "This is rat eat rat, dog eat dog. I'll kill 'em and I'm going to kill 'em before they kill me."?
   (*a*) Howard D. Johnson (*b*) Ray Kroc
   (*c*) Joe Baum (*d*) Earl Prince.
8. What is 'sitophobia'?
   (*a*) Morbid dislike of alcohol (*b*) Morbid dislike of lunch
   (*c*) Morbid dislike of dinner (*d*) Morbid dislike of food.
9. Of which country was Pedro Antonis de Alarcon a poet and novelist?
   (*a*) Brazil (*b*) Colombia (*c*) Spain (*d*) Portugal.

10. In which country is *khedive* a title?
(*a*) Egypt (*b*) Syria (*c*) Sudan (*d*) Israel.

11. Which country is known as the 'Land of the White Cloud'?
(*a*) Canada (*b*) New Zealand (*c*) UK (*d*) Japan.

12. Charon is the moon of which planet?
(*a*) Jupiter (*b*) Saturn (*c*) Uranus (*d*) Pluto.

13. Which disease is known as 'paralysis agitans'?
(*a*) Schizophrenia (*b*) Parkinson's disease
(*c*) Small pox (*d*) Leprosy.

14. Which country is famous for sheep and kangaroos?
(*a*) Kibrati (*b*) Australia (*c*) Ireland (*d*) Tonga

15. In which American state would you find 'The Valley of Ten Thousand Smokes'?
(*a*) Alaska (*b*) North Dakota
(*c*) North Carolina (*d*) Minnesota.

16. Who is the author of *Bad Blood* ?
(*a*) Kuldip Nayyar (*b*) Lewis Wallace
(*c*) Chester Bowles (*d*) Ernest Hemingway.

17. When did Nigeria achieve independence peacefully from the British?
(*a*) 1950 (*b*) 1955 (*c*) 1960 (*d*) 1965.

18. Which gaseous element did Scheele isolate in 1774 by the action of manganese dioxide in hydrochloric acid?
(*a*) Nitrogen (*b*) Oxygen (*c*) Hydrogen (*d*) Chlorine.

19. Among the following, which is not a function of money?
(*a*) Stabilization of price level
(*b*) Standard of deferred payments
(*c*) Unit of account
(*d*) Medium of exchange.

20. What do you mean by ponder?
(*a*) Jolly remembrance (*b*) Think
(*c*) Rural building (*d*) Debt.

QUIZ 116

1. When did Bell Labs invent the negative-feedback amplifier, significantly improving telecom quality?
   (*a*) 1924 (*b*) 1927 (*c*) 1930 (*d*) 1933.
2. Who wrote *The Big Test*?
   (*a*) Nicholas Lemann (*b*) J.K. Rowling
   (*c*) James Gleick (*d*) Susan Tifft.
3. Who was the famous son of Charles Merrill, the founder of Merrill Lynch & Co., who later became one of America's finest poets?
   (*a*) James Merrill (*b*) George Merrill
   (*c*) Arthur Merrill (*d*) Matthew Merrill.
4. To which country do the national airlines UTA and Air Inter belong?
   (*a*) UK (*b*) Germany (*c*) France (*d*) Austria.
5. In which country would you find *Ainu*, a native race?
   (*a*) China (*b*) Japan (*c*) Korea (*d*) Mongolia.
6. How many letters or alphabets are used in the Roman system of numerals?
   (*a*) Ten (*b*) Nine (*c*) Eight (*d*) Seven.
7. What is ochlophobia?
   (*a*) Fear of open spaces (*b*) Fear of enclosed places
   (*c*) Fear of religious temples (*d*) Fear of crowds.
8. What pen-name did writer Samuel L. Clemens use to write his books?
   (*a*) George Eliot (*b*) Elia (*c*) Mark Twain (*d*) His Own.
9. Which American city is known as the 'City of Magnificent Distances'?
   (*a*) Washington D.C. (*b*) San Francisco
   (*c*) Chicago (*d*) New York

10. "A good husband should be deaf and a good wife blind". To which country does this proverb belong?
(*a*) Sweden (*b*) France (*c*) UK (*d*) Germany

11. With which country are *Edam* and *Gouda* Cheese associated?
(*a*) Italy (*b*) France (*c*) Switzerland (*d*) Holland.

12. Among the following airports, which is farthest from Paris?
(*a*) Manila (*b*) New Delhi (*c*) Wellington (*d*) Melbourne.

13. Who is the US democrat who lost 3 times in the race for presidency?
(*a*) William J. Bryan (*b*) Harry Truman
(*c*) Ulysseys Grant (*d*) Adlai Stevenson.

14. Lilangeni is the currency of which African country?
(*a*) Tanzania (*b*) Swaziland (*c*) Gabon (*d*) Chad.

15. As of 1996, which are the two countries where winter Olympic games have been held for 3 times each?
(*a*) Japan and USA (*b*) Austria and France
(*c*) France and USA (*d*) Switzerland and Japan.

16. What is the official language of Zambia?
(*a*) French (*b*) Dutch (*c*) German (*d*) English.

17. Sidney and Beatrice Webb founded a well-known organization in 1884. Name it.
(*a*) Fabian Society (*b*) Owenites
(*c*) St. Simonians (*d*) Tolpuddle Martyrs.

18. What do seeds of apples contain that can cause poisoning?
(*a*) Malic acid (*b*) Cyanide (*c*) Chloride (*d*) Sulfur.

19. Who propounded the theory of social dualism?
(*a*) P.T. Bauer (*b*) Bertil Ohlin
(*c*) J. H. Boeke (*d*) James Tobin.

20. What do you mean by affects?
(*a*) Untrue pride (*b*) Property
(*c*) Emotions related with an idea (*d*) Belongings.

QUIZ 117

1. Rod Glaser is a former Micorsoft executive. Whom was he referring to when he stated : "He's relentless, Darwinian. Success is defined as flattering competition, not creating excellence".
   (*a*) Steve Jobs (*b*) David Bowie
   (*c*) Bill Gates (*d*) Donald Trump.
2. Who wrote the book *The Future in Plain Sight : Nine Clues to the Coming Instability*?
   (*a*) Eugene Linden (*b*) Harry Figgie
   (*c*) Paul Erdman (*d*) T.S. Eliot.
3. From which country does River Adige flow into the Adriatic Sea?
   (*a*) France (*b*) Italy (*c*) Spain (*d*) Portugal.
4. "In God we trust; all others must pay cash." To which country does this adage belong?
   (*a*) UK (*b*) Canada (*c*) Australia (*d*) USA.
5. Which is the highest active volcano in the world?
   (*a*) Chimoborzo (*b*) Etna (*c*) Fujiyama (*d*) Cotopaxi.
6. Which city is called the 'City of Skyscrapers'?
   (*a*) Chicago (*b*) New York (*c*) London (*d*) Tokyo.
7. Which islands were formerly called Sandwich Islands?
   (*a*) Caribbean Islands (*b*) Canary Islands
   (*c*) Hawaiian Islands (*d*) Channel Islands.
8. What is the form of government in which power is in the hands of a few people called?
   (*a*) Oligarchy (*b*) Autocracy (*c*) Plutocracy (*d*) Theocracy.
9. In the 1924 Winter Olympics, Charles Jewtraw won the men's 500 metres in speed skating. What was his native country?
   (*a*) UK (*b*) USA (*c*) Poland (*d*) New Zealand.

10. In Russia, what is a 'kolkhoz'?
(*a*) A national zoo (*b*) A unit of currency
(*c*) A common building (*d*) A collective farm.

11. Of which country was Ismet Inonu a soldier and statesman?
(*a*) Iran (*b*) Iraq (*c*) Turkey (*d*) Cyprus.

12. The film, *The Wild One,* was the success of which American actor?
(*a*) Paul Newmann (*b*) Robert Redford
(*c*) Dustin Hoffman (*d*) Marlon Brando.

13. What name is more commonly used for the disease *variola*?
(*a*) Small pox (*b*) Typhoid (*c*) Measles (*d*) Malaria.

14. Approximately, how far can a giant tortoise crawl in 1 minute?
(*a*) 3 yards (*b*) 5 yards (*c*) 7 yards (*d*) 9 yards.

15. Within how many years of each other did Buddha and Confucius die?
(*a*) 4 years (*b*) 8 years (*c*) 12 years (*d*) 16 years.

16. How many lines are there in a Spenserian stanza?
(*a*) Six (*b*) Seven (*c*) Eight (*d*) Nine.

17. In which century BC did the Mayan civilization began to develop in Central America?
(*a*) 3rd (*b*) 4th (*c*) 5th (*d*) 6th.

18. Of the following, which does not contain carbohydrates?
(*a*) Starch (*b*) Wax (*c*) Cellulose (*d*) Wheat flour.

19. How is money defined when its commodity value and its value as money are equal?
(*a*) Fiat money (*b*) Quasi-money
(*c*) Full-bodied money (*d*) Token money.

20. What do you mean by patchouli?
(*a*) Perfume (*b*) Disease
(*c*) Underwear (*d*) Trousers.

QUIZ 118

1. Which is the second largest island in the world?
   (*a*) New Guinea (*b*) Madagascar (*c*) Borneo (*d*) Baffin.
2. What was the name of the US steamer bound from Havana to New York burned off Asbury Park on September 8, 1934?
   (*a*) Vestris (*b*) Morro Castle
   (*c*) Grandcamp (*d*) Yarmouth.
3. Where is Coober Pedy?
   (*a*) New Zealand (*b*) Australia (*c*) UK (*d*) Canada.
4. What was the name of Alexander the Great's father?
   (*a*) Philip I (*b*) Darius (*c*) Cyrus (*d*) Philip II.
5. What is Caper-spurge?
   (*a*) Kinds of precious stones
   (*b*) Wooden furnitures
   (*c*) Family of herbs, shrubs and trees
   (*d*) Carpets and curtains.
6. On what day is the Russian October Revolution celebrated?
   (*a*) October 24 (*b*) October 31
   (*c*) November 7 (*d*) November 14.
7. During the South African War, Winston Churchill was a war correspondent. Which paper did he represent?
   (*a*) Morning Post (*b*) Sun (*c*) Star (*d*) Financial Times.
8. When did King Edward III found the Order of the Garter?
   (*a*) 1339 (*b*) 1349 (*c*) 1359 (*d*) 1369.
9. Who first won international fame in a film entitled *Gosta Berling*?
   (*a*) Marlene Dietrich (*b*) Elizabeth Taylor
   (*c*) Marilyn Monroe (*d*) Greta Garbo.
10. Which is the longest river in United Kingdom?
    (*a*) Thames (*b*) Avon (*c*) Mersey (*d*) Severn.

11. Who was the first of the Lancastarian Kings?
(*a*) Richard I (*b*) Henry IV (*c*) James I (*d*) Henry II.

12. Of what vitamin does rose-hip syrup have a plentiful supply?
(*a*) Vitamin A (*b*) Vitamin B
(*c*) Vitamin C (*d*) Vitamin D.

13. In which European city is *The Third Man* set?
(*a*) Vienna (*b*) Paris (*c*) London (*d*) Prague.

14. When was the first US satellite, Explorer I, launched?
(*a*) 1956 (*b*) 1958 (*c*) 1960 (*d*) 1962

15. Approximately, how many pints of air does an adult inhale in one normal breath?
(*a*) One (*b*) Two (*c*) Three (*d*) Four.

16. What type of insect is a 'devil's coach-horse'?
(*a*) Caterpillar (*b*) Snail (*c*) Ant (*d*) Beetle

17. When did the Chou dynasty start in China?
(*a*) 1300 BC (*b*) 1200 BC
(*c*) 1100 BC (*d*) 1000 BC.

18. Proteins are polymers (long chains) of amino acids. Of the following, which is not a protein?
(*a*) DNA (genetic material) (*b*) Finger-nails
(*c*) Wool (*d*) Hair

19. Among the following theories of trade cycle, which one was propounded by W.S. Jevons?
(*a*) Innovation Theory
(*b*) Sunspot Theory
(*c*) Saving — Investment Theory
(*d*) Monetary Theory.

20. What do you mean by blasé?
(*a*) Believable (*b*) Beautiful (*c*) Empty (*d*) Indifferent.

QUIZ 119

1. Who succeeded Harold Macmillan as Prime Minister of UK in 1963?
   (*a*) Harold Wilson (*b*) Alec Douglas-Home
   (*c*) Anthony Eden (*d*) Edward Heath.
2. Which is the largest state in Australia?
   (*a*) Western Australia (*b*) South Australia
   (*c*) Queensland (*d*) Victoria.
3. Which African country has pula as the monetary unit?
   (*a*) Botswana (*b*) Niger (*c*) Gabon (*d*) Cameroon.
4. Sandro Botticelli was an Italian Renaissance painter who lived and worked in a certain city. Which one?
   (*a*) Venice (*b*) Florence (*c*) Turin (*d*) Pisa.
5. When did Brazil declare war on Germany in World War I ?
   (*a*) 1914 (*b*) 1915 (*c*) 1916 (*d*) 1917.
6. In which country is the Eiffel Bridge?
   (*a*) France (*b*) UK (*c*) Portugal (*d*) Netherlands
7. When was the cable — stayed bridge at Yokohama Bay in Japan opened?
   (*a*) 1992 (*b*) 1991 (*c*) 1990 (*d*) 1989.
8. Brunei is surrounded by one county. Which one?
   (*a*) Indonesia (*b*) Thailand
   (*c*) Malaysia (*d*) Philippines.
9. Which county has the national anthem, *Kaba Makye* ('Our Free Homeland')?
   (*a*) Thailand (*b*) Vietnam
   (*c*) Kampuchea (*d*) Myanmar.
10. Which chief family includes the following : *skipper, metalmarks, satyrs* and *wood nymphs*?
    (*a*) Owls (*b*) Butterflies (*c*) Parrots (*d*) Eagles.

11. Which language did the Byzantines speak?
(*a*) Greek (*b*) Turkish (*c*) Bulgarian (*d*) English.

12. Whom did Charlotte Corday assassinate in 1793?
(*a*) Georges Danton (*b*) Maximilien Robespierre
(*c*) Jean Paul Marat (*d*) Louis XVI.

13. Who wrote the play *Romanoff and Juliet* ?
(*a*) William Shakespeare (*b*) Charles Dickens
(*c*) Peter Ustinov (*d*) George Eliot.

14. Captain Nemo appears in which of Jules Verne's novel?
(*a*) *Around the World in Eighty Days*
(*b*) *Twenty Thousand Leagues Under the Sea*
(*c*) *Journey to the Center of the Earth*
(*d*) *From the Earth to the Moon.*

15. Who was murdered at Berkely Castle, Gloucestershire in 1327?
(*a*) Edward I (*b*) Charles II (*c*) Henry IV (*d*) Edward II.

16. Gertude Ederle of USA was the first woman to swim the English Channel on August 6. Which year?
(*a*) 1924 (*b*) 1925 (*c*) 1926 (*d*) 1927.

17. Who assisted Egypt in the construction of Aswan Dam?
(*a*) USA (*b*) Germany (*c*) UK (*d*) Russia.

18. What do we acquire when limestone is heated in a lime kiln?
(*a*) Quicklime and carbon dioxide
(*b*) Milk of lime
(*c*) Slaked lime and carbon dioxide
(*d*) Calcium hydroxide and carbon dioxide.

19. According to Ricardo, which one of the following would form a bottleneck to economic growth?
(*a*) Soaring wage bills (*b*) Paucity of land
(*c*) Increasing rent (*d*) Paucity of gold and silver.

20. What do you mean by alcopop?
(*a*) Oriental music (*b*) Home-made juice
(*c*) Ready-mixed drink (*d*) Waltz.

QUIZ 120

1. Which is often called the 'Steel City' in USA?
(*a*) Detroit (*b*) Gary (*c*) St. Paul (*d*) Bismarck.
2. What do you mean by a trade name of a drug?
(*a*) It describes its chemical name
(*b*) It is usually an abbreviated chemical name
(*c*) It is the name given to a drug by the company that sells it
(*d*) It is the name given to drug during its preparation.
3. What is a 'dugong'?
(*a*) It is a plant-eating mammal
(*b*) It is a kind of a shark
(*c*) It is another name for platypus
(*d*) It is related to crocodile.
4. Duodecimal numerals form a numeration system based on which number?
(*a*) 10 (*b*) 12 (*c*) 14 (*d*) 16.
5. How many rivers are there in Saudi Arabia?
(*a*) None (*b*) One (*c*) Two (*d*) Three.
6. What was Rimsky — Korsakov's original job?
(*a*) Doctor (*b*) Plumber (*c*) Engineer (*d*) Sailor.
7. How many legs has a daddy-long-legs?
(*a*) Twelve (*b*) Ten (*c*) Eight (*d*) Six.
8. About how many red corpuscles of the blood stacked upon each other would make an inch?
(*a*) 5,500 (*b*) 7,500 (*c*) 9,500 (*d*) 11,500.
9. 'Pipistrelle' is a variety of what?
(*a*) Sparrows (*b*) Bats (*c*) Owls (*d*) Eagles.
10. For how long has the cockroach, in its modern form, existed on earth?
(*a*) 50 million years (*b*) 250 million years
(*c*) 450 million years (*d*) 650 million years.

11. What is the pen name of Hector Hugh Munro, the writer of satirical short stories and novels?
(*a*) Saki (*b*) Lisa (*c*) Michael Titmarsh (*d*) George Eliot.

12. In USA, the Verrazano-Narrows Bridge connects Brooklyn and Staten Island. It is also the longest and heaviest single span suspension bridge in the world. When was it opened?
(*a*) 1972 (*b*) 1968 (*c*) 1964 (*d*) 1960.

13. In which city was Interpol founded?
(*a*) Paris (*b*) Rome (*c*) Geneva (*d*) Vienna.

14. When Alexander died, his General, Ptolemy I, took over the government of a certain country. Which one?
(*a*) Babylon (*b*) Mesopotamia (*c*) Egypt (*d*) Persia.

15. Simone de Beauvoir won the Goncourt prize in 1954. Name the novel.
(*a*) *The Mandarins* (*b*) *She Came to Stay*
(*c*) *The Prime of Life* (*d*) *The Second Sex.*

16. Who led the Lollards who spread his ideas throughout the countryside in the late fourteenth century?
(*a*) Joseph Smith (*b*) Joseph Conrad
(*c*) John Locke (*d*) John Wycliffe.

17. Which Korean Leader did the Japanese coerce to flee to Hawaii in 1911?
(*a*) Park Chung Hee (*b*) Syngman Rhee
(*c*) Kim Ok-Kyun (*d*) Park Young-Hyo.

18. Around when did man begin to use copper metal?
(*a*) 4000 BC (*b*) 3000 BC (*c*) 2000 BC (*d*) 1000 BC.

19. Of the following, which is not an indicator of economically underdeveloped countries?
(*a*) High illiteracy level
(*b*) Low share of labour force in the agricultural sector
(*c*) High mortality rate
(*d*) Low per capita income.

20. What is the meaning of prion?
(*a*) Baby (*b*) Pulse (*c*) Small insect (*d*) Protein particle.

QUIZ 121

1. Who wrote the autobiography entitled *My Bondage and My Freedom*?
(*a*) Booker T. Washington (*b*) Frederick Douglas
(*c*) Ralph Bunche (*d*) Andrew Young.

2. Down's syndrome, formerly called *Mongolism,* is a disorder that is present at birth. It promotes mental retardation and possesses physical features such as a flat nose and a small head. What are the chances of it occurring in birth?
(*a*) 1 out of every 1,000 births
(*b*) 2 out of every 1,000 births
(*c*) 3 out of every 1,000 births
(*d*) 4 out of every 1,000 births.

3. Which is the largest grape-growing country in the world?
(*a*) USA (*b*) Spain (*c*) Italy (*d*) France.

4. Jean Buridan, the French philosopher's ass, referred to one specific psychological trait. Name it.
(*a*) Meekness (*b*) Presumption
(*c*) Resignation (*d*) Indecision.

5. When did the Cultural Revolution start in China?
(*a*) 1961 (*b*) 1966 (*c*) 1971 (*d*) 1976.

6. In which country was Pabolo Picasso, the painter of *Guernica*, born?
(*a*) Spain (*b*) Portugal (*c*) France (*d*) Italy.

7. From which place in the New World was potato introduced in the Old World?
(*a*) USA (*b*) Ecuador (*c*) Chile (*d*) Uruguay.

8. At what height are the baskets hung in basketball?
(*a*) 7 feet (*b*) 8 feet (*c*) 9 feet (*d*) 10 feet

9. In which country lies the largest deposits of tin?
(*a*) Malaysia (*b*) China (*c*) Brazil (*d*) Philippines.

10. In which country is the largest railway network in Asia located?
(*a*) India (*b*) Malaysia (*c*) Indonesia (*d*) Japan.

11. Who made the highest ever runs in Test Cricket at Lord's?
(*a*) Imran Khan (*b*) Kapil Dev
(*c*) Don Bradman (*d*) Graham Gooch.

12. Which is the least populated state in India?
(*a*) Assam (*b*) Meghalaya (*c*) Sikkim (*d*) Mizoram.

13. Switzerland has a number of official languages. Of the following, which is *not* an official language?
(*a*) Italian (*b*) English (*c*) German (*d*) French.

14. In which country was sauna (hot steam bath) first introduced?
(*a*) Japan (*b*) Turkey (*c*) China (*d*) Finland.

15. Among the following African cities, which has the highest population?
(*a*) Cairo (*b*) Nairobi (*c*) Khartoum (*d*) Lusaka.

16. When did the ancient Olympic games start in Greece?
(*a*) 976 BC (*b*) 876 BC (*c*) 776 BC (*d*) 676 BC.

17. What is the name of the first Japanese political party, which, since 1900, boasted of leaders like Hirobumi, Saionji and Harakei?
(*a*) Doshikai (*b*) Seiyukai
(*c*) Minsieto (*d*) Liberal Democratic Party.

18. Noble gases are inert, that is, under normal conditions, they do not react. Of the following, which is not a noble gas?
(*a*) Argon (*b*) Neon (*c*) Lithium (*d*) Helium.

19. Which is not a necessary feature of a socialist economy?
(*a*) Government implementation
(*b*) Deployment of centralized planning
(*c*) Ownership of production means
(*d*) Independent enterprise.

20. What do you mean by prebuttal?
(*a*) Response (*b*) High wall
(*c*) Pocket money (*d*) Debate.

QUIZ 122

1. Among many others, who published *Daily Bread* (1910) and *Thoroughfares* (1914)?
   (*a*) Jane Austin (*b*) Jonathan Swift
   (*c*) Wilfred W. Gibson (*d*) Oscar Wilde.
2. When did King Edward VI introduce 'The Book of Common Prayer'?
   (*a*) 1559 (*b*) 1549 (*c*) 1539 (*d*) 1529.
3. Robert Fulton tried out the first submarine in a certain river in France in 1801. Name the river.
   (*a*) Loire (*b*) Vistula (*c*) Tagus (*d*) Seine.
4. Who Created Rip Van Winkle?
   (*a*) Washington Irving (*b*) Alexander Dumas
   (*c*) Robert L.Stevenson (*d*) Mark Twain.
5. During the First World War, the French soldier was known as a 'Poilus'; what name was give to the British soldier?
   (*a*) Tommy (*b*) Desert rat (*c*) Jerry (*d*) Desert fox.
6. The Biblical Solomon was the son of Bathsheba; who was his father?
   (*a*) Saul (*b*) Peter (*c*) David (*d*) Paul.
7. What is a 'brumby'?
   (*a*) Giraffe (*b*) Zebra
   (*c*) Kangaroo (*d*) Horse.
8. What is the geographical distinction of the island of Muckleflagar?
   (*a*) The most southerly point in the Shetlands
   (*b*) The most northerly point in the Shetlands
   (*c*) The most westerly point in the Shetlands
   (*d*) The most easterly point in the Shetlands.

9. In the Revelation of St. John the Divine, how many horsemen of the Apocalypse are there?
(*a*) Eight (*b*) Six (*c*) Four (*d*) Two

10. Mozambique was formerly an overseas territory belonging to which country?
(*a*) Portugal (*b*) Spain (*c*) France (*d*) Belgium.

11. In a car, what name is given to the device in which air and petrol are mixed, before being fed to the engine?
(*a*) Gear (*b*) Brake (*c*) Accelerator (*d*) Carburettor.

12. Bouillabaisse is a popular French dish. What is its main component?
(*a*) Chicken (*b*) Fish (*c*) Ham (*d*) Beef.

13. Which Shakespearian character spoke these lines, "Cowards die many times before their death. The valiant never taste of death but once"?
(*a*) King Lear (*b*) Macbeth (*c*) Julies Caesar (*d*) Hamlet.

14. For how long can a bed-bug exist without eating?
(*a*) One year (*b*) Two years (*c*) Three years (*d*) Four years.

15. In tennis, how far are the service lines from the net?
(*a*) 19 feet (*b*) 21 feet (*c*) 23 feet (*d*) 25 feet.

16. How many brain cells does an average person lose per day from the age of about thirty?
(*a*) 40,000 (*b*) 70,000
(*c*) 100,000 (*d*) 130,000.

17. Who set up the anti-communist regime in South Vietnam in 1954 but alienated the United States alliance by his authoritarian rule?
(*a*) Norodom Sihanouk (*b*) Lon Nol
(*c*) Vo Nguyen Giap (*d*) Ngo Dinh Diem.

18. Sodium and sulfur can be melted through heating. Of the following, which is the use of molten sodium and molten sulfur?
(*a*) As electrodes in battery
(*b*) For refining lead
(*c*) As a medium for extracting metals
(*d*) As catalysts.

19. What is the outcome of contraction of demand?
(*a*) Fall in the number of consumers
(*b*) Augmentation in the price of the goods concerned
(*c*) Augmentation in the prices of other commodities
(*d*) Fall in the income of buyers.

20. What do you mean by advent ?
(*a*) Victor (*b*) Highly intelligent
(*c*) Arrival (*d*) Beer.

QUIZ 123

1. Which country uses the most soap per capita?
   (*a*) UK (*b*) China (*c*) France (*d*) Germany.
2. Which card game's name means 'discarded'?
   (*a*) Poker (*b*) Flush (*c*) Bridge (*d*) Ecarte.
3. Between 1928 and 1968, the Olympic men's hockey gold medal invariably went to two countries. One was India, which was the other?
   (*a*) Australia (*b*) Holland (*c*) Pakistan (*d*) Canada.
4. Where did apples and pears originate?
   (*a*) Nepal (*b*) Bangladesh (*c*) Bhutan (*d*) Afghanistan.
5. For chopping off which part of the body was the guillotine originally invented?
   (*a*) Legs (*b*) Hands (*c*) Neck (*d*) Stomach.
6. Expand the middle initial of Jerome K. Jerome.
   (*a*) Klapka (*b*) Ken (*c*) Kris (*d*) Keith.
7. Who is the author of *Ascent of Everest*?
   (*a*) Tenzing Norgay (*b*) Junko Tabei
   (*c*) Edmund Hillary (*d*) John Hunt.
8. Who invented the motorcar?
   (*a*) Swan (*b*) Austin (*c*) Ford (*d*) Cygnet.
9. With which sport is the Argentinean Marie Kempes associated?
   (*a*) Tennis (*b*) Football (*c*) Rugby (*d*) Horse-riding.
10. Which American President abolished slavery?
    (*a*) Abraham Lincoln (*b*) Andrew Jackson
    (*c*) James Monroe (*d*) George Washington.
11. What is 'El-Alamein'?
    (*a*) A Roman amphitheatre
    (*b*) Scene of great Allied victory in World War II
    (*c*) French name for an UN agency
    (*d*) A fort in Corsica.

12. Geriatrics is a branch of medicine, which deals with the problem, and disease of :
(*a*) Dogs (*b*) Skin (*c*) Children (*d*) Old age.

13. When was Prince Sihanouk of Cambodia overthrown by the Communists?
(*a*) 1975 (*b*) 1974 (*c*) 1973 (*d*) 1972.

14. What is GNAT?
(*a*) Aircraft Carrier (*b*) Military Tank
(*c*) Fighter Aircraft (*d*) Supersonic Jet Airplane.

15. What is 1 ohm equal to?
(*a*) 1x106 o.m.u. (*b*) 1x107 o.m.u.
(*c*) 1x108 o.m.u. (*d*) 1x109 o.m.u.

16. Harley Street is famous as a :
(*a*) Center of film industry in Los Angeles
(*b*) London street where expert medical advice is obtainable
(*c*) Well-known movie theatre
(*d*) Stamp-collecting center in Prague.

17. This dynasty was established by the Mongols from 1264 to 1368 and had Peking as its capital. Name it.
(*a*) Chun (*b*) Sung (*c*) Yuan (*d*) Tang.

18. Nearly 500 antibiotics, including streptomycin, aureomycin and terramycin have been isolated from :
(*a*) The bacteria, actinomycetes
(*b*) Kentucky bluegrass
(*c*) The bacteria, rhizobium
(*d*) Alluvial soil.

19. Among the following, which is not an essential situation for an economic problem to arise?
(*a*) Alternative uses of scarce resources
(*b*) Scarcity of resources
(*c*) Unlimited wants
(*d*) Use of money.

20. What do you mean by concupiscent?
(*a*) Obscure (*b*) Lustful (*c*) Snickering (*d*) Smart.

QUIZ 124

1. When was the 1976 Commonwealth Prime Ministers' conference held?
   (*a*) Nairobi (*b*) New Delhi (*c*) Wellington (*d*) Kingston.
2. Who was the hero of the 'American War of Independence'?
   (*a*) George Washington (*b*) Benjamin Franklin
   (*c*) Thomas Jefferson (*d*) Abraham Lincoln.
3. What is coronary insufficiency the disease of?
   (*a*) Skin (*b*) Intestine (*c*) Heart (*d*) Lung.
4. What is used in a rocket?
   (*a*) Only oxidizer (*b*) Only fuel
   (*c*) Both fuel and oxidizer (*d*) Neither fuel nor oxidizer.
5. Statistically, if the class marks of a frequency are 6, 12, 18, 24, 30, 36, then the class size is :
   (*a*) 36 (*b*) 12 (*c*) 06 (*d*) 03.
6. What is the protein present in the body, which prevents coagulation of blood in the blood vessels called?
   (*a*) Heparin (*b*) Fibrinogen (*c*) Globulin (*d*) Albumin
7. What is the length of a cricket pitch?
   (*a*) 20 yards (*b*) 22 yards (*c*) 24 yards (*d*) 26 yards.
8. Who was the first person to float in space?
   (*a*) Michael Collins (*b*) Alan Shepherd
   (*c*) Yuri Gagarin (*d*) Alexi Leonov.
9. Which of the following is a great circle?
   (*a*) Tropic of Equator (*b*) Tropic of Capricorn
   (*c*) Tropic of Cancer (*d*) Arctic Circle
10. Which Pakistani leader wrote *Friends, not Masters*?
    (*a*) Nawaz Sharif (*b*) Yahya Khan
    (*c*) Zulfikar Ali Bhutto (*d*) Ayub Khan

11. What is a calorimetry?
(*a*) Term employed for equal expansion of different gases
(*b*) Measurement of calories
(*c*) Measurement of heat
(*d*) Vitamin.

12. What is the principal religion of Ivory Coast in West Africa?
(*a*) Hinduism (*b*) Animism (*c*) Buddhism (*d*) Islam.

13. The normal sea-route from Black Sea to Bombay passes through the :
(*a*) Kiel Canal (*b*) Suez Canal
(*c*) Cape of Good Hope (*d*) Panama Canal.

14. What title is given to Herodotus?
(*a*) The Father of Philosophy (*b*) The Father of Democracy
(*c*) The Father of Medicine (*d*) The Father of History.

15. What is the average weight of the human liver?
(*a*) 3½ pounds (*b*) 2½ pounds
(*c*) 1½ pounds (*d*) ½ pound.

16. Which of the following do not lay eggs?
(*a*) Pigeons (*b*) Ants (*c*) Bats (*d*) Frogs.

17. When did the Jallianwala Bagh massacre occur in India?
(*a*) 1909 (*b*) 1919 (*c*) 1929 (*d*) 1939.

18. What is the purest form of carbon?
(*a*) Graphite (*b*) Diamond (*c*) Coal (*d*) Wood charcoal.

19. What is the feature of capital-output ratios in developed countries?
(*a*) Slowly augmenting (*b*) Rigidly stationary
(*c*) Normally fluctuating (*d*) Fairly stable.

20. What is the meaning of red top?
(*a*) Tabloid newspaper (*b*) Acid
(*c*) Soldier (*d*) Truck.

QUIZ 125

1. With what kind of novel is Edger Alan Poe associated?
   (*a*) Non-fiction (*b*) Horror (*c*) Fiction (*d*) Drama.
2. Which instrument is used for determining the purity of milk?
   (*a*) Penumbra (*b*) Seismograph
   (*c*) Tachometer (*d*) Speedometer.
3. Which is the eighth largest country in the world in area?
   (*a*) Sudan (*b*) Brazil (*c*) India (*d*) Argentinas.
4. When was the first satellite used?
   (*a*) 1957 (*b*) 1960 (*c*) 1963 (*d*) 1966.
5. Who invented microscope?
   (*a*) Zickerman (*b*) Faraday (*c*) Galileo (*d*) Janson.
6. With which game is Davis Cup associated?
   (*a*) Tennis (*b*) Billiards (*c*) Cricket (*d*) Hockey.
7. In England, which language prevailed throughout the Middle Ages as a language of religion and scholarships?
   (*a*) English (*b*) Irish (*c*) Latin (*d*) Welsh.
8. What is a persimmon?
   (*a*) Vegetable (*b*) Fruit (*c*) Alcoholic drink (*d*) Cereal.
9. In the first century AD, Flavius Josephus wrote history of which people?
   (*a*) The Egyptians (*b*) The Palestinians
   (*c*) The Syrians (*d*) The Jews.
10. The bird known as Pica Pica is very fond of bright things. What is its more common name?
    (*a*) Kingfisher (*b*) Nightingale (*c*) Magpie (*d*) Swallow.
11. Septuagint is the name given to which translation of the Old Testament?
    (*a*) The Greek Translation (*b*) The French Translation
    (*c*) The Latin Translation (*d*) The German Translation.

12. Which part of the body would be affected by cutaneous disease?
(*a*) The liver (*b*) The lungs (*c*) The heart (*d*) The skin.

13. In which play by Shakespeare is the character Launcelot Gobbo found?
(*a*) *Hamlet* (*b*) *The Merchant of Venice*
(*c*) *Two Gentlemen of Verona* (*d*) *As you like It.*

14. When did Henrik Ibsen publish his first play, *Catalina*?
(*a*) 1840 (*b*) 1850 (*c*) 1860 (*d*) 1870.

15. British physicists devised Zero Energy Thermonuclear Assembly (Zeta). When?
(*a*) 1955 (*b*) 1956 (*c*) 1957 (*d*) 1958

16. In which gaol did John Bunyan write *The Pilgrim's Progress* in 1675?
(*a*) Bedford (*b*) Reading (*c*) Southampton (*d*) Dover.

17. Which communist dictator was overthrown and executed in Romania during the bloody uprising of 1989?
(*a*) Edward Benes (*b*) Imre Nagy
(*c*) Wladyslaw Gomulka (*d*) Nicolai Ceauesescu.

18. Who discovered parachute?
(*a*) Herschel (*b*) Ross (*c*) Garnerin (*d*) Harvey.

19. Who is the author of *An Introduction to Positive Economics*?
(*a*) William Nordhaus (*b*) James Tobin
(*c*) Richard Quandt (*d*) R.G. Lipsey.

20. What do you mean by occult?
(*a*) Serious (*b*) Secret (*c*) Story (*d*) Shabby.

ANSWERS

QUIZ 1

(1)	b	(6)	c	(11)	a	(16)	a
(2)	d	(7)	d	(12)	d	(17)	c
(3)	a	(8)	b	(13)	b	(18)	c
(4)	d	(9)	b	(14)	b	(19)	b
(5)	b	(10)	c	(15)	b	(20)	b

QUIZ 2

(1)	a	(6)	d	(11)	d	(16)	b
(2)	b	(7)	c	(12)	c	(17)	b
(3)	d	(8)	d	(13)	a	(18)	c
(4)	a	(9)	d	(14)	a	(19)	b
(5)	a	(10)	b	(15)	d	(20)	d

QUIZ 3

(1)	d	(6)	d	(11)	c	(16)	b
(2)	a	(7)	a	(12)	b	(17)	a
(3)	a	(8)	d	(13)	a	(18)	b
(4)	b	(9)	a	(14)	d	(19)	c
(5)	c	(10)	c	(15)	c	(20)	a

QUIZ 4

(1)	b	(6)	c	(11)	a	(16)	a
(2)	b	(7)	d	(12)	c	(17)	c
(3)	c	(8)	a	(13)	b	(18)	d
(4)	a	(9)	b	(14)	c	(19)	a
(5)	d	(10)	d	(15)	a	(20)	c

QUIZ 5

(1)	c	(6)	d	(11)	d	(16)	b
(2)	a	(7)	b	(12)	d	(17)	a
(3)	b	(8)	a	(13)	c	(18)	b
(4)	d	(9)	b	(14)	d	(19)	c
(5)	c	(10)	c	(15)	a	(20)	c

QUIZ 6

(1)	b	(6)	c	(11)	a	(16)	a
(2)	b	(7)	b	(12)	c	(17)	c
(3)	a	(8)	c	(13)	d	(18)	c
(4)	c	(9)	a	(14)	b	(19)	d
(5)	d	(10)	b	(15)	b	(20)	a

QUIZ 7

(1)	a	(6)	c	(11)	d	(16)	b
(2)	c	(7)	a	(12)	c	(17)	d
(3)	b	(8)	d	(13)	d	(18)	b
(4)	d	(9)	b	(14)	c	(19)	c
(5)	b	(10)	a	(15)	a	(20)	a

QUIZ 8

(1)	a	(6)	d	(11)	d	(16)	c
(2)	b	(7)	b	(12)	b	(17)	c
(3)	c	(8)	a	(13)	a	(18)	d
(4)	d	(9)	b	(14)	c	(19)	c
(5)	a	(10)	c	(15)	a	(20)	d

QUIZ 9

(1)	a	(6)	b	(11)	a	(16)	c
(2)	c	(7)	c	(12)	b	(17)	d
(3)	d	(8)	a	(13)	b	(18)	c
(4)	b	(9)	a	(14)	c	(19)	d
(5)	d	(10)	c	(15)	d	(20)	b

QUIZ 10

(1)	c	(6)	b	(11)	d	(16)	a
(2)	d	(7)	a	(12)	a	(17)	b
(3)	a	(8)	a	(13)	d	(18)	a
(4)	d	(9)	b	(14)	d	(19)	c
(5)	c	(10)	c	(15)	b	(20)	b

QUIZ 11

(1)	c	(6)	d	(11)	d	(16)	d
(2)	b	(7)	b	(12)	b	(17)	c
(3)	a	(8)	a	(13)	c	(18)	d
(4)	b	(9)	c	(14)	b	(19)	a
(5)	d	(10)	a	(15)	a	(20)	a

QUIZ 12

(1)	d	(6)	c	(11)	d	(16)	b
(2)	c	(7)	a	(12)	b	(17)	c
(3)	b	(8)	a	(13)	a	(18)	a
(4)	b	(9)	b	(14)	c	(19)	d
(5)	d	(10)	c	(15)	b	(20)	b

QUIZ 13

(1)	a	(6)	c	(11)	b	(16)	a
(2)	c	(7)	b	(12)	d	(17)	b
(3)	d	(8)	c	(13)	a	(18)	a
(4)	a	(9)	d	(14)	d	(19)	c
(5)	b	(10)	a	(15)	c	(20)	c

QUIZ 14

(1)	b	(6)	b	(11)	a	(16)	c
(2)	a	(7)	c	(12)	c	(17)	d
(3)	c	(8)	d	(13)	b	(18)	a
(4)	a	(9)	a	(14)	d	(19)	b
(5)	b	(10)	c	(15)	d	(20)	c

QUIZ 15

(1)	b	(6)	a	(11)	a	(16)	b
(2)	c	(7)	c	(12)	d	(17)	d
(3)	a	(8)	d	(13)	b	(18)	c
(4)	d	(9)	b	(14)	c	(19)	a
(5)	b	(10)	c	(15)	a	(20)	d

QUIZ 16

(1)	a	(6)	c	(11)	d	(16)	b
(2)	d	(7)	d	(12)	b	(17)	a
(3)	b	(8)	b	(13)	d	(18)	c
(4)	b	(9)	b	(14)	c	(19)	d
(5)	a	(10)	c	(15)	a	(20)	a

QUIZ 17

(1)	c	(6)	b	(11)	d	(16)	a
(2)	b	(7)	c	(12)	a	(17)	b
(3)	d	(8)	d	(13)	c	(18)	d
(4)	a	(9)	a	(14)	d	(19)	c
(5)	a	(10)	c	(15)	b	(20)	d

QUIZ 18

(1)	a	(6)	a	(11)	a	(16)	b
(2)	b	(7)	d	(12)	b	(17)	d
(3)	d	(8)	a	(13)	d	(18)	c
(4)	c	(9)	c	(14)	c	(19)	a
(5)	b	(10)	b	(15)	a	(20)	a

QUIZ 19

(1)	b	(6)	c	(11)	c	(16)	b
(2)	d	(7)	d	(12)	b	(17)	d
(3)	c	(8)	a	(13)	d	(18)	a
(4)	a	(9)	b	(14)	a	(19)	b
(5)	b	(10)	c	(15)	c	(20)	c

QUIZ 20

(1)	b	(6)	c	(11)	a	(16)	a
(2)	a	(7)	b	(12)	c	(17)	d
(3)	d	(8)	d	(13)	d	(18)	c
(4)	c	(9)	a	(14)	b	(19)	a
(5)	a	(10)	b	(15)	a	(20)	d

QUIZ 21

(1)	b	(6)	c	(11)	a	(16)	d
(2)	c	(7)	a	(12)	d	(17)	b
(3)	a	(8)	d	(13)	b	(18)	c
(4)	d	(9)	b	(14)	c	(19)	a
(5)	b	(10)	c	(15)	a	(20)	d

QUIZ 22

(1)	a	(6)	a	(11)	a	(16)	b
(2)	c	(7)	a	(12)	b	(17)	c
(3)	b	(8)	b	(13)	c	(18)	b
(4)	d	(9)	c	(14)	d	(19)	d
(5)	c	(10)	d	(15)	a	(20)	a

QUIZ 23

(1)	b	(6)	d	(11)	a	(16)	d
(2)	a	(7)	a	(12)	c	(17)	b
(3)	d	(8)	c	(13)	b	(18)	a
(4)	c	(9)	b	(14)	a	(19)	c
(5)	b	(10)	d	(15)	c	(20)	d

QUIZ 24

(1)	b	(6)	b	(11)	b	(16)	a
(2)	d	(7)	d	(12)	a	(17)	b
(3)	a	(8)	a	(13)	c	(18)	d
(4)	a	(9)	c	(14)	d	(19)	c
(5)	c	(10)	d	(15)	b	(20)	a

QUIZ 25

(1)	b	(6)	d	(11)	d	(16)	d
(2)	d	(7)	a	(12)	d	(17)	b
(3)	a	(8)	c	(13)	b	(18)	c
(4)	c	(9)	b	(14)	c	(19)	a
(5)	b	(10)	a	(15)	a	(20)	d

QUIZ 26

(1)	a	(6)	a	(11)	d	(16)	a
(2)	b	(7)	b	(12)	c	(17)	c
(3)	d	(8)	c	(13)	d	(18)	d
(4)	c	(9)	a	(14)	a	(19)	d
(5)	d	(10)	b	(15)	b	(20)	b

QUIZ 27

(1)	d	(6)	d	(11)	a	(16)	a
(2)	c	(7)	c	(12)	c	(17)	c
(3)	b	(8)	c	(13)	b	(18)	b
(4)	b	(9)	b	(14)	b	(19)	d
(5)	a	(10)	d	(15)	d	(20)	c

QUIZ 28

(1)	a	(6)	b	(11)	b	(16)	a
(2)	c	(7)	c	(12)	a	(17)	a
(3)	b	(8)	a	(13)	c	(18)	d
(4)	d	(9)	b	(14)	c	(19)	c
(5)	a	(10)	d	(15)	b	(20)	c

QUIZ 29

(1)	a	(6)	c	(11)	b	(16)	b
(2)	b	(7)	a	(12)	c	(17)	c
(3)	c	(8)	b	(13)	d	(18)	a
(4)	d	(9)	d	(14)	a	(19)	d
(5)	c	(10)	a	(15)	d	(20)	c

QUIZ 30

(1)	a	(6)	b	(11)	d	(16)	d
(2)	d	(7)	d	(12)	c	(17)	c
(3)	c	(8)	c	(13)	b	(18)	b
(4)	b	(9)	b	(14)	a	(19)	a
(5)	a	(10)	a	(15)	b	(20)	d

QUIZ 31

(1)	d	(6)	c	(11)	c	(16)	c
(2)	a	(7)	b	(12)	d	(17)	a
(3)	b	(8)	d	(13)	a	(18)	d
(4)	a	(9)	b	(14)	b	(19)	b
(5)	c	(10)	a	(15)	d	(20)	b

QUIZ 32

(1)	b	(6)	a	(11)	d	(16)	c
(2)	c	(7)	c	(12)	c	(17)	b
(3)	a	(8)	d	(13)	b	(18)	a
(4)	b	(9)	b	(14)	a	(19)	d
(5)	d	(10)	a	(15)	d	(20)	c

QUIZ 33

(1)	a	(6)	c	(11)	c	(16)	d
(2)	b	(7)	d	(12)	d	(17)	b
(3)	d	(8)	d	(13)	b	(18)	a
(4)	c	(9)	b	(14)	a	(19)	b
(5)	a	(10)	a	(15)	c	(20)	c

QUIZ 34

(1)	c	(6)	d	(11)	a	(16)	d
(2)	c	(7)	b	(12)	b	(17)	c
(3)	d	(8)	a	(13)	c	(18)	b
(4)	b	(9)	c	(14)	b	(19)	a
(5)	c	(10)	d	(15)	a	(20)	a

QUIZ 35

(1)	b	(6)	c	(11)	a	(16)	b
(2)	a	(7)	b	(12)	d	(17)	d
(3)	d	(8)	d	(13)	a	(18)	a
(4)	c	(9)	b	(14)	c	(19)	b
(5)	a	(10)	c	(15)	c	(20)	c

QUIZ 36

(1)	b	(6)	a	(11)	a	(16)	b
(2)	a	(7)	d	(12)	a	(17)	a
(3)	d	(8)	b	(13)	c	(18)	c
(4)	b	(9)	c	(14)	d	(19)	a
(5)	c	(10)	b	(15)	c	(20)	d

QUIZ 37

(1)	a	(6)	a	(11)	a	(16)	a
(2)	b	(7)	b	(12)	b	(17)	c
(3)	b	(8)	c	(13)	c	(18)	c
(4)	d	(9)	d	(14)	d	(19)	d
(5)	c	(10)	a	(15)	b	(20)	a

QUIZ 38

(1)	a	(6)	c	(11)	a	(16)	c
(2)	d	(7)	b	(12)	a	(17)	b
(3)	b	(8)	c	(13)	b	(18)	d
(4)	c	(9)	d	(14)	c	(19)	a
(5)	a	(10)	b	(15)	d	(20)	c

QUIZ 39

(1)	b	(6)	c	(11)	a	(16)	a
(2)	c	(7)	b	(12)	c	(17)	b
(3)	c	(8)	a	(13)	b	(18)	a
(4)	a	(9)	b	(14)	d	(19)	d
(5)	d	(10)	d	(15)	c	(20)	c

QUIZ 40

(1)	c	(6)	b	(11)	b	(16)	a
(2)	a	(7)	c	(12)	a	(17)	b
(3)	b	(8)	c	(13)	b	(18)	a
(4)	a	(9)	d	(14)	d	(19)	d
(5)	d	(10)	a	(15)	c	(20)	c

QUIZ 41

(1)	d	(6)	a	(11)	b	(16)	b
(2)	b	(7)	b	(12)	a	(17)	d
(3)	c	(8)	c	(13)	c	(18)	b
(4)	d	(9)	b	(14)	d	(19)	c
(5)	a	(10)	d	(15)	a	(20)	a

QUIZ 42

(1)	c	(6)	c	(11)	d	(16)	d
(2)	b	(7)	b	(12)	d	(17)	d
(3)	a	(8)	c	(13)	c	(18)	c
(4)	a	(9)	b	(14)	b	(19)	b
(5)	d	(10)	a	(15)	a	(20)	c

QUIZ 43

(1)	a	(6)	c	(11)	d	(16)	c
(2)	a	(7)	d	(12)	a	(17)	b
(3)	b	(8)	a	(13)	d	(18)	a
(4)	d	(9)	b	(14)	b	(19)	d
(5)	d	(10)	c	(15)	c	(20)	b

QUIZ 44

(1)	b	(6)	b	(11)	c	(16)	b
(2)	a	(7)	c	(12)	d	(17)	a
(3)	b	(8)	b	(13)	a	(18)	d
(4)	c	(9)	c	(14)	c	(19)	c
(5)	d	(10)	a	(15)	d	(20)	d

QUIZ 45

(1)	a	(6)	a	(11)	d	(16)	c
(2)	b	(7)	b	(12)	b	(17)	b
(3)	c	(8)	d	(13)	b	(18)	a
(4)	d	(9)	c	(14)	c	(19)	d
(5)	d	(10)	a	(15)	d	(20)	c

QUIZ 46

(1)	d	(6)	a	(11)	a	(16)	a
(2)	a	(7)	d	(12)	b	(17)	d
(3)	b	(8)	b	(13)	d	(18)	b
(4)	a	(9)	c	(14)	b	(19)	d
(5)	c	(10)	c	(15)	c	(20)	a

QUIZ 47

(1)	c	(6)	b	(11)	d	(16)	b
(2)	c	(7)	c	(12)	d	(17)	d
(3)	a	(8)	a	(13)	c	(18)	c
(4)	b	(9)	b	(14)	c	(19)	a
(5)	d	(10)	a	(15)	a	(20)	d

QUIZ 48

(1)	d	(6)	d	(11)	c	(16)	a
(2)	c	(7)	a	(12)	c	(17)	a
(3)	a	(8)	d	(13)	a	(18)	b
(4)	b	(9)	b	(14)	d	(19)	c
(5)	c	(10)	b	(15)	d	(20)	d

QUIZ 49

(1)	c	(6)	b	(11)	c	(16)	c
(2)	c	(7)	b	(12)	d	(17)	a
(3)	d	(8)	c	(13)	a	(18)	b
(4)	a	(9)	a	(14)	d	(19)	d
(5)	d	(10)	b	(15)	a	(20)	c

QUIZ 50

(1) b	(6) c	(11) c	(16) d
(2) a	(7) a	(12) a	(17) a
(3) d	(8) d	(13) d	(18) c
(4) a	(9) d	(14) c	(19) b
(5) c	(10) b	(15) b	(20) c

QUIZ 51

(1) b	(6) c	(11) c	(16) c
(2) b	(7) b	(12) d	(17) a
(3) a	(8) a	(13) a	(18) b
(4) d	(9) d	(14) b	(19) c
(5) c	(10) b	(15) d	(20) a

QUIZ 52

(1) c	(6) d	(11) c	(16) a
(2) b	(7) d	(12) b	(17) c
(3) a	(8) c	(13) a	(18) b
(4) c	(9) a	(14) c	(19) b
(5) b	(10) a	(15) d	(20) d

QUIZ 53

(1) d	(6) c	(11) b	(16) c
(2) b	(7) a	(12) c	(17) a
(3) a	(8) d	(13) a	(18) b
(4) d	(9) d	(14) b	(19) a
(5) b	(10) b	(15) d	(20) d

QUIZ 54

(1) a	(6) c	(11) c	(16) d
(2) b	(7) a	(12) b	(17) d
(3) c	(8) d	(13) d	(18) b
(4) b	(9) b	(14) a	(19) a
(5) d	(10) a	(15) a	(20) c

QUIZ 55

(1)	a	(6)	d	(11)	d	(16)	d
(2)	d	(7)	c	(12)	a	(17)	d
(3)	b	(8)	b	(13)	b	(18)	c
(4)	d	(9)	c	(14)	c	(19)	a
(5)	a	(10)	b	(15)	b	(20)	a

QUIZ 56

(1)	a	(6)	d	(11)	a	(16)	a
(2)	c	(7)	a	(12)	d	(17)	d
(3)	c	(8)	a	(13)	c	(18)	c
(4)	b	(9)	d	(14)	b	(19)	b
(5)	b	(10)	b	(15)	c	(20)	a

QUIZ 57

(1)	c	(6)	a	(11)	b	(16)	a
(2)	a	(7)	b	(12)	d	(17)	a
(3)	b	(8)	d	(13)	c	(18)	c
(4)	c	(9)	c	(14)	d	(19)	b
(5)	d	(10)	a	(15)	b	(20)	d

QUIZ 58

(1)	b	(6)	b	(11)	c	(16)	d
(2)	c	(7)	c	(12)	a	(17)	a
(3)	a	(8)	a	(13)	c	(18)	b
(4)	d	(9)	b	(14)	b	(19)	c
(5)	d	(10)	d	(15)	d	(20)	a

QUIZ 59

(1)	a	(6)	b	(11)	a	(16)	b
(2)	c	(7)	a	(12)	c	(17)	c
(3)	a	(8)	c	(13)	d	(18)	b
(4)	b	(9)	d	(14)	a	(19)	c
(5)	d	(10)	b	(15)	b	(20)	a

QUIZ 60

(1)	c	(6)	c	(11)	c	(16)	d
(2)	b	(7)	b	(12)	d	(17)	c
(3)	b	(8)	c	(13)	c	(18)	b
(4)	a	(9)	d	(14)	b	(19)	a
(5)	d	(10)	a	(15)	a	(20)	d

QUIZ 61

(1)	a	(6)	a	(11)	b	(16)	d
(2)	c	(7)	b	(12)	a	(17)	b
(3)	c	(8)	c	(13)	b	(18)	b
(4)	b	(9)	a	(14)	d	(19)	a
(5)	d	(10)	d	(15)	c	(20)	c

QUIZ 62

(1)	b	(6)	d	(11)	d	(16)	b
(2)	c	(7)	b	(12)	c	(17)	b
(3)	a	(8)	b	(13)	b	(18)	c
(4)	d	(9)	a	(14)	a	(19)	a
(5)	a	(10)	a	(15)	d	(20)	d

QUIZ 63

(1)	a	(6)	c	(11)	c	(16)	c
(2)	c	(7)	a	(12)	a	(17)	a
(3)	d	(8)	d	(13)	a	(18)	d
(4)	a	(9)	b	(14)	d	(19)	c
(5)	b	(10)	d	(15)	b	(20)	b

QUIZ 64

(1)	b	(6)	b	(11)	c	(16)	b
(2)	a	(7)	b	(12)	d	(17)	c
(3)	d	(8)	d	(13)	d	(18)	a
(4)	a	(9)	b	(14)	a	(19)	d
(5)	c	(10)	a	(15)	c	(20)	a

QUIZ 65

(1)	c	(6)	b	(11)	a	(16)	a
(2)	b	(7)	c	(12)	c	(17)	c
(3)	d	(8)	d	(13)	d	(18)	b
(4)	a	(9)	a	(14)	d	(19)	c
(5)	c	(10)	b	(15)	b	(20)	a

QUIZ 66

(1)	b	(6)	b	(11)	b	(16)	a
(2)	d	(7)	c	(12)	d	(17)	b
(3)	c	(8)	d	(13)	b	(18)	c
(4)	a	(9)	b	(14)	c	(19)	d
(5)	a	(10)	c	(15)	a	(20)	a

QUIZ 67

(1)	c	(6)	b	(11)	b	(16)	c
(2)	b	(7)	a	(12)	d	(17)	d
(3)	a	(8)	d	(13)	a	(18)	d
(4)	d	(9)	c	(14)	c	(19)	b
(5)	a	(10)	a	(15)	b	(20)	a

QUIZ 68

(1)	a	(6)	a	(11)	c	(16)	d
(2)	b	(7)	c	(12)	b	(17)	b
(3)	d	(8)	b	(13)	b	(18)	a
(4)	d	(9)	d	(14)	a	(19)	c
(5)	c	(10)	d	(15)	c	(20)	c

QUIZ 69

(1)	a	(6)	a	(11)	a	(16)	a
(2)	c	(7)	a	(12)	d	(17)	c
(3)	b	(8)	c	(13)	c	(18)	d
(4)	d	(9)	d	(14)	b	(19)	a
(5)	b	(10)	b	(15)	d	(20)	b

QUIZ 70

(1)	a	(6)	a	(11)	d	(16)	b
(2)	b	(7)	b	(12)	b	(17)	a
(3)	c	(8)	c	(13)	c	(18)	c
(4)	a	(9)	c	(14)	c	(19)	a
(5)	d	(10)	a	(15)	d	(20)	d

QUIZ 71

(1)	b	(6)	b	(11)	b	(16)	a
(2)	c	(7)	a	(12)	a	(17)	b
(3)	a	(8)	c	(13)	c	(18)	c
(4)	b	(9)	b	(14)	b	(19)	a
(5)	d	(10)	d	(15)	d	(20)	c

QUIZ 72

(1)	b	(6)	b	(11)	c	(16)	b
(2)	a	(7)	b	(12)	d	(17)	b
(3)	c	(8)	c	(13)	d	(18)	c
(4)	d	(9)	a	(14)	a	(19)	c
(5)	a	(10)	b	(15)	c	(20)	c

QUIZ 73

(1)	b	(6)	b	(11)	c	(16)	c
(2)	a	(7)	d	(12)	d	(17)	d
(3)	c	(8)	a	(13)	b	(18)	d
(4)	d	(9)	c	(14)	a	(19)	b
(5)	c	(10)	b	(15)	d	(20)	a

QUIZ 74

(1)	a	(6)	b	(11)	c	(16)	a
(2)	b	(7)	a	(12)	b	(17)	c
(3)	d	(8)	d	(13)	d	(18)	b
(4)	a	(9)	d	(14)	a	(19)	d
(5)	c	(10)	c	(15)	d	(20)	c

QUIZ 75

(1)	b	(6)	d	(11)	c	(16)	a
(2)	a	(7)	a	(12)	a	(17)	c
(3)	a	(8)	b	(13)	b	(18)	d
(4)	b	(9)	d	(14)	b	(19)	b
(5)	c	(10)	c	(15)	d	(20)	a

QUIZ 76

(1)	a	(6)	c	(11)	d	(16)	b
(2)	c	(7)	b	(12)	b	(17)	c
(3)	d	(8)	c	(13)	c	(18)	d
(4)	a	(9)	c	(14)	a	(19)	b
(5)	b	(10)	a	(15)	b	(20)	a

QUIZ 77

(1)	a	(6)	a	(11)	b	(16)	b
(2)	b	(7)	d	(12)	d	(17)	d
(3)	d	(8)	c	(13)	c	(18)	a
(4)	b	(9)	b	(14)	c	(19)	c
(5)	c	(10)	a	(15)	a	(20)	a

QUIZ 78

(1)	a	(6)	c	(11)	b	(16)	d
(2)	c	(7)	a	(12)	a	(17)	a
(3)	d	(8)	d	(13)	d	(18)	d
(4)	a	(9)	b	(14)	b	(19)	c
(5)	b	(10)	c	(15)	b	(20)	b

QUIZ 79

(1)	c	(6)	c	(11)	b	(16)	d
(2)	a	(7)	b	(12)	a	(17)	a
(3)	d	(8)	c	(13)	c	(18)	d
(4)	a	(9)	a	(14)	b	(19)	b
(5)	b	(10)	d	(15)	a	(20)	c

QUIZ 80

(1)	b	(6)	a	(11)	a	(16)	a
(2)	a	(7)	b	(12)	b	(17)	c
(3)	d	(8)	d	(13)	d	(18)	d
(4)	c	(9)	c	(14)	c	(19)	b
(5)	b	(10)	b	(15)	b	(20)	c

QUIZ 81

(1)	b	(6)	d	(11)	b	(16)	a
(2)	a	(7)	b	(12)	c	(17)	b
(3)	c	(8)	c	(13)	b	(18)	c
(4)	a	(9)	a	(14)	a	(19)	d
(5)	d	(10)	d	(15)	d	(20)	b

QUIZ 82

(1)	b	(6)	b	(11)	a	(16)	c
(2)	d	(7)	a	(12)	c	(17)	a
(3)	c	(8)	d	(13)	d	(18)	b
(4)	a	(9)	b	(14)	a	(19)	d
(5)	c	(10)	c	(15)	b	(20)	c

QUIZ 83

(1)	c	(6)	b	(11)	c	(16)	d
(2)	b	(7)	c	(12)	b	(17)	d
(3)	a	(8)	a	(13)	c	(18)	b
(4)	c	(9)	d	(14)	a	(19)	c
(5)	d	(10)	b	(15)	b	(20)	a

QUIZ 84

(1)	a	(6)	b	(11)	b	(16)	b
(2)	b	(7)	b	(12)	d	(17)	d
(3)	a	(8)	a	(13)	c	(18)	c
(4)	c	(9)	c	(14)	a	(19)	b
(5)	d	(10)	d	(15)	c	(20)	a

QUIZ 85

(1) b
(2) a
(3) c
(4) b
(5) a
(6) d
(7) c
(8) c
(9) d
(10) b
(11) b
(12) a
(13) d
(14) c
(15) a
(16) b
(17) d
(18) b
(19) c
(20) d

QUIZ 86

(1) b
(2) c
(3) d
(4) a
(5) b
(6) c
(7) b
(8) c
(9) d
(10) b
(11) a
(12) a
(13) d
(14) c
(15) b
(16) d
(17) a
(18) a
(19) d
(20) a

QUIZ 87

(1) d
(2) a
(3) c
(4) b
(5) c
(6) a
(7) d
(8) b
(9) a
(10) b
(11) c
(12) d
(13) a
(14) c
(15) b
(16) a
(17) d
(18) c
(19) b
(20) d

QUIZ 88

(1) b
(2) c
(3) b
(4) a
(5) d
(6) c
(7) b
(8) a
(9) c
(10) d
(11) a
(12) b
(13) c
(14) a
(15) d
(16) b
(17) c
(18) a
(19) b
(20) d

QUIZ 89

(1) b
(2) c
(3) d
(4) a
(5) a
(6) b
(7) d
(8) c
(9) c
(10) a
(11) b
(12) b
(13) d
(14) c
(15) a
(16) a
(17) d
(18) b
(19) c
(20) a

QUIZ 90

(1)	a	(6)	b	(11)	c	(16)	b
(2)	d	(7)	d	(12)	a	(17)	a
(3)	b	(8)	c	(13)	b	(18)	c
(4)	a	(9)	c	(14)	d	(19)	b
(5)	c	(10)	a	(15)	c	(20)	a

QUIZ 91

(1)	b	(6)	b	(11)	b	(16)	b
(2)	a	(7)	a	(12)	a	(17)	d
(3)	d	(8)	d	(13)	d	(18)	c
(4)	d	(9)	c	(14)	c	(19)	a
(5)	c	(10)	b	(15)	a	(20)	b

QUIZ 92

(1)	a	(6)	c	(11)	d	(16)	c
(2)	c	(7)	a	(12)	b	(17)	b
(3)	b	(8)	b	(13)	a	(18)	d
(4)	d	(9)	d	(14)	a	(19)	a
(5)	b	(10)	c	(15)	a	(20)	d

QUIZ 93

(1)	b	(6)	a	(11)	d	(16)	d
(2)	a	(7)	c	(12)	b	(17)	a
(3)	c	(8)	b	(13)	a	(18)	c
(4)	b	(9)	d	(14)	c	(19)	d
(5)	d	(10)	c	(15)	b	(20)	c

QUIZ 94

(1)	a	(6)	c	(11)	c	(16)	b
(2)	c	(7)	a	(12)	b	(17)	b
(3)	b	(8)	b	(13)	a	(18)	c
(4)	b	(9)	d	(14)	d	(19)	a
(5)	d	(10)	c	(15)	c	(20)	d

QUIZ 95

(1)	b	(6)	a	(11)	a	(16)	c
(2)	a	(7)	d	(12)	d	(17)	a
(3)	c	(8)	b	(13)	b	(18)	d
(4)	b	(9)	a	(14)	c	(19)	a
(5)	d	(10)	c	(15)	b	(20)	b

QUIZ 96

(1)	a	(6)	b	(11)	c	(16)	c
(2)	b	(7)	c	(12)	a	(17)	b
(3)	d	(8)	a	(13)	b	(18)	d
(4)	a	(9)	b	(14)	d	(19)	c
(5)	c	(10)	d	(15)	a	(20)	a

QUIZ 97

(1)	a	(6)	c	(11)	a	(16)	d
(2)	b	(7)	a	(12)	d	(17)	c
(3)	c	(8)	a	(13)	c	(18)	a
(4)	b	(9)	b	(14)	a	(19)	d
(5)	d	(10)	d	(15)	b	(20)	b

QUIZ 98

(1)	a	(6)	b	(11)	d	(16)	a
(2)	b	(7)	a	(12)	a	(17)	c
(3)	d	(8)	c	(13)	c	(18)	c
(4)	a	(9)	b	(14)	d	(19)	a
(5)	d	(10)	c	(15)	b	(20)	b

QUIZ 99

(1)	c	(6)	c	(11)	b	(16)	c
(2)	b	(7)	b	(12)	c	(17)	b
(3)	b	(8)	d	(13)	d	(18)	c
(4)	a	(9)	a	(14)	a	(19)	d
(5)	d	(10)	c	(15)	b	(20)	a

QUIZ 100

(1)	b	(6)	a	(11)	d	(16)	a
(2)	a	(7)	c	(12)	c	(17)	d
(3)	c	(8)	b	(13)	b	(18)	c
(4)	b	(9)	d	(14)	d	(19)	b
(5)	d	(10)	a	(15)	b	(20)	a

QUIZ 101

(1)	c	(6)	a	(11)	b	(16)	b
(2)	a	(7)	c	(12)	a	(17)	d
(3)	d	(8)	b	(13)	c	(18)	c
(4)	c	(9)	d	(14)	d	(19)	a
(5)	b	(10)	c	(15)	a	(20)	b

QUIZ 102

(1)	c	(6)	c	(11)	b	(16)	b
(2)	d	(7)	a	(12)	a	(17)	a
(3)	a	(8)	b	(13)	b	(18)	c
(4)	b	(9)	c	(14)	c	(19)	d
(5)	d	(10)	d	(15)	d	(20)	b

QUIZ 103

(1)	b	(6)	b	(11)	d	(16)	d
(2)	c	(7)	c	(12)	a	(17)	c
(3)	a	(8)	b	(13)	c	(18)	a
(4)	d	(9)	d	(14)	b	(19)	a
(5)	a	(10)	b	(15)	d	(20)	d

QUIZ 104

(1)	d	(6)	d	(11)	d	(16)	c
(2)	a	(7)	b	(12)	b	(17)	d
(3)	c	(8)	a	(13)	a	(18)	b
(4)	b	(9)	b	(14)	b	(19)	a
(5)	a	(10)	c	(15)	d	(20)	c

QUIZ 105

(1)	a	(6)	c	(11)	a	(16)	b
(2)	c	(7)	b	(12)	d	(17)	d
(3)	b	(8)	d	(13)	b	(18)	b
(4)	d	(9)	a	(14)	c	(19)	a
(5)	a	(10)	c	(15)	d	(20)	b

QUIZ 106

(1)	c	(6)	c	(11)	a	(16)	b
(2)	b	(7)	b	(12)	c	(17)	d
(3)	a	(8)	d	(13)	a	(18)	c
(4)	d	(9)	c	(14)	b	(19)	d
(5)	a	(10)	b	(15)	b	(20)	c

QUIZ 107

(1)	a	(6)	d	(11)	b	(16)	b
(2)	b	(7)	a	(12)	a	(17)	c
(3)	b	(8)	c	(13)	c	(18)	b
(4)	c	(9)	b	(14)	a	(19)	a
(5)	a	(10)	d	(15)	d	(20)	c

QUIZ 108

(1)	a	(6)	d	(11)	b	(16)	b
(2)	d	(7)	c	(12)	c	(17)	d
(3)	b	(8)	a	(13)	a	(18)	a
(4)	b	(9)	d	(14)	d	(19)	c
(5)	c	(10)	a	(15)	c	(20)	b

QUIZ 109

(1)	d	(6)	d	(11)	b	(16)	b
(2)	a	(7)	c	(12)	c	(17)	c
(3)	c	(8)	b	(13)	a	(18)	c
(4)	b	(9)	a	(14)	d	(19)	d
(5)	a	(10)	d	(15)	a	(20)	a

QUIZ 110

(1)	a	(6)	a	(11)	c	(16)	a
(2)	b	(7)	c	(12)	b	(17)	d
(3)	b	(8)	b	(13)	c	(18)	b
(4)	c	(9)	d	(14)	a	(19)	c
(5)	d	(10)	d	(15)	b	(20)	a

QUIZ 111

(1)	a	(6)	b	(11)	b	(16)	a
(2)	b	(7)	a	(12)	d	(17)	c
(3)	c	(8)	d	(13)	b	(18)	b
(4)	c	(9)	c	(14)	a	(19)	d
(5)	d	(10)	a	(15)	c	(20)	c

QUIZ 112

(1)	d	(6)	c	(11)	a	(16)	d
(2)	a	(7)	d	(12)	d	(17)	a
(3)	a	(8)	a	(13)	a	(18)	b
(4)	c	(9)	c	(14)	b	(19)	b
(5)	b	(10)	b	(15)	c	(20)	d

QUIZ 113

(1)	a	(6)	d	(11)	c	(16)	d
(2)	b	(7)	c	(12)	c	(17)	a
(3)	a	(8)	b	(13)	b	(18)	b
(4)	c	(9)	a	(14)	c	(19)	c
(5)	d	(10)	d	(15)	a	(20)	d

QUIZ 114

(1)	d	(6)	d	(11)	a	(16)	b
(2)	c	(7)	c	(12)	c	(17)	a
(3)	b	(8)	b	(13)	a	(18)	c
(4)	c	(9)	d	(14)	d	(19)	d
(5)	a	(10)	b	(15)	d	(20)	c

QUIZ 115

(1)	a	(6)	a	(11)	b	(16)	b
(2)	b	(7)	b	(12)	d	(17)	c
(3)	d	(8)	d	(13)	b	(18)	d
(4)	c	(9)	c	(14)	b	(19)	a
(5)	d	(10)	a	(15)	a	(20)	b

QUIZ 116

(1)	b	(6)	d	(11)	d	(16)	d
(2)	a	(7)	d	(12)	c	(17)	a
(3)	a	(8)	c	(13)	a	(18)	b
(4)	c	(9)	a	(14)	b	(19)	c
(5)	b	(10)	b	(15)	c	(20)	c

QUIZ 117

(1)	c	(6)	b	(11)	c	(16)	d
(2)	a	(7)	c	(12)	d	(17)	c
(3)	b	(8)	a	(13)	a	(18)	b
(4)	d	(9)	b	(14)	b	(19)	c
(5)	d	(10)	d	(15)	a	(20)	a

QUIZ 118

(1)	a	(6)	c	(11)	b	(16)	d
(2)	b	(7)	a	(12)	c	(17)	c
(3)	b	(8)	b	(13)	a	(18)	a
(4)	d	(9)	d	(14)	b	(19)	b
(5)	c	(10)	d	(15)	a	(20)	d

QUIZ 119

(1)	b	(6)	c	(11)	a	(16)	c
(2)	a	(7)	d	(12)	c	(17)	d
(3)	a	(8)	c	(13)	c	(18)	a
(4)	b	(9)	d	(14)	b	(19)	b
(5)	d	(10)	b	(15)	d	(20)	c

QUIZ 120

(1)	b	(6)	d	(11)	a	(16)	d
(2)	c	(7)	c	(12)	c	(17)	b
(3)	a	(8)	d	(13)	d	(18)	a
(4)	b	(9)	b	(14)	c	(19)	b
(5)	a	(10)	b	(15)	a	(20)	d

QUIZ 121

(1)	b	(6)	a	(11)	d	(16)	c
(2)	a	(7)	c	(12)	c	(17)	b
(3)	c	(8)	d	(13)	b	(18)	c
(4)	d	(9)	b	(14)	d	(19)	d
(5)	b	(10)	a	(15)	a	(20)	a

QUIZ 122

(1)	c	(6)	c	(11)	d	(16)	c
(2)	b	(7)	d	(12)	b	(17)	d
(3)	d	(8)	b	(13)	c	(18)	a
(4)	a	(9)	c	(14)	a	(19)	b
(5)	a	(10)	a	(15)	b	(20)	c

QUIZ 123

(1)	a	(6)	a	(11)	b	(16)	b
(2)	d	(7)	d	(12)	d	(17)	c
(3)	c	(8)	c	(13)	c	(18)	a
(4)	d	(9)	b	(14)	a	(19)	d
(5)	b	(10)	a	(15)	d	(20)	b

QUIZ 124

(1)	d	(6)	b	(11)	c	(16)	c
(2)	a	(7)	b	(12)	b	(17)	b
(3)	c	(8)	d	(13)	a	(18)	b
(4)	a	(9)	a	(14)	d	(19)	d
(5)	c	(10)	d	(15)	a	(20)	a

QUIZ 125

(1)	b	(6)	a	(11)	a	(16)	a
(2)	c	(7)	c	(12)	d	(17)	d
(3)	d	(8)	b	(13)	b	(18)	c
(4)	a	(9)	d	(14)	b	(19)	d
(5)	d	(10)	c	(15)	c	(20)	b